A PROTEST MOVEMENT BECALMED:

A Study of Change in the CCF

What ever became of the Socialist Party?

A PROTEST MOVEMENT BECALMED

A Study of Change
in the CCF

by Leo Zakuta

———

UNIVERSITY OF TORONTO PRESS

© *University of Toronto Press, 1964*
Printed in Canada

To my parents
from whom I first acquired my interest
in politics

CANADIAN STUDIES IN SOCIOLOGY

Editor: S. D. CLARK

1. *A Protest Movement Becalmed: A Study of Change in the CCF.*
   By Leo Zakuta

FOREWORD

THE ESTABLISHMENT by the Social Science Research Council of Canada, through a grant from the Canada Council, of a new series, Canadian Studies in Sociology, represents an important move forward in the support of scholarly work in the social sciences in Canada. There are now series sponsored by the Council in economics, history and politics, and sociology. It was not so long ago when publications in sociology in Canada could be counted on one hand. The pressing problems of a new country like ours appeared largely to be of an economic or political character. When sociology first made its appearance as a teaching discipline there were in almost every university in Canada strong departments of economics and politics and a mounting flow of scholarly publications in these fields gave an indication of the importance of the work being done. Indeed, by the time the first third of the century had passed Canada could boast scholars in economics and politics of such standing as James Mavor, Stephen Leacock, H. A. Innis and R. MacG. Dawson.

It would be a foolish boast to claim that the second third of the century belonged to sociology, but two devastating world wars, rapid industrialization and urbanization and sweeping technological developments brought such changes that the social world we came to know was one very different from the social world we had known not more than a third of a century ago. No longer could all the answers to the problems which faced us be found in economics and political science. We needed to think sociologically much more than we once had about what was happening in our society. Sociology became securely established alongside economics and political science as a field of scholarly work in the Canadian university. In laying a firm foundation for such work through research and publication much is owing to the late Carl A. Dawson.

It would be my hope that the series, Canadian Studies in Sociology, will not only bring strength in a general way to scholarly work in sociology in Canada but that it will serve to direct the attention of Canadian sociologists more to the examination of that society of which they are a part. There is still only a corporal's guard of sociologists in Canada. With such few numbers, we cannot afford to spread ourselves over a vast front. This is not to say that diversity in the interests of Canadian sociologists in any way should be discouraged. We want sociologists who are specialists in societies other than our own. But it is Canadian society that we know best and it is, therefore, in the seeking of an understanding of this society that we can make the greatest contribution. What we need is a much more concerted effort to examine the character of development and the changing shape of Canadian social institutions, forms of social organization, community groupings, value systems and ways of life. It was when there was a turning to the study of the economy and political system of Canada as such that the "break through" occurred in the development of economics and political science in this country. It is upon similar foundations of work on the Canadian society that Canadian sociology must be built.

S. D. CLARK

ACKNOWLEDGMENTS

MY FOREMOST DEBT is to Professor Herbert Blumer, the most inspiring of my teachers. It is almost twenty years since his well-known article, "Social Movements," converted me almost instantly from a participant in to an observer of the CCF. Some years later, in discussing my proposal for a thesis on the CCF, he suggested that I concentrate on "emotional enthusiasm" in the party. His advice seemed more intriguing than feasible at the time and for some years was virtually forgotten. However, the further the study proceeded, the clearer it became that its main focus had to be "emotional enthusiasm." The penetrating criticism and the advice of Professors Everett C. Hughes and Peter M. Blau were extremely helpful. It was the former's suggestion that led me to look beyond the CCF and to undertake the comparisons in the final chapter. Several of my colleagues at the University of Toronto read and commented on the manuscript. I am especially grateful to Professors Jean Burnet and S. D. Clark, both of whom endured several readings of the entire manuscript in its various stages. The study owes much to their criticism and advice, to that of the editorial readers, and to the skill of Miss Jean Jamieson of the University of Toronto Press.

A Rockefeller grant gave me a year free from teaching. The study could not have been completed without it. This work has been published with the help of a grant from the Social Science Research Council, using funds provided by the Canada Council.

The leaders and officers of the Ontario Section of the CCF were remarkably co-operative and generous. They not only gave me free access to their records, including many which were confidential, but also space in their office for many months so that I could examine these records fully. I am grateful to Ken Bryden, former Provincial Secretary of the Ontario CCF and now New Democratic member for Woodbine in the Legislative Assembly, for reading the manuscript and correcting a number of inaccuracies in it. I owe a special debt to Miss Ellen Adams, Secretary of the New Democratic Caucus in the Legislative Assembly of Ontario. Without her thorough knowledge of the CCF I should have been quite lost. The great contribution made by the CCF leaders whom I interviewed will be readily apparent: regrettably, they must remain anonymous. I have disguised personal names by using fictitious given names and omitting surnames. The few surnames which do appear are all real, however.

L.Z.

CONTENTS

PART I

Introduction

1. Aim and Method

WHEN THE TWENTIETH CENTURY OPENED, socialist parties were already well established in Continental Europe and were just getting under way throughout the English-speaking world. In Canada, however, three further decades elapsed before the CCF's numerous progenitors, aroused by an acute economic and political crisis at home and abroad, drew together in order to form a socialist party on a national scale.

The Co-operative Commonwealth Federation was born on the Canadian prairies in the summer of 1932. It began as a loose federation of existing parties—agrarian, labour and socialist—from the four western provinces, but other groups, including eastern and trade union bodies, displayed an interest in it from the outset. During the next few years, the new party experienced a good deal of coming and going as many of these groups entered its fold, several left, some hovered uncertainly on the sidelines and still others sought in vain to make common cause with it. Of these numerous bodies, those which left and those which were denied entry indicate the range of the CCF's ideology. The first set valued major reform above socialism while the other prized socialism well above the parliamentary system. (Throughout its history, the CCF was to court the former groups and to be courted by the latter.)

If the west brought the new party to life, the east did much to shape its character. Its initial "braintrust" was the League for Social Reconstruction, led by Fabian-oriented professors at McGill and Toronto. The LSR contributed significantly not only to the CCF's philosophy and programme but also to the recruitment of its future leaders and to its solvency during its faltering infant years.

Although survival was precarious at first, the CCF immediately became—and remained—the dominant force in "left of centre" Canadian politics. In the early 1940's it gained sudden popularity across the country, sweeping Saskatchewan in 1944 and surging to the threshold of power in Ontario and later in British Columbia. But by 1945 the party's fortunes had begun to ebb, and thereafter, despite the occasional resurgence and an unbroken hold on Saskatchewan, they receded slowly but steadily.[1] In 1961, the CCF came officially to an end when, with the support of the Canadian Labour Congress, it formed the New Democratic party.

In addition to these changes in strength, the party underwent considerable change in character during its life span. It began as a rather radical and spontaneous political movement but eventually developed much of the outlook and structure of the "old parties." It became, in brief, a somewhat conventional political party itself.

The CCF was an established hunting ground for social scientists. Underhill and Lipset wrote provocatively and illuminatingly about it; McHenry and Engelmann contributed valuable accounts of its formal structure and history, and its explosive rise inspired numerous MA theses.[2] Most of these studies displayed a touch of enchantment, attempting to show that the CCF was a "genuinely" democratic party based on mass participation and control. In addition, many CCF leaders and sympathizers were highly articulate and wrote voluminously on it until about 1945, especially in the *Canadian Forum* which was their chief medium during that period.

The CCF served its investigators primarily as a gauge of the Canadian scene. They saw in its birth and growth evidence of serious discontent among certain groups, whose changing sentiments they measured according to the shifts in the party's support. In his *Agrarian Socialism* Lipset applied this perspective skilfully to Saskatchewan. However, except for his brief but illuminating discussion of changing CCF policies in that province,[3] these studies usually took the party as given and regarded the voters' reactions to it as the variable for investigation. This study reverses that perspective. It focuses on the party, not the public, by taking as its theme the process known familiarly, if awkwardly, as "institutionalization" and examining both its common and its distinctive aspects in the CCF.

Institutionalization refers to that sequence of changes in which a new crusading group loses its original character[4] as it becomes enmeshed

[1]For the statistical record of CCF popular support in federal and Ontario elections, see App. A.

[2]Underhill, "The Canadian Party System in Transition," "The Development of National Parties in Canada," "The Party System in Canada," "Political Parties in Canada"; Lipset, *Agrarian Socialism*; McHenry, *The Third Force in Canada*; Engelmann, "The Cooperative Commonwealth Federation of Canada."

[3]Chaps. VII, XI, XII and Epilogue.

[4]Throughout this study, "character" refers to the group's prevailing type of ideology, structure and membership involvement.

in the surrounding society and develops an increasing resemblance to the established bodies against whose very nature it initially arose in protest. To analyse this sequence of change in the CCF, the study divides the party's history into three phases—political movement, major party and minor party—based on the CCF's changing character and strength.

My initial mode of procedure stemmed from my original aim, which was to observe sectarian behaviour at first hand and, as a secondary objective, how it turns into the more conventional type. These interests grew out of my experience and observations as a deeply involved "CCFer" from 1942 to 1945, years of enormous excitement and change for the party. But when this study began, in 1952, the CCF had long shed its sectarian character, and its early stages of "institutionalization," the only ones I knew, were well over. After what now seems an incredibly long time, I eventually concluded that my original priorities should be reversed and that I would have to reconstruct the past from interviews and the written records.

My initial aim, however, made "participant observation" seem the most suitable method of research. Since I was familiar with CCF thinking and history, this method was particularly inviting. Entry into the CCF is not difficult. The simplest way is to join the riding association in one's neighbourhood (in my case, in Toronto), and, with the kind assistance of a colleague, I did so and participated regularly in its affairs for five years and very occasionally for the next five.

This method offered considerable advantages. The riding association met regularly, which provided an opportunity for sustained observation of the rank and file. In addition, as a member of my local group, I attended many meetings at higher levels as a delegate or simply as a participant quite as a matter of course without any questions being asked or special arrangements required. Membership in the local group was therefore a useful base of operations and of identification throughout the party; it facilitated unobtrusive access to many places. In fact, for several years I reluctantly consented to serve on the executive of my local group, although it became evident that to my fellow executive members I exemplified what the top CCF leaders were constantly bemoaning—"deadwood" among the local "leadership." In retrospect, this does not seem too high a price for the additional opportunities for observation.

Throughout the study, the members of my local group and many others, including the top leaders in Ontario, knew about my research interest. It is unlikely that the knowledge caused much apprehension.

The CCF always had so many friends in the universities and was studied so often and sympathetically that its reaction to its academic investigators was much more friendly and co-operative than wary.

My new research objective created one very perplexing problem—on which body to focus this study, the national party, the provincial organization or the local groups? None of these levels was satisfactory by itself but none could be ignored. The fortunes and character of the party everywhere were inseparable from those of the national body. The latter was also the source of the major policy decisions and therefore the focus for the examination of the CCF's official ideology. On the other hand, this large, sprawling body was quite unsuitable for the close observation and types of data required to understand the party's structure, especially its informal aspects, and the involvement of its members.

With no perfect solution to this problem in sight, the CCF's organization into provincial sections provided what seemed an acceptable compromise. The provincial sections had considerable autonomy and operated as the party's main administrative units. For two reasons, besides my obvious convenience, the Ontario Section seemed a satisfactory choice for the focus of much of this study. Because of the size and varied character of the province, it contained local groups which were reasonably representative of the party across Canada. These ranged all the way from some which were nearly as strong as any in the west to others which were almost as weak as any in the east.

The second reason was the significance of Ontario to the national CCF's political ambitions and organizational strength. The former can hardly be overestimated. No party can hope to take office in Ottawa without extensive support in Quebec or Ontario, which together hold three-fifths of the seats in the House of Commons. Since Quebec never showed any interest in the CCF, the party's hopes for national victory or even prominence depended all the more heavily on Ontario. As if to underline that importance, the two main turning points in the CCF's history occurred there. The first was a spectacular by-election victory in Toronto early in 1942, which gave an enormous impetus to the party's upsurge, and the other was the disastrous setback in the Ontario provincial election three years later, which virtually snuffed out the CCF's immediate chances of displacing the Liberals or the Conservatives nationally, a shock from which the party never fully recovered.

The party's national organization depended heavily on Ontario. No other province contributed as many votes or dollars to the CCF; only Saskatchewan provided more members; and, after the party's first few years, its leaders from Ontario wielded more influence within it than those from any other province. Finally, many of the detailed data here report on the CCF in Toronto, the great core and clearly dominant centre of the party in Ontario.

Thus, instead of settling on one specific body for investigation, the study uses several, depending on the problem or the available data. From the national to the provincial to the metropolitan, the focus sometimes narrows to the riding association level for a closer view of the rank and file.

PART II

The Unchanging Aspects of the CCF

II. Ideology

TO EXAMINE HOW THE CCF CHANGED, some familiarity with its basic beliefs and organization is necessary because they constituted the durable framework within which the alterations took place. The most stable beliefs were those general principles and policies which commanded the widest agreement among CCFers, but one major issue which divided them permanently into two camps was equally enduring.

COMMON GROUND

Like any political group, the CCF believed that the superiority of its doctrines compelled it morally to seek power. These doctrines embraced both official policy and its underlying principles, the latter constituting an unwritten creed, expressed primarily on ceremonial occasions. The creed was based on the following premises: that the fullest realization of "the good life," whatever it might be, required liberty, equality of opportunity, brotherhood and economic security; that the quest for these conditions constituted the central course of human history and that it necessarily led to political action through bodies which, like the CCF, were intelligently dedicated to these goals.

Its intelligence, the party believed, was manifest in the logic of its policies, but its sincerity, it felt, was even more clearly shown by its structure. It insisted proudly that it alone, among Canada's parties, was organized, financed and controlled on the genuinely democratic basis to which the others paid only lip service. These convictions of the moral excellence of its beliefs and practices, of their harmony with the inevitable course of human events and, consequently, of ultimate triumph constituted the foundation blocks of CCF faith.

Followers expect declarations of faith to come from their leaders. Hence, in the CCF, the latter provided most of the examples below.

In three years we have built the most effective socialist movement in Canadian history, and defeats, discouragements, difficulties of every sort

have failed to weaken, on the contrary, they have strengthened the determination to carry on. Growth has been recorded. Growth will be recorded.
The stars in their courses are fighting for the cause of socialism.

That was in 1936, in the Report of the Ontario Executive to the
Provincial Convention. Sixteen years later, at a large gathering marking
the tenth anniversary of the death of the CCF's first leader and most
revered figure, J. S. Woodsworth, Premier Douglas of Saskatchewan
told the audience that

"there are times when all of your effort does not result in any progress
for your cause. At times, it may even seem to be slipping in popularity.
But these things aren't really the important ones. If your cause is just and
right, sooner or later you will win. It must triumph because it is part of
the warp and woof of the universe. . . . No matter how long it takes, no
matter how many setbacks there may be along the road, you may be sure
that some day the right and just will prevail. It must prevail simply because
it is right and just."

The following conversation between two rank and file members in 1952
expresses the same theme:

First member: "I think we'll win the next federal election." (*general
demurral*)
First member (*angrily*): "Some people have no faith. I'm sure we'll be
in within the next ten years."
Second member: "It's the ones who think we'll be in within the next ten
years who have no faith."

At Christmastime the party's newspapers and club bulletins usually
contained messages from the leaders in which they linked the CCF's
ideals with the Christian Gospels. The following is an example:

Did the jingling bells of the shivering Salvation Army volunteer induce
you to drop a little change in his "Christmas pot" outside some big
department store or on some windy corner in your small town?
And did that clear your conscience for Christmas?
Or did you think of the Child whose birthday we are supposed to be
celebrating?
Did you think of the Man who told us to feed the hungry and clothe the
naked and comfort the widowed and fatherless, not on our doorsteps but
wherever we could reach them and whether or not they were of our own
blood?
Did you ask yourself whether you had some responsibility to help change
the world?
If we worked together we could replace slums with decent housing.
We could get rid of unemployment and fear of crop failures or glutted
markets.
We could see that every child gets all the food it can eat, all the milk
and orange juice it can drink, and all the education it can absorb, and

that all the Tiny Tims everywhere get all the assistance known to medical science.

All men could be brothers, sharing a common freedom and a common responsibility.

The CCF is not anti-anything. It is pro-something.

It holds fast by no theological or economic dogma. It is, as all good politics should be, simply applied religion.

We would like to keep that pot boiling all the year round.[1]

Why the party merited this praise, in contrast to its rivals, was explained by Donald C. MacDonald, Ontario Leader, to a riding association meeting in 1956.

"We've been having educational conferences throughout the province. That's a wonderful thing because people have sat down for a whole day and sometimes two to sweat out an answer to the question, What is the CCF? That may sound like a strange thing to you. But it isn't if you try to imagine the Liberals and Conservatives trying to do that. Because if they did find out what the Liberal and Conservative parties were, if they had a conscience, they'd go mad. It's a good thing then for us to refresh our convictions."

One of these convictions, it will be recalled, was that only the CCF practised the democracy which all preached. Because it regarded this as an effective selling point, the party stressed it in its leaflets, of which the following is a sample:

IS THE CCF DEMOCRATIC?

Completely. Consider its origin, development, organization and aims.

1. *Origin.* The CCF grew out of various people's movements which preceded it, such as the Progressive Party which swept the prairies and Ontario in the 1920's, labor and farmer parties which had existed in many parts of Canada, and the Socialist Party of Canada.

2. *Development.* The CCF has been built by the voluntary efforts of its members. It continues to depend on the rank and file for fund-raising activities of its members. It is therefore controlled only by its members and is free from any obligation to private interests.

3. *Organization.* The CCF is built from the ground up. Clubs and constituency associations meet regularly throughout the year. Conventions have supreme authority. They too meet regularly and frequently to hammer out party policy and are composed of democratically elected delegates from the local associations. *Officers do not make policy. They carry out the program laid down by the conventions. Further, they are always answerable to the movement and come up for election or re-election at every convention, both provincial and national.*[2]

[1]"Keep the Pot Boiling," *CCF News*, Jan. 1956.
[2]From *They'll Ask You*, a leaflet published by the CCF National Office, May 1948.

Finally, the following remarks, all by rank and file members of the CCF's "left wing," give simple testimony to the party's sense of superiority over its rivals:

In an informal conversation about the CCF and French Canada, one participant remarked that the CCF has not tried "to woo" the French Canadians. "Our trouble," he said ruefully but proudly, "is that we're too honest."

At a riding association executive meeting in 1956, the conversation turned to the recent provincial elections, which really meant only the Saskatchewan contest, in which the CCF government had been returned. The Quebec and New Brunswick elections were ignored. One veteran member remarked: "I always like to read about Saskatchewan, it peps me up." She mentioned Saskatchewan's health plan and its enormous advantages and suggested that there might be a diminishing need for its services because it had made the people of the province healthier. "Isn't it just wonderful that they got in again," she concluded. "It's wonderful."

At another riding association meeting, a right wing member concluded her remarks by saying ". . . why assume that the people won't recognize that fact? Why assume that we're superior to them?" A left winger replied emphatically, "As socialists we are superior." (*No reaction by any of the others*)

By far the most important source of official policy was the CCF's National Convention and especially its major policy pronouncements.[3] Its most celebrated statement was the Regina Manifesto, the party's foundation document and its closest approximation to a sacred text. By comparing its opening sentences with those of the Winnipeg Declaration (1956), the CCF's last major statement of policy, one can measure, at a glance, the degree of permanence—and of change—in general policy over the party's life span.[4] The Regina Manifesto began:

The CCF is a federation of organizations whose purpose is the establishment in Canada of a Co-operative Commonwealth in which the principle regulating production, distribution and exchange will be the supplying of human needs and not the making of profits.

We aim to replace the present capitalist system, with its inherent injustice and inhumanity, by a social order from which the domination and exploitation of one class by another will be eliminated, in which economic planning will supersede unregulated private enterprise and competition, and in which

[3]The National Convention had ultimate authority over the entire party as the provincial conventions did over their sections. These gatherings were held either annually or biennially.

The CCF constantly cited the frequency and regularity of these conventions as the most obvious proof of its genuine democracy and of its superiority, in this respect, to the Liberal and Conservative parties, which held them only very occasionally, usually to choose a new leader.

[4]For the full texts of the Regina Manifesto and the Winnipeg Declaration, see App. B.

genuine democratic self-government, based upon economic equality will be possible. The present order is marked by glaring inequalities of wealth and opportunity, by chaotic waste and instability; and in an age of plenty it condemns the great mass of the people to poverty and insecurity. . . . We believe that these evils can be removed only in a planned and socialized economy in which our natural resources and the principal means of production and distribution are owned, controlled and operated by the people.

The Winnipeg Declaration opened as follows:

The aim of the Co-operative Commonwealth Federation is the establishment in Canada by democratic means of a co-operative commonwealth in which the supplying of human needs and the enrichment of human life shall be the primary purpose of our society. Private profit and corporate power must be subordinated to social planning designed to achieve equality of opportunity and the highest possible living standards for all Canadians.

Common ground in the CCF, as elsewhere, lay in its more general beliefs and in the appearance which it tried to present to the public. But in a closer view of the party, especially within its own confines, this picture of solidarity naturally receded and revealed among the fissures one much deeper and more pervasive than the rest—the split between "left" and "right."

BATTLEGROUND

When the Book of Genesis of human organizations is written, its author may be tempted to remark, "Purist and politician created he them." The words themselves are of little importance; others would do equally well. Fundamentalist and revisionist, radical and moderate, and orthodox and modernist are among the many acceptable synonyms. In politics, the CCF included, the terms "left" and "right" refer to corresponding differences in outlook.

These two words had quite unequal standing in the CCF. "Left" was a title of honour and sentiment while "right" was a term of accusation. But, in internecine combat, the two factions used these words somewhat differently. One proudly called itself "left wing" or "leftist" and disparagingly referred to the other as "right wing." The latter naturally rejected that epithet and retaliated, somewhat defensively perhaps, by labelling its accusers as "doctrinaire" or as "purists" or as "the lunatic fringe" or, ultimately, as "the real reactionaries," on the grounds that they clung rigidly to outmoded doctrines.[5]

[5]The terms "left" and "right" appear henceforth as convenient forms of identification. Because they often evoke emotion, they have been set in quotation marks until now, a practice too awkward to continue.

Within the framework of common CCF beliefs, and regardless of shifts in the entire framework, a deep division persisted between these two factions. Not every member could be neatly classified as one or the other[6] and some of the specific issues between the two groups changed; but certain fundamental distinctions between them remained.

At bottom, these turned on different feelings about the existing social order and on different conceptions of its power structure. The left wing, rejecting it more completely, wanted to change it immediately and drastically, but, like any extreme group, it attributed to its principal foe enormous intelligence, unity, ruthlessness and strength. The capitalist puppet-masters, it explained, tolerated the parliamentary system only when it served their interests by concealing class domination behind the illusion of popular control. Therefore, even if they failed to ensnare a socialist government in parliamentary entanglements, was it reasonable to expect that they would watch passively—witness Germany, Italy, Austria and Spain—while the very basis of their existence was being dismantled? These considerations made the left wing highly sceptical about the effectiveness of parliamentary democracy as a vehicle of fundamental social change. Thus, although it was formally committed to constitutional procedure and unquestionably saw it as the long-run ideal, this faction made the private reservation, "by constitutional means, *if possible*," and it considered the right wing's total commitment to that possibility extremely naive and dangerous.

The latter, less outraged by the world, proposed to alter it more moderately and gradually. Nor did it endorse whole-heartedly the left wing's constant scriptural references to Marx, its forbidding picture of the enemy or its Armageddon-like vision of an inevitable "final conflict." With its more moderate aims and less embattled views, the right wing maintained its faith in parliamentary democracy as the vehicle of change and took as its models the Labour and Social Democratic parties of the Commonwealth, Scandinavia, and especially of Great Britain. (Eventu-

---

[6]The difficulties of classification are nowhere more apparent than in the following passage, cited by K. McNaught (*A Prophet in Politics*, p. 269), which quotes two statements by G. H. Williams, the former Leader of the CCF in Saskatchewan. The first, a letter to M. J. Coldwell, Jan. 30, 1935, says, " . . . the sooner we reconcile ourselves to out and out socialism and all the abuse that term means, the sooner we will be worthy of the crown of success." The second was in the debate at the CCF National Convention, Aug. 1936: "Some say the only way to attain socialism is by being pure socialist and having no truck nor trade with anyone who is not a pure socialist. Now, as a matter of idealism that is fine, but as a matter of practicality it may be political futility. There is only one way to have socialism in Canada and that is to have a socialist government. . . . We learned a good lesson in the last [federal] election. . . ."

ally the left wing also identified closely with the British Labour party, though naturally with its "Bevanite" faction.)[7]

The invariable debate on "how far" and "how fast" socialism should proceed led to sharply contrasting views about party strategy and organization in addition to programme. The left wing considered the dissemination of socialist doctrine as the CCF's most urgent task, higher in priority than winning elections. A CCF government elected by a public unsympathetic to socialism would not, it believed, succeed in implementing a genuinely socialist programme, a failure which would be disastrous to the socialist cause. Therefore the CCF must regard itself not as "another political party" but as a crusading movement interested in socialism first and power second. The leaders had reversed these priorities and so had lost sight of the party's original objectives. When returned to their proper order, these aims would require a "movement" organized around a small core of the trustworthy, whose deep commitment to socialism would ensure their effectiveness. The speaker below, a campaign manager, expressed this viewpoint forcibly in a conversation on a quiet evening in an election committee room.

Bob: "I'm not sure it wouldn't be a good idea to have a small, disciplined cadre instead of trying to build a mass organization. This way never gets you anywhere. We'll never be elected on this basis. All that happens is that your programme gets as diluted as hell until you're nothing but an advance guard for the Liberal party. That's what's been happening to us for years now.

"No, I'm not in favour of letting every one in. That's our trouble now. Did you see who comes into the committee room to work? Not our members but guys off the street. The trouble with [our riding] is that we're just full of teachers and theorists who just like to talk and never get off their asses when there's work to be done. They're full of ideas about what to do and never do a goddam bit of real work. And most of their ideas are harebrained anyway because they're so out of touch with reality and with how the great mass of the people think and live.

"No, I think a small well-knit group would be a far better idea than our present kind of organization. I think two categories of membership is a damn fine idea.[8] I wouldn't accept these talkers who do nothing as full members."

Betty: "Well, what about the people who just come in and work during the elections and we never see at any other time?"

Bob: "No, them neither. Being a member isn't a game. It's not a game to me—I hate the goddam capitalists—it's a full time, year round job. What I'm afraid of is that the way things are now, by the time we do get to be in a position to implement our programme, it will have become so diluted that we'll be just like the Liberals. That's what's happening

[7]Of the two wings, the left was always the much greater admirer of the Soviet Union.

[8]The conversation had started with my scornful reference to such an organization in the CCF Youth Movement in Quebec a decade earlier.

now. The right wing runs this party and calls all the shots. They run it because they happen to be better organizers."

Author: "Happen to be? Is it an accident? You make it sound that way."

Bob (who is himself a union organizer): "No, it's the labour movement. The unions are usually more right wing in a capitalist society and the union organizers know how to do it. The left wingers just do the talking and the other guys run the party because they're the organizers. They think in terms of how to get more votes.

"Christ, if there's one thing that makes me sick, it's all of these guys who say, 'I'll give you money but I can't do any work.' We don't need their goddam money that badly; to hell with it. Or else [*laughing*], we could take their money but I still wouldn't accept them as full members.

"The organizers are oriented towards getting another hundred votes. Hell, we'll never get elected that way. That's not what most of us joined the CCF for. The great majority didn't join to get more votes. No, I still think a limited membership would be a good idea."

Author: "What would the purpose of such an organization be?"

Bob: "Educational—to educate people."

Betty: "Bob, if you like such an organization, why don't you join the Trotskyites?"

Bob: "I would gladly forsake the CCF and join the Trotskyites except that I don't like being presented with the revealed truth."

Betty: "Don't you agree with Marx?"

Bob: "Oh sure, I think he was a great economist, but I don't agree with everything of his. He's no god."

Betty: "They don't say he is."

Bob: "No, but they imply as much."

Betty: "[My husband] says he wishes that at least they wouldn't quote him on biology."

The right wing, however, contended that the measures enacted by a CCF government would be the most effective way of making Canadians favourable towards socialism and that therefore electoral success must have a very high priority. To obtain that success the party must be as large as possible and organized to achieve maximum efficiency in elections. To the left wing's charges that these arguments were mere rationalizations to conceal an excessive fondness for power, prestige and the conventional social order, the right wing replied scornfully that the former were the "real conservatives." A top leader remarked, in a private conversation,

"You know we can be just as conservative as anyone else and spend our time looking inward instead of outward. We've made Woodsworth a saint and the Regina Manifesto the Scriptures. . . . We've developed such a rigid structure [concerning Woodsworth and the Regina Manifesto] in the course of only twenty five years. . . .

"It's interesting to see that many of those who profess to have little or no use for religion are among those who go furthest in making a religion of it—dogmas, saints, symbols and all the trappings. One of the things I have no use for are the Woodsworth worshippers. There's no doubt he was an unusual person, but he had his failings and weaknesses like all the rest of us. He may have had more courage which was what got him where it did, but I refuse to get down and worship him. And [*heatedly but with a laugh*] the Regina Manifesto! As if we're not as intelligent now as they were then. But it's become sacred and. . . .

"The notion of continually referring to the CCF as a movement doesn't appeal to me. As if there's something to be ashamed of in being a political party. I believe there's much more sense in trying to appeal to lots of decent people [than to be exclusive]. After all, not everybody can be doctrinaire fanatics, can they? I think it's a great deal better to be a downright political party embracing many different people and trying to raise the standards of political knowledge and political morality as widely as possible."

The great problem was how to reach these "decent people." Their closest counterpart in the party, most CCF leaders felt, was the reform-minded rather than the socialist members. The leaders saw the former as the advance guard of many who shared the CCF's objectives but failed to join or even support it because of unwarranted fears of socialism and the party's failure to appeal to them in their own language. To the left wing's arguments that the CCF's first task should be to dispel these false fears, the right wing replied that the public's conception of socialism had become distorted beyond redemption by the many bitter attacks in which it had been lumped together with communism and Hitler's National Socialism. Consequently, insistent emphasis on "socialism" was, in the private words of one top leader, "playing the enemy's game."

"This is heresy. I won't say it, but it's heresy if you question the usefulness of the word socialism. I think that that label on the North American continent does us more harm than good. People may agree with your objectives, but the label socialism can be and has been used to scare them away from you because the term has come to be associated with regimentation. Take Adlai Stevenson, for example. His programme embraces many of the same things as ours does. But he always says, 'This isn't socialism and has nothing to do with socialism.'

"Still the term socialism refers to something of worldwide significance and loyalty. And to question or oppose the use of that label would be construed as lacking in that loyalty. But it's playing the enemy's game. They attach a label to you so that people who want the same things as you do will oppose you. Perhaps there is something to the other view that if you persist, you can explain the true meaning of the word to the people, but . . . ."

This distinctly right wing view can be balanced against the sentiments expressed in a proposed letter to the CCF membership from a number of left wingers who called themselves the "Ginger Group," after the name given to the group of MPs who had helped found the CCF.

DEAR COMRADES,

. . . We in the Ginger Group believe that the CCF would benefit from the existence of a group which would recapture some of the old enthusiasm and missionary zeal we used to have; a group which, through education and constructive action within the party, would activate the rank and file membership to more active participation in our party's affairs, and a more informed and therefore more enlightened attitude toward domestic and world events.

We believe that our conventions should be more democratic; that members of the National Council should not make policy-making statements a day before a convention; that the resolutions committee should not have the power to move concurrence and non-concurrence to club resolutions; that as many riding associations as possible should strive to be represented by elected rather than by appointed delegates. We believe that we should be on guard against any watering down of our essential socialist principles, and keep them in full public view as long range aims alongside any short range reforms which we may advocate for the moment. We believe that we should develop a distinctive foreign policy of our own, instead of "me tooing" the foreign policy of the Liberal government.

We believe that our aims can only be accomplished by working constructively in and through the CCF. We are not a splinter group. We declare that we will never co-operate with any party which seeks to achieve its aims by undemocratic and unconstitutional methods. Our purpose is a constructive one. We hope to arouse the members who are apathetic or bewildered to do some concrete work in their clubs, and to encourage critical thinking by our members toward a stronger CCF, which will take a clearer socialist stand on foreign policy.

We welcome all CCF members in good standing who wish to make "keep left" their watchword and to work with us through education and the building of our clubs, in staying on the road to socialism that Woodsworth followed.

> Yours comradely,
> Executive Committee
> The Ginger Group

It is hoped to hold an all Ontario Meeting within the next few months. If you support our efforts, please write to us:

c/o The Ginger Group
565 Jarvis St. [the address of the CCF Provincial Office]
Toronto 5, Ontario.[9]

The flavour of the disputes between the two factions appears in the following remarks and exchanges, prompted by several controversial resolutions at the Ontario Provincial Convention in 1953. One resolution

[9]Provincial Council, Minutes, Oct. 21, 1950. The Council turned down the Ginger Group's request to have this open letter published (as a paid advertisement) in the *CCF News*, the official organ of the Ontario CCF.

stated: "Resolved that CCF election platforms stress immediate implementation of basic CCF principles and objectives outlined in the First
Term Program, rather than sniping at minor political issues." The debate
on this resolution included the following remarks (each by a different
speaker):

Left Winger: "I wonder if it isn't time for the CCF to stop doing nothing
but pointing to the Russian bear and instead look over our shoulder at the
capitalist wolf."

Prominent Right Winger (genially): "We in [X Riding] consider ourselves
twice as radical and progressive as those old fogies from [Y Riding]. I'm very
fond of the people from [Y Riding], but anything that they can do, our
riding can do and any other group in the CCF can do. Let's not each try
to show that we are the most radical and progressive group in the CCF."

Left Winger: "I am supporting this resolution because we must support
basic socialist principles. It's as simple as that."

Right Winger: "I am against this resolution because it seems to suggest
that some of us are better socialists than others. If there is one perfect
socialist here, then perhaps he can criticize the others. . . . This resolution
infers that some of us are better socialists than others. Socialism means
humanitarianism."

Left Winger: "The job of socialists is not to form governments but to
change people's minds. When a party begins to get concerned about getting
power it becomes cautious and careful."

Other resolutions elicited the following remarks:

Right Winger: "I think that it's the ultimate of conservatism—the ultimate
of conservatism—to say that because we took a stand fifteen years ago we
should never change it."

Left Winger: "I do feel very strongly that we should put before the people
the fact that we are a movement and not just another political party. I'll
give you just one example of what we should do. We should never publish
an advertisement without a quotation from Mr. Woodsworth."

Left Winger: "This convention is the biggest steamroller that has ever
been perpetrated. I notice that every time that there is a controversial
question—one to which the right wing would object [*derisive laughter by
some delegates*], it's referred back [to the Resolutions Committee for re-
drafting]."

Convention chairman (replying to the last speaker): "I won't ask you to
withdraw that remark. But I will ask you to be careful."

The relation between the two groups presents an apparent paradox.
The left wing was on the defensive, its position jeopardized by changing
times and decreasing numbers, but it conducted this defence chiefly by
attacking the right wing. The minority faction was the more frequent
aggressor, precisely because of its minority position. The majority, like
all stronger groups, took less account of its weaker rival. It knew that it

could have its way when it wished, though the minority's clamour, real or anticipated, often had some effect on the course that was chosen.[10] The weaker faction, like all self-conscious minority groups, had to jab and stab to make its voice heard and to prevent itself from being dragged along by the more powerful group.

The struggle between the left and right resembled a boxing match in which the smaller, lighter and more lively fighter, though always attacking, was constantly forced back by his stronger opponent. The contest between these two factions was also constantly on the move, but the relation between them remained essentially unchanged as they traversed a considerable stretch of ground in the direction of the "world."

[10]Although the left wing's view rarely prevailed, it carried at least nominal weight, as the remarks of a Provincial Council member demonstrate. Questioned as to whether the "administration slate" for Provincial Council ever included left wingers, he mentioned several people, "who have been tried but didn't work out—G, J and C. I would vote for C but she's such a trial." He related how C had once persuaded Council to spend half a day in a "soul-searching session not because anyone was in favour of it but because they figured 'all right, let her get it off her chest.' I voted against it because it was a waste of time. You know, everybody showed up for it. No one wanted to be accused of ducking out of it. We talked and talked but of course nothing was accomplished."

III. Structure

ALTHOUGH ITS POLICIES ARE BEST EXAMINED on the national level, the CCF was administered chiefly through its provincial sections. Since most of these were organized rather similarly, at least officially, the discussion of the party's structure will be based on the Ontario Section.

THE BASIC CONSTITUTIONAL STRUCTURE

The basic unit of organization was the riding association; every member belonged officially to the one in his locality. Its membership total determined how many delegates the riding association was entitled to send to the annual Provincial Convention, the supreme governing body in provincial affairs. Affiliated organizations, mainly trade union locals, also sent delegates to the Convention, although they were rarely numerous. The remainder of the Convention consisted of the outgoing Provincial Council, the governing body between conventions.

The Provincial Council was elected by the preceding Convention, although, beginning in 1945, many of the larger ridings and groups of ridings were given direct representation on it. Because the Council met only about five times a year, the day to day administration of CCF affairs was in the hands of its Executive, which the Council chose from its own ranks.[1]

About a dozen standing committees, responsible to the Executive, and the party's salaried staff carried out the great bulk of administrative activities. Although the constitution did not mention these committees, they were always very important. The specific committees varied somewhat but they always included three major ones—Finance, Organization

[1]Nationally, the ridings, the National Convention, the National Council and Executive and the affiliated organizations were linked in much the same way as were the corresponding provincial bodies. The national office usually dealt with the ridings through the provincial offices partly as a matter of convenience, but also to avoid trespassing on the latter's jurisdiction.

and Membership Education. Other committees, such as Trade Union, Farm, Women's, Youth, Ethnic Council and Publicity, did specialized organizational work, while the Literature and Research committees were responsible for special educational tasks.

The party's administrative personnel were mainly voluntary. The exceptions were the clerical staff, the editor of the newspaper and such full-time officials as the Provincial Secretary, the organizers and, latterly, the Provincial Leader. In addition, organizers were employed on a part-time basis or for special jobs. In earlier times, notably the 1930's, some of these positions were filled on a voluntary basis, with expenses reimbursed when possible.

THE TOP LEADERS

The CCF's top officers in every province were the members of the national and provincial executives and councils and the senior salaried officials, many of whom were on these bodies as well. Other important figures were its members of Parliament and of the provincial legislatures, almost all of whom had served on the party's top councils.

The composition and selection of this leadership were not studied in detail, but several aspects are worth noting. First, the overwhelming majority came from the middle class. Of the 152 top officers[2] between 1934 and 1957 who lived in Toronto, all but seven were in "non-manual" occupations. The occupations of the senior officials who lived elsewhere in Ontario were not checked systematically but they seemed to correspond, at least roughly, to the pattern in Toronto.

Although most of these officers were elected rather than appointed, they were chosen in somewhat the same way as cabinets are. Like the government, the party sought to maximize competence and representativeness in its top councils, although each of these objectives necessarily limited the attainment of the other. It wanted acceptable representatives from as many important groups and regions as possible, but especially from the large groups among whom it was very weak, such as French Canadians, Roman Catholics, immigrants and, above all, farmers. Consequently, it tended to cultivate its members from these groups, as the following passage indicates:

One executive member remarked about another, "He's our only Roman Catholic [on the Provincial Executive], and don't forget we're especially

[2]Unless specified otherwise, the term "top officers" refers throughout the study to the members of the Ontario Provincial Council, to the chairmen of its standing committees and to the National Council members who were from Ontario. (Members of the Ontario Provincial Council who were elected by the ridings are excluded on the grounds that they were generally minor figures in the party.)

kind to our only RC and to our only farmer. With most members of the executive, they're listened to only if they have something worth while to say. You don't *have to* listen to them. But with P and E. . . ."

Turning to the subject of French Canadians in the CCF's leadership, the speaker continued, "The largest vote for the position of ———— went to M, though he wasn't present and isn't especially active. But he was the only French Canadian nominated. . . .

"Did you know L? He used to be on National Council. He was a real nut, a rabble rouser and a windbag. At first people found him amusing and entertaining, partly because of his broad French-Canadian accent, but then he became tiresome. You could just see that [the National Leader] was getting more and more annoyed."

A smoother path to the top for some meant a more difficult one for others. For example, so many potential leaders were concentrated in Toronto that their individual chances of "making Council" were slimmer than most. Explaining how one Provincial Council member, whom his colleagues regarded as a tedious nuisance, happened to be on that body, a fellow Council member declared off-handedly, "Outside of Toronto and Hamilton almost anyone can get on the Provincial Council as a riding representative."

THE UNOFFICIAL LEADERSHIP

The unofficial leadership was more homogeneous, more spontaneously chosen and, on the whole, more influential than the official set. The top officers played a major, if indirect, role in selecting both sets of leaders, but they chose the former simply as friends without having to consider either the public or the general membership. Several of these interlocked groups of friends formed the core of the CCF's leadership in Ontario from the mid-1930's and later in the national organization. They had many things in common, of which perhaps the most important for the party were a right wing orientation and close connections with the trade unions.

The innermost of these groups, during the 1950's, comprised, at the outside, a dozen men and their wives, most of whom lived in Toronto. (All, except for some of the wives, were or had been top officers in the provincial and national organizations.) Despite some turnover in personnel, this nucleus remained remarkably intact for over two decades. Similarities in age, education, occupation and interests made friendship easy.[3] In addition, many of the wives were very "active" and had considerable stature of their own in the party. The prominence of women

[3]For a more detailed discussion of the composition of this group see chap. IV, pp. 35–36.

in the CCF and the many avenues of participation that were open to them meant that the personality and activities of a man's wife could affect his standing more than they would have in most organizations and that she was less likely to object to his participation.[4]

Like similar groups in most organizations, this inner circle had neither an official existence nor a formal structure. It did not meet behind closed doors to plot coldly and methodically. It consisted, instead, of top leaders, who were preoccupied with CCF operations and welfare, and whose mutual interests, frequent contact and close friendship made discussions about the party an inevitable and vital aspect of their daily lives. In informal telephone conversations, during sociable evenings and on many other occasions, they arrived at common understandings about the conduct of CCF affairs. In so doing, they maintained a firm hand on the party's direction because these understandings usually found their way into formal proposals to the Executive and Council, many of whose leading members had already formed their opinions in these informal conversations. The virtual certainty that these bodies would ratify the proposals can be attributed more to this network of personal relations than to deliberate manipulation.

The inner circle did not control the party. It was simply the most influential of the various informal groups and it owed much of that influence to its close links, both personal and professional, with several other groups of top CCF leaders whose lives centred less exclusively on the party. The closest and most important of these groups consisted largely of salaried trade union officials mainly from the unions most friendly to the party. The inner circle itself contained no union men except for one of its veteran members who eventually joined the staff of a large and friendly union. A distinction, however subtle, existed between the inner circle and these other groups, as the following indicates:

An inner circle member was asked whether the Ts belonged to the group. [Arthur T was an important leader in the CCF and in the————workers, a friendly major union. His wife was also very active in the party.] The speaker replied that they were not really members of the group and, in answer to another question, tried to explain why.

"Well, somehow they just don't seem to fit in. Nor do the Rs [a couple in an almost identical position]. They're very sociable. Everyone has been to their place but somehow neither they nor the Ts would be at the [Provincial Leader's] unless it was some kind of special occasion.

"On the other hand, the————workers–CCF group would be at an affair at the Gs' [members of the inner circle with closer union connections than most]. But once again, as at all such affairs, the union people would all be the CCF ones. . . . I'm afraid we're a terribly ingrown little group."

[4]See in partial contrast A. Gouldner's discussion of trade union officers and their wives in "Attitudes of 'Progressive' Trade Union Leaders," pp. 389–92.

The inner circle and these closely associated groups were often referred to, sometimes bitterly, as "the administration." This was also an informal body. Probably even its own members could not agree completely on its composition because it coincided with no official body. The administration also maintained a strong guiding hand in CCF affairs. A case in point was its role at the annual conventions. Since the CCF's policies and leaders were officially determined by the Convention, both were theoretically subject to drastic changes on these occasions. Although the party's general consensus ordinarily ensured a predictable Convention, the administration, nevertheless, did what it could to maintain continuity in policy and leadership, regarding the two as inseparable. While this objective did require some conscious planning, its achievement depended much more on the unplanned consequences of the close association and prestige of the administration's members.

The established leadership influenced policy formation at the conventions in various ways. The most direct was by presenting Provincial Council resolutions, most of which had originated in the Executive. These statements were aimed at the public as well, but, as pronouncements of the top official bodies, they were ordinarily assured of overwhelming acceptance by the Convention and they helped to set the tone of its proceedings.

More important was the role of the Resolutions Committee. It was appointed by the Executive (Council and Convention had to approve) to sort and edit all the resolutions submitted to the Convention and to draft composite resolutions in cases of duplication or overlapping. It was also empowered to redraft resolutions which the Convention "referred back" to it. Many of the latter were among the most controversial and had been "referred back" in the hope that the Committee could produce a satisfactory compromise.[5] For many years, the Committee's members or its appointees introduced all resolutions on the Convention floor. But probably its greatest influence stemmed from its authority, which it exercised constantly during those years, to move the acceptance or rejection of resolutions upon their introduction. In so doing, the Resolutions Committee generally expressed the administration's opinion before the debate began.[6]

By dominating the Provincial Council, the administration gained additional strength at the Convention. All Council members had the status of delegates at the Convention and together they constituted from one-

[5]See the last remarks of the Left Winger, chap. II, p. 21.
[6]McHenry reports an essentially similar role for the Resolutions Committee at national conventions. See McHenry, *The Third Force in Canada*, p. 36.

sixth to one-fifth of all the delegates. Because each delegate had only one vote,[7] the administration and its followers theoretically could cast a sizable portion of the Convention ballots themselves. Because many of the Council members were selected directly by the ridings rather than by the Convention, it would be misleading to regard the Council as a monolithic administration body.

At national conventions, a similar, though much less important, result arose from the Provincial Council's practice of circulating lists of members who were available to act as delegates to those ridings which had not selected any.[8] The riding associations could choose representatives from this list, although they were under no obligation to do so. The effect, though probably not the intention, of this procedure was usually to reinforce the administration, since the people chosen to represent the ridings were likely to be sympathetic to it. They were picked more because of their willingness to attend than for their views. But these two attributes often coincided. Some of these members were the wives of CCF leaders, officers or delegates and "would be going anyway" to accompany their· husbands; some were minor officers of the party. They were all drawn to the conventions because of sociability, deep involvement in party affairs or, usually, both. (Unlike the delegate who knew very few CCFers outside his own riding, members closer to the administration were certain to meet many friends and acquaintances.) The result, however unplanned, was some additional support for the administration.

The selection of officers is a matter of some moment in any organization since its future course and their prestige and careers may be involved. The leaders are likely to take whatever steps they believe warranted to protect their position, policies or both. The nominating committee is probably the most common of these methods. The Ontario Convention had no official nominating committee, but there was a *de facto* one which drew up and circulated, more or less openly, what its opponents angrily called "the administration slate."[9] The following

[7]There was no proxy system as in the British Labour party.

[8]The great distances discouraged the less prosperous riding associations from sending delegates to the national conventions.

[9]"The slate" and many of the other ways in which the administration influenced conventions came in for much outspoken criticism from the left wing minority. For a brief summary of some of these grievances, see the second paragraph of the "Ginger Group's" letter, chap. II, p. 20.

A conspicuous exception to this pattern of administration dominance occurred in 1960 when the National Convention rejected a National Council proposal which would have prevented Hazen Argue from becoming full National Leader and, instead, conferred that status upon him. However, on this occasion the administration was itself divided.

comments suggest, however, that unofficial organization existed within both factions at conventions, and give an idea of their relative strength:

Conversation at a table of university students, all left wingers: "so far six out of six [elected] of the administration slate. . . . That's one of our slate." Then turning to an observer, one of them said: "Did you know that there were two slates? There were private caucuses, especially on the part of the administration. They've got the convention sewed up. You saw that even P was defeated. The P group was completely beaten."

Regarding these charges of semi-secret caucusing, a right wing leader remarked in private conversation, "They [the left wing] do maintain some separate organization. At the convention they all supported P and wore buttons which were passed out. They all voted the P ticket as they were told to; so I suppose they do retain some organization among themselves." His lack of concern put him in sharp contrast to the speaker above.

How the administration drew up its "slate" was explained by one of its members.

"Haven't you ever heard of the PAC[10] Room? H [the PAC chairman] makes up the slates and passes them around. He can deliver the union vote. . . ."

Then, answering a question about the operation of the PAC Room, "You know what it was like last night [at a sociable gathering of some inner circle members]. Well, it's the same way—outspoken and uninhibited. They begin with a list of about forty names and then weed out about half."

Questioned as to who was usually present at these sessions, he replied, "Oh, people just drop in. H is there. D and L come around and A, B, C and so on [all members of the inner circle or administration]. [The Provincial Leader] stays away now and so do X, Y and Z." (All these are senior trade union leaders once very active in CCF administrative affairs and still staunch supporters.)

In reply to a question as to what would happen if an outsider to the group showed up, he paused, surprised and slightly puzzled, and said, "I don't know what they would do. It's never happened. People don't just come in by themselves. You've got to be invited. They would make you feel pretty unwelcome. Of course, if you came with me or D or L, that would be different. That would show you were a *bona fide* person. . . .

"If you want to run for Council, you just let H know. Once when I decided to run, I told H at the last moment. He said, 'Why didn't you let me know earlier? The slate's already gone out. I don't know what I can do but I'll try.'

"Actually, the slate isn't really as important as it sounds. I've compared my vote to the slate several times—I voted without looking at the slate—and I've discovered that there's never a difference of more than one or two names between my choice and the slate.

"You know there's really considerable similarity in the thinking of lots of the people at the top not only here but in the other provinces as well, and there really isn't much need for arranging everything in advance." He commented scornfully about R, a right wing Council member who, in discussing the selection of an important committee, implied privately that prob-

[10]The Political Action Committee, set up by the trade unions sympathetic to the CCF.

ably it had already been "arranged." According to the speaker, it hadn't been and it wasn't necessary to do so. Replying to the question, "Did R figure the mysterious 'they' had everything neatly arranged and organized?" he said, "Yes, that's just it. And he, of all people, should have known better."

Later in the conversation, the speaker referred to the slate at national conventions. Asked who chooses it, he replied that it is drawn up mainly by the provincial secretaries. Then, after remarking that Ontario really dominates these conventions, he added, "Usually these people think sufficiently alike that no organization is really required [at national conventions]."

These remarks indicate that, whatever the specific methods of the established leadership, its real power lay much more in its own deeper consensus and close personal relations than in any of its deliberate arrangements.

LOCAL OFFICERS AND THE RANK AND FILE

A survey of the CCF's local officers and general membership in Toronto showed almost no change in the broad occupational pattern between 1945 and a decade later.[11] At both times, the former were evenly divided between "manual" and "non-manual" jobs while almost three-quarters of the latter were in "manual" work. (By comparison, five-eighths of Toronto's male labour force were in "manual" occupations,[12] but almost none of the CCF's top officers.[13])

Tables I and II provide a rough idea of the party's ethnic composition in Ontario and Toronto. The general pattern is one of stability, Anglo-Saxons and Jews being more inclined to become CCF members than were French Canadians or other groups.[14]

[11]The term "local officer" refers to the members of the riding association executive. The survey included all local officers in Toronto in 1945 and in 1956, about 200 in each year.

The general membership figures are based on 20 per cent random samples of the total Toronto membership in 1945 and in 1954. As in the local officer survey, women were classified according to husband's occupation. Unmarried women, constituting about 10 per cent of the membership, were excluded from the samples to permit comparison with Toronto's male labour force. All members of a family living at the same address were counted as one membership so that the samples actually covered more than 25 per cent of the members.

The absence of membership card files prevented occupational and ethnic comparisons to be extended back beyond 1945. Information on occupations came mainly from the *Toronto City Directory*. In the few instances in which it could be checked, the *Directory* proved to be very reliable.

[12]Census of Canada, 1951.

[13]See above, p. 24.

[14]In this connection, see the detailed study of the CCF's local leadership in Saskatchewan in Lipset, *Agrarian Socialism*, chaps. IX and X.

TABLE I*

ETHNIC COMPOSITION OF THE CCF IN ONTARIO, 1951, 1956

| By origins | Population 1951† % | CCF members | |
		1951‡ %	1956§ %
British	67	77	78
French	10	3	4
Jewish	2	5	4
Others	21	16	15

*The accuracy of these figures is very questionable because they were based on guessing the ethnic identity of names. In a few cases, membership in an ethnically organized club was used to establish identity, but these were a small minority. The hazards of this method are too obvious to require elaboration; however, no other seemed available.
†Census of Canada, 1951.
‡Based on a 25 per cent random sample.
§Based on a complete count in which 2 per cent of the members were not classified.

TABLE II*

ETHNIC COMPOSITION OF THE CCF IN TORONTO, 1945, 1951, 1956

| By origins | Population 1951† % | CCF members | | |
		1945‡ %	1951§ %	1956‖ %
British	73	80	80	82
French	3	2	1	1
Jewish	5	8	9	8
Others	19	11	10	9

*See Table I, note *.
†Census of Canada, 1951.
‡Based on a 20 per cent random sample.
§Based on a 25 per cent random sample.
‖Based on a complete count in which 2 per cent of the members were not classified.

PART III

The Changes in the CCF

IV. Protest Movement
1932-41

THE CCF CAME TO LIFE amidst an almost world-wide depression and an emerging threat of war. In Canada, unemployment was at record heights; farm markets had collapsed, and drought, dust and repeated crop failures were devastating the prairies. On all sides, dissatisfaction and questioning of the established social order were mounting. The apparent failure of "capitalist democracy" and the growth of totalitarianism in Europe were polarizing political convictions everywhere towards both the extreme left and right, making each side more militant and determined to destroy the other.

Among the Canadians most deeply stirred by these events were two groups which soon became the nuclei of the CCF. The larger, centred on the prairies, was led by men long prominent in the farmers' movements, particularly the co-operatives and the organizations of political protest.[1] Every aspect of the early CCF, including its name, reflected the background and dominance of this group. Most of its members had previously stopped short of socialism, but the new climate of opinion carried them towards the socialists of the cities, with whom they made common cause against a mutual set of villains, "the exploiting moneyed interests" who, conveniently, were located in the east.[2]

The second, and ultimately dominant, group consisted of a set of young men and women, concentrated in a few large eastern cities, who entered the CCF within its first five years and, at least in Ontario, rapidly took over its control.[3] This group was predominantly Anglo-

[1]See Lipset, *Agrarian Socialism*, chaps. IX and X.

[2]A significant variation on this pattern occurred in Alberta where most of the farmers' top leaders went to the CCF but the rank and file became the backbone of the Social Credit movement. For an account of these events see Irving, *The Social Credit Movement in Alberta*.

[3]Almost identical changes took place in the United States Socialist party at

Saxon, Protestant and middle class. Most were recent university graduates and had first come into contact with socialism and the CCF as students. Many were the children of ministers, chiefly of the United Church. (In the west, however, many Protestant clergymen themselves were among the CCF's most influential leaders.) The group included a noteworthy number of Rhodes scholars, who had become well acquainted with the British Labour party and had been much influenced by the Fabians. Thus, the heritages of the Social Gospel, of British Fabianism and, in some cases, of European radicalism blended in the university atmosphere to become the most formative influence on the future leaders of the CCF.

Occupationally, this group also had much in common. The teachers, welfare workers and children of clergymen were thoroughly familiar with non-profit institutions, which had strong "service" orientations, paid notoriously low salaries, and brought their employees into contact with a wide segment of the public, often with the groups hardest hit by the depression. In addition, many members of this group failed to find attractive jobs. Under these circumstances, their common antipathy to the "profit system" is hardly surprising.

Since they could not find satisfying jobs, the time at their disposal was more plentiful and with family burdens few and their closest intimates equally ardent CCFers, these newcomers to the "movement"[4] were able to plunge whole-heartedly into its activities. Their deep involvement and their concentration in Toronto and Ottawa made them the CCF's most cohesive, stable and influential groups.

The party made a respectable showing in its initial election campaigns. It demonstrated impressive strength throughout the west except in Alberta, where Social Credit had risen even more dramatically.[5] However, whereas in the west, socialism was a long additional step on a familiar road, in the east it constituted a radical departure from the main paths. Consequently, east of the Toronto area the CCF was virtually non-existent. The prevailing view throughout eastern Canada barely distinguished socialism from communism, associated the latter with Bolshevism, and rejected all three as unthinkable. Many were less violently opposed but dismissed socialism as a noble but impractical

---

the same time. They are vividly described by Daniel Bell in "Marxian Socialism [in the United States]."

Among the many striking parallels in the Canadian and American socialist movements during the 1930's were similar amalgams of leadership groups and sources of popular support in the east and west.

[4]Most of its members referred to the CCF by this term during its first period. Some continued to do so after, often deliberately to distinguish it from "party."

[5]For a detailed account of that rise see Irving, *The Social Credit Movement in Alberta.*

dream. Even among the more sympathetic, many doubted that it could ever win a significant following in the east. Allies were negligible; the eastern farmers wanted no part of socialism, and the trade unions, although dissatisfied with their position and that of the industrial worker, either dismissed socialism as the solution or else the CCF as a useful ally.

Under these circumstances, the CCF's initial electoral performances in Ontario were not unpromising. In its first major contest, the provincial election of 1934, it won 7 per cent of the vote and one seat in the legislature. A year later, in its first federal campaign, it gained 8 per cent of the Ontario ballots, one per cent below its national average. However, after 1935, the party registered no further advances anywhere, except in Saskatchewan, until October 1941, when a large gain in British Columbia (where it had polled a plurality of the votes as early as 1935) signalled the start of its nation-wide upsurge. The intervening elections had been particularly depressing for the Ontario Section. In the 1937 provincial campaign, it failed to increase its popular support over that of 1934 and lost its only seat in the legislature, and in its second federal contest, in 1940, it lost considerable ground.

The general climate of opinion, the particular views and characteristics of the CCF's members and the relative weakness of its popular support constitute the starting points for an examination of the CCF's initial viewpoint and structure and the incentives of its members.

IDEOLOGY

No belief bound the new movement together more firmly than did the conviction that capitalism, in the words of the Regina Manifesto, was a "cancer which is eating at the heart of our society." The records of the CCF in Ontario contain not one sympathetic word written or spoken on capitalism's behalf nor the slightest doubt that it would never work again. Instead, with a single voice, CCFers blamed it for the social order's most alarming ailments—war, the depression and the growth of Fascism. Whatever use it had once served, its day was long since done and its "eradication" was urgent. The hazards of that task and the tough-minded resolution it would require were set forth in the following official statement:

. . . every CCF member should insist and understand that in no sense is the socialism of the CCF mere reformism, mere gradualism, or compromise with capitalism of any kind. A CCF government attaining power must proceed promptly, drastically, thoroughly to liquidate the power of capitalist forces and secure for the socialist party in control of the organs of the state the most ample assurance that capitalist interests could not sabotage, weaken or overthrow socialism. The CCF must recognize and prepare for the most ruthless opposition . . . [we] must be fully conscious of the opposition that will seek to destroy our efforts and of the danger of the final stages of the struggle. Anyone who does not understand the nature of the struggle has no place in the CCF as a candidate, delegate, officer of a club or any other position of the most minimum importance. The CCF is on the uttermost left in objective and understanding or it is nowhere.[6]

CCFers strove to match these words with deeds. The movement's newspapers[7] of the 1930's were full of accounts of CCF street corner and other open air meetings, of meetings that were banned, of CCFers who were prominent in organizing the unemployed, of others who led dramatic strikes, some of which resulted in violence and suppression by the police, and of party stalwarts who, despite the depression, defiantly supported the CCF and lost their jobs. The movement scandalized public opinion by its admiration of the Soviet Union,[8] and, most

[6]Report of Executive to Ontario Provincial Convention, 1936.

[7]The Ontario Section's newspaper mirrored the changes which overtook the party. In the CCF's first phase, its name, the *New Commonwealth*, expressed the movement's ultimate goal. Weekly publication and extensive coverage of the political news made it much more like a conventional newspaper than it became later. It was more absorbed in world than in party affairs, and it voiced the outraged minority viewpoint on the issues, such as trade unionism, Fascism and the Spanish Civil War, which split Canada and many other countries.

Very soon after the party's initial success in 1942, the paper's name was changed to *CCF News* and it turned its gaze inward to become a typical house organ. It was published monthly and concentrated almost exclusively on organizational news and views. (Upon the foundation of the New Democratic party, it was renamed the *New Democrat*.)

[8]Under the heading "The Political Situation and Economic Conditions" the Report of the Executive to the 1936 Ontario Convention began its doctrinal section as follows: "There is no independent national political situation. Each national situation may have its own peculiarities, and must be dealt with according to those peculiarities, but in the inter-dependent world of today national political situations as well as national economic conditions reflect the world trends. In attempting to plot the strategy and tactics of a socialist movement, even in one province in one nation, international trends cannot be ignored. For, in the last analysis, they determine the pattern.

"Treating the economic and political conditions together, what are the vital trends that must be weighed in estimating the future course of a socialist movement in Canada, or indeed, for that matter, any other country?

"First, the outstanding political factor in the world today is the economic success of the Union of Socialist Soviet Republics in Russia. No other long-term factor is so potent in its influence. Here is a nation that has, under workers' and socialist government, become one of the greatest industrial powers in the world, that has attained a rate of industrial progress unknown before, and that has ended depressions, mass unemployment and capitalism. Within a decade, to quote Sidney and Beatrice Webb, "the U.S.S.R. will have become the wealthiest country in the world, and at the same time the community enjoying the greatest

provocatively, by its pacifist assertion that Canada must never again go to war "to save the British Empire."

These heresies, coupled with the CCF's general intolerance of the prevailing social order, provoked a reciprocal hostility on the part of the public, which attacked CCFers as "Bolsheviks" or derided them as "crackpots" and "dreamers." But the movement's continued espousal of unpopular causes illustrates its initial reluctance to move with some of the main currents of Canadian opinion.

Despite all this, by accepting the established parliamentary rules as the only appropriate means of attaining power, the CCF had committed itself more deeply to "the world" than most of its founders and early members perhaps realized. It had thereby placed its fate entirely in the hands of the voters and from then on it steadily intensified its efforts to reach them. When it did, it had to persuade them not only that its policies had merit but, often more difficult, that its voice would be strong enough to be heeded.[9]

Throughout its first phase, which coincided with the depression, the CCF's main appeal to the public was that "poverty in the midst of plenty" was indefensible because socialism made it unnecessary. Although the opportunity to prove that belief by winning office was nowhere in sight, the movement, nevertheless, insisted that every CCF vote counted. Like any party it dramatized the choice between itself and its rivals as a contest between good and evil, but like minor parties without hope of immediate victory, it assured the public that a substantial CCF vote would be the sharpest prod to a callous government.

However, many CCFers, especially in the east, where victory was very remote, gave only qualified approval to this approach. Socialism, to them, meant not so much a specific set of reforms as a totally different way of life that had to be grasped at the root to be understood. To disseminate that understanding to "the masses," small élites must first receive a "basic socialist education." Thus, in characteristic evangelical

aggregate of individual freedom." Add to this fact the success of socialist democracies, using parliamentary methods, such as Sweden, Norway and Demark, and there is unanswerable enduring proof that socialism can create at once security and freedom."

[9]The *raison d'être* of any organization combines its policies and prospects. Since support is always solicited on both grounds, they constitute the twin threads of analysis of the CCF's changing appeals to the public. For convenience, this combination will be called "strategy," although the word often suggests greater manœuvrability than is ordinarily possible at this level.

Organizations do, of course, speak differently to the public than to their own members. But the maintenance of radically divergent public and private objectives requires an authoritarian and conspiratorial structure far removed from that of the CCF.

fashion, these members were more interested in people's inner convictions than in their outward behaviour, in conversions rather than
votes, and, consequently, in intensive work with small groups rather
than in superficial contact with the general public.

Perhaps the most specific gauge of a party's "socialism" is its official
policy on social ownership. The belief in social ownership as the key
to the classless society has always distinguished socialist from reform
parties, and the CCF's advocacy of such a policy was long its chief
badge of identity. Nevertheless, the official statements on this issue
reveal that it was always a delicate one. Their invariable vagueness
stemmed partly from the leaders' reluctance to tie their hands before
taking office but also from a desire for unity. Ambiguity gave them
room to manœuvre in office, on the public platform and in internal party
debates. If general statements shunned specific commitments to nationalization, they also avoided specific exemptions, and gave the critics
on either side little solid ammunition.

Divided opinions and the general temptation to speak cautiously on
social ownership doubtless explain the cloudy inconsistency of the
passages from the Regina Manifesto, the national party's strongest
socialist pronouncement, which, though they have already been quoted,
may usefully be repeated here for the purpose of illustration. The Manifesto opened on a clear note:

> The C.C.F. is a federation of organizations whose purpose is the establish-
> ment in Canada of a Co-operative Commonwealth in which the principle
> regulating production, distribution and exchange will be the supplying of
> human needs and not the making of profits.
> *We aim to replace the present capitalist system*, with its inherent injustice
> and inhumanity, by a social order from which the domination and exploita-
> tion of one class by another will be eliminated. . . . [italics added]

And it concluded on even more unequivocal terms: "No C.C.F. Government will rest content until it has eradicated capitalism and put into
operation the full programme of socialized planning which will lead
to the establishment in Canada of the Co-operative Commonwealth."
But its intermediate passages were more moderate; one specified quite
clearly that "we believe that these evils can be removed only in a
planned and socialized economy in which our natural resources and the
principal means of production and distribution are owned, controlled
and operated by the people" (italics added), a view with which the
sections on social ownership and finance agree.

This exegetic procedure, however tedious, illuminates the division
and uncertainty in the CCF from the very beginning regarding "how
fast" and "how far" the march of socialism should proceed. Although

the party could never take a stand on this issue that was both clear and united, the milder of these approaches marked its eventual path.

STRUCTURE

What form should the new movement take best to pursue its high ideals? Should it seek a large membership of men of goodwill and a substantial vote in the hope of effecting immediate improvements? Or should it try to forge small, tight bands of thoroughgoing socialists capable of giving leadership on a perhaps more distant and tumultuous occasion when the way would be open for revolutionary changes?

A minority, it will be recalled, warned that a party of the conventional form would either become mired in a parliamentary morass or, if it escaped that trap, would be defenceless against the ruthlessness of its now desperate foes. Political "realism" dictated the creation of a more effective instrument, towards which Lenin's model of tightly disciplined élites might be a useful guide.

But if some opposed the conventional party structure as too weak, even more rejected it as too strong. The latter included many of the influential agrarian leaders whose movements for popular democracy had reflected the west's endemic suspicion of parties and the party system as agents of eastern and capitalist exploitation. Political parties, they argued, thwarted democracy and change because, in their desire for power, they stifled the expression of the popular will by curbing the freedom of its parliamentary spokesmen.[10] Therefore, although these western agrarians seconded the left wing's repudiation of "party," they advocated a more, rather than a less, "democratic" alternative. Instead of a keenly honed instrument of revolutionary violence, they proposed

[10]Less than a decade earlier, this aversion to the centralized controls of party had led to the disintegration of the Progressive party, one of the CCF's antecedents. In dissociating themselves from the Progressive caucus, a number of its MPs, some of whom later helped to found the CCF, explained, "There was, we believe, nothing further from the minds of our constituents than the building of another party machine on the model of the old. . . . there are two species of political organization—one the 'Political Party' that aspires to power, and in so doing inevitably perpetuates that competitive spirit in matters of legislation and government generally which has brought the world wellnigh to ruin; the other is the democratically organized group which aims to co-operate with other groups to secure justice rather than to compete with them for power. It is as representatives of this latter type that we take our stand. . . ." Open letter, undated, to the *U.F.A.*, July 2, 1924, pp. 12–13, as quoted in Morton, *The Progressive Party in Canada*, p. 195.

How these views contributed to the Progressive party's disintegration is described fully by Morton in the same book. For thorough accounts of this general viewpoint, see also Macpherson, *Democracy in Alberta*; Rolph, *Henry Wise Wood of Alberta*; and Sharp, *The Agrarian Revolt in Western Canada*.

the traditional prairie solution, a popular movement of such magnitude as to make peaceful and orderly change irresistible.

Some of the CCF's founders and early adherents favoured still another form of organization. As admirers of the Labour and Social Democratic parties, they were not against parties *per se*, and they considered these to be appropriate models. Their view prevailed in the long run, but it was the agrarian stand that governed the founders, who, accordingly, created a loosely connected body. The first CCF Constitution described that body's aim and form as follows:

The object of the Federation shall be *to coordinate* the activities of member organizations in order to promote through political action and other appropriate means the establishment in Canada of a Co-operative Commonwealth. . . .
Membership in the Federation shall consist of approved provincial organizations which accept the Co-operative Commonwealth Federation Program.[11]

A decentralized structure, the founders hoped, would help to achieve a broad, popular and genuinely democratic movement because local autonomy would simultaneously encourage rank and file participation and avoid the central domination which was allegedly the scourge of the other parties. Accordingly, the CCF's initial constitutions, national and provincial, designed formal machinery with these ends in view. They set up clubs in order to maximize the general membership's participation, required annual conventions to ensure its control, and limited the role of the central bodies, composed of the representatives of the component units, to "co-ordinating" or "correlating" the activities of these units, which thereby retained considerable autonomy. An editorial in a newspaper sympathetic to the CCF explained, "The new movement is not a political party, it is a federation of groups which in their own sphere retain their autonomy and identity, but in support of a common national program, which will make common cause from coast to coast."[12] J. S. Woodsworth expressed a similar view in the following letters:

It is absurd to say that the CCF Clubs constitute a new political party. Some have taken the ground that the CCF itself was a new party. Strictly speaking it was only a federation in which each party or group maintains its identity. The CCF Clubs were organized simply as a third group which, together with Farmer and Labor, would constitute the federation in Ontario.

[11]Constitution of the CCF, adopted at the First National Convention, Regina, July 1933, (italics added).
[12]Editorial, "People Want a Radical Change," *U.F.A.*, Dec. 1, 1932, p. 3, quoted in Morton, *The Progressive Party in Canada*, p. 282.

The proposed constitution [for Ontario] would recognize individual membership in the CCF. This, in my judgment, is not in harmony with the Constitution as adopted at Regina.[13]

The desire for local autonomy doubtless reflected another invariable aspect of the federation process—the prior existence of separate organizations[14] reluctant to surrender their viewpoints and identities completely and not free from mutual suspicion.[15] But, however mixed the founders' motives were, they led to the same conclusion—opposition to central control.

That conclusion became apparent almost at once in Ontario, to which we now turn for a more detailed picture of the CCF organization in the 1930's. The life of the federated structure in Ontario was singularly short and unhappy. Conceived in November 1932, it lay demolished sixteen months later. It began as a loose alliance of three bodies, the Ontario Labor Conference,[16] the Associated CCF Clubs[17] and the once

[13]Woodsworth to Ald. John Mitchell, later Ontario CCF President, March 31, 1933; and to Arthur Mould, Chairman of the Labor Conference of Ontario, Oct. 2, 1933.

[14]The founding meeting in Calgary was the annual one of the Western Conference of Labour Political Parties, described by Lewis and Scott (*Make This Your Canada*, p. 117) as a "co-ordinating body of the various farmer and labour parties in the west. [It was] composed of the Socialist Party of British Columbia, the Canadian Labour Party, the Dominion Labour Party of Alberta and the Independent Labour parties of Saskatchewan and Manitoba. In 1931 the Conference decided to invite representatives of farmer groups. The 1932 convention of the United Farmers of Alberta . . . made a similar decision to cooperate with labour. In the . . . same year Saskatchewan political labour, under the leadership of M. J. Coldwell, and the farmers, under the leadership of G. H. Williams, formed the Saskatchewan Farmer-Labour Party." Lewis and Scott were, respectively, CCF National Secretary and National Chairman when they wrote *Make This Your Canada* in 1943.

The following groups were represented at the Calgary Conference (see Minutes, Aug. 1932), although not all affiliated subsequently: *Alberta*, United Farmers of Alberta, Canadian Labour party, Dominion Labour party; *British Columbia*, Socialist party of Canada; *Manitoba*, Independent Labour party; *Saskatchewan*, United Farmers of Canada (Saskatchewan Section), Independent Labour party, Cooperative Labour party; *National*, Canadian Brotherhood of Railway Employees.

[15]"There was unavoidable suspicion and strangeness [at the Calgary Conference]. There were provincial parties which had achieved some political success and were determined to retain their identity. There were differences in social philosophy, ranging all the way from pure reformism to doctrinaire socialism." Lewis and Scott, *Make This Your Canada*, p. 119.

[16]It included the Socialist party of Canada (Ontario Section) and the Ontario Labor party, consisting largely of trade unionists.

[17]These clubs, which began to form in the various provinces as early as 1932, constituted the beginning of a non-affiliated type of organization. They were not, however, envisioned in the original plans for the new federation and were at first affiliated bodies themselves because there was no other basis of membership.

powerful United Farmers of Ontario, the last affiliating without accepting the full CCF programme.

Within a year, mutual suspicion turned into outright accusation. The UFO, in some alarm, charged the Ontario Labor Conference with, in effect, being "soft on Communism," more precisely, with failure to discipline leaders who allegedly were prominent in Communist party front organizations. The CCF Clubs' leaders sided with the UFO, but a Labor Conference faction retaliated with a sharp attack of its own. It criticized the formation and imperialistic ambitions of the CCF Clubs —names of potential recruits should have been turned over to the existing bodies, it claimed—and denounced the CCF Clubs' leaders as middle class and anti-labour.[18] Letters flowed back and forth between all three organizations and J. S. Woodsworth, to whom all appealed as a mediator. Their letters grew more frequent and agitated; his, though concerned, remained calm and firm. Finally, concluding that the conflicts were irreconcilable, the National Council first suspended and then dissolved the Ontario Provincial Council and immediately called a new Provincial Convention to reorganize the CCF in Ontario.[19] In the meantime, the UFO had reached the end of its long tailspin from the political heights by withdrawing permanently from the CCF and political life.

TABLE III

CCF MEMBERSHIP IN ONTARIO, 1934–41*
(Total in June,† 1945 = 100)

1934	16
1935	26
1936	15
1937	12
1938	9
1939	12
1940	13
1941	8

*The figures for the entire first period are not very reliable. For some years several sets exist, none of which inspires great confidence. This casual attitude to the keeping of records seems to be typical of new organizations.

†All figures are for June, except those of 1934 and 1941, which are for April, the nearest month to June for which figures were available.

The Ontario Section of the CCF was reorganized at once (April 1934) on a basis which remained fundamentally unchanged until the end.[20]

[18]Toronto Labor party statement, issued in 1933; no further date given (from the Archives in the National CCF Office, Ottawa).

[19]The above history of the initial CCF organization in Ontario is based on documents in the Archives of the National CCF Office, Ottawa.

[20]See the description in chap. III, pp. 23–24.

Membership in the new body grew quickly (see Table III), rising to a peak of 7,500 by the end of 1935. But it declined abruptly immediately thereafter, an indication that the movement's initial impetus was spent. By September 1938, two-thirds of the clubs which had existed in 1935 were reported defunct,[21] and by 1941, just before the CCF's great upsurge, its membership in Ontario sank to the lowest point in its entire history.[22]

Finances were a constant and desperate problem throughout the first period but especially after the serious decline in membership. The new movement began without funds and, for years, staggered from one financial crisis to the next under an accumulating load of debt. The following excerpts from its minutes[23] are typical:

Jolliffe accepted the position as Provincial Campaign Manager for the federal election. . . . [He was] allowed $10 a week as and when available.

The Provincial Executive set the following salary scale: Provincial President $15 per week; Provincial Secretary $7.50 per week; Assistant Secretary $5 per week; Stenographer $5 per week.

Financial Situation of Ontario CCF. The Secretary explained that the finances of the movement were in an extremely low state, there being approximately $15 in the treasury and pressing debts amounting to over $300; that the pledges as well as the Provincial Office dues were falling considerably in arrears and needed close attention; that many of the pledges were not renewing their pledges and so the revenue of the CCF was gradually decreasing, while there were very few new pledges being added to the list to counteract those dropping out; that if this state of affairs continued much longer, it might become necessary to close up the office and that therefore something drastic had to be done; that organization work had to be done and done now if Ontario was to be ready to do its proper share in respect to the coming federal election and that money had to be found for this purpose also; that both the New Commonwealth and the Stafford Printers were sadly in need of efficient business managership if they were to be maintained.

The shortage of money and the loose structure tended to perpetuate each other. Without a tighter organization, money was hard to collect, but without money, it was difficult to tighten the organization.

The movement's poverty and general weakness can, however, also be attributed to the absence of strong allies. The trade unions, whose support was so important to social democratic parties elsewhere, were, on the whole, neither strong nor sympathetic to the CCF. Many individual trade unionists were members of the party, but no union bodies

[21]Provincial Council, Minutes, Sept. 6, 1938.
[22]For the entire membership record of the Ontario CCF, see Figure 1, p. 110.
[23]Provincial Council, June 30, 1935, Provincial Executive, Aug. 9, 1937, and Aug. 22, 1938, respectively.

were formally associated with it. Most of the unions were AFL—the CIO unions were just beginning—and the Canadian trade union movement in general was torn between the conflicting British and American union traditions regarding political action. Nor were all CCFers anxious for such an alliance. Many on both the left and right opposed trade unions affiliating as bodies on the grounds that the CCF would become as conservative and union-dominated as the British Labour party. They proposed instead that the CCF continue to welcome trade unionists, but only as individual members. However, a majority eagerly sought closer relations with the unions. One reason was the desire for financial support:

a precondition to an adequate financial position [is] to secure the regular support of organized labor. The Finance Committee realizes that this has long been the endeavour of the CCF. . . . They cannot emphasize too strongly, however, the importance which they attach from the financial side to securing this support.[24]

Weakness and poverty, however trying, were not the most aggravating of the difficulties which beset the early CCF. Rejected by the world, the movement turned in on itself, and its senior administrative bodies became more preoccupied with handling internal dissension than with any other single activity. On countless occasions, year after year, the Provincial Council and Executive were called upon to arbitrate disputes, consider charges, conduct hearings or defend or rescind expulsions, and, whatever their decision, some animosity against the "provincial office" was inevitable.

The problem arose in part from the CCF's peculiar structure and relatively weak central controls. The basic constitutional units were clubs. Although each of these had a territorial base, many constituencies contained more than one but had no co-ordinating body. The result was a lack of concerted effort at elections and many jurisdictional and ideological battles within ridings as well as much friction and irritation which never reached the official record. Commenting many years later on the existence of two clubs in her riding during the 1930's, a long-time CCF officer said, "The people in the south [of the riding] had no use for the group in the north—they thought they were a bunch of snobs. And the group in the north felt that the others were just a bunch of ragtag and bobtail."[25]

24Provincial Executive, Minutes, Oct. 19, 1940.
25The subsequent merging of the two clubs into one riding association undoubtedly alleviated some problems, but the formation of groups on a purely territorial basis, especially where the members were of very different social

Of the various sources of internal dispute, one, however, over-shadowed all the rest, the question of co-operation with "other pro-gressive groups" or, more simply, with the Communists. No issue aroused as much animosity between the CCF's two wings as this one invariably did, and, in the 1930's, it was forever in the forefront. Its prominence, intensity and duration and its illumination of the CCF's authority struc-ture warrant a thorough examination of this expression of factionalism.

After this issue had contributed to the wrecking of the CCF's initial organization in Ontario, the Communists' violent attacks upon the CCF and social democracy in general left a wide gap between the two parties. But a world-wide reversal of Communist strategy in 1935 intensified the internal strife in the CCF. The Communists abruptly ceased attack-ing other left wing groups and, instead, called for a United Front with all "progressive forces," as the recipients of these overtures were sud-denly renamed. Although these persistent, coaxing appeals were rejected indignantly by the CCF's official bodies, they did attract many members and thereby alarmed or infuriated many more. The passages below cover one brief period in the recurrent factional struggle which centred on the question of the United Front:

On April 11, 1936 the Provincial Council instructed all CCF units not to participate in an organization which had been set up to celebrate May Day.

About a month later, a "Continuing Committee" of CCFers issued a statement, "May Day in Toronto", which defended participation in the 1936 May Day celebration and attacked the Provincial Council for prohibiting participation and for expelling the participants. The statement explained, "The issue is much greater than that of disobedience to an official order. It is not the maintaining of 'discipline'. It goes right to the very foundation principle of the CCF movement.

"Is the CCF to become simply another political 'party', with a party 'machine' that demands party 'regularity'? Or, shall we assume our rightful place in the leadership of the cause of social justice? Shall we establish comradeship with the exploited class through joining with them in their aspirings and strivings? Or shall our efforts be to build an organization?"

The June 15th Provincial Council meeting received a letter from a club in one of the larger ridings stating its intention to cooperate with the Com-munist Party "when we think it is in our best interest to do so". The same Council meeting heard an appeal from the units which had been expelled for May Day cooperation with the Communists. The minutes report:

". . . After considerable discussion, the following resolution was moved . . .: We, the Provincial Council of the CCF after hearing the delegation

---

position, created many others. In the case above, for example, closer association did not necessarily lead these groups to change their opinions of each other. The more significant consequences of this change are discussed in subsequent chapters.

representing the expelled units and reading their statements submitted in writing to the Provincial Council, herewith reaffirm our previous decision and maintain the expulsions, but, in view of the possibility that the members of the said units acted in good faith though mistakenly, we wish the delegation to be informed that we shall welcome back into the movement those units that have been expelled, if, on application for affiliation, they reaffirm their loyalty to the CCF and agree to abide by the policy and decisions of the CCF. . . . Carried."

The United Front debate dominated the next two Provincial Council meetings on Aug. 2 and Sept. 5. There were further hearings and expulsions. At the latter meeting the following resolutions were carried:

"Co-operation with other Organizations. After considerable discussion, the following resolution was finally moved . . .: CCF units may extend or accept invitations to participate in economic action and immediate issues provided that such invitations are not to or from other political parties and that they are on immediate issues of a non-permanent character.

". . . that the following be added to the above resolution: This Council feels strongly that such co-operation with other organizations is not the best policy to pursue permanently and is only a temporary measure until such time as our organization has developed its own machinery to handle these matters so that the CCF becomes the focal point for the attack and defence of the working class."

On the question of co-operation on May Day, the following resolution was adopted . . . "That our units may, if they so desire, participate in May Day demonstrations brought into being by a neutral non-partisan committee providing that the general policy of the Provincial Council is followed in such participation; and in the event of such participation, our units are instructed to insist on no political banners being carried or displayed."[26]

The continuing struggle between the two factions over the United Front appears in the following characteristic resolutions submitted to the Provincial Convention in April 1939.

Be it therefore resolved that we call upon the National Convention to the end that Ontario CCF units can be permitted when it is expedient to co-operate politically with all democratic and progressive organizations with a view to combatting the reactionary drive of Hepburn, Duplessis, Drew, and their gold and power baron masters.

Spadina North CCF

Be it resolved that where one or more [labour] candidates are available to contest a parliamentary or municipal seat, in addition to a CCF candidate, the CCF take the initiative in endeavouring to arrive at a mutual arrangement whereby the strongest left wing candidate will enter the field unopposed by the others, and that this resolution be forwarded by the Provincial Council to the National Convention for consideration.

Danforth CCF

[26]The portions within quotation marks are from Provincial Council, Minutes, April 11, June 15, Aug. 2, Sept. 5, 1936.

(a) The CCF, Ontario Section, reaffirms its policy of prohibiting the co-operation of its affiliated groups, or members thereof, with the Communist or any other parties in Federal, Municipal, or Provincial elections.
(b) The CCF, Ontario Section, forbids any of its affiliated groups, or members thereof, to extend to or accept from the Communist Party any invitation to co-operate on any specific matter, political or otherwise.
(c) This convention instructs the Provincial Council to expel any CCF member or group which violates the provisions of this resolution.

Provincial Executive

The protracted bitterness which this issue inevitably aroused, especially when combined with accusations of responsibility for the CCF's failure, pervaded an exchange in the *New Commonwealth*, which is given here partly in summary and partly in direct quotation. (The United Front, though not mentioned until the end, was indirectly involved in the whole controversy.)

In a letter to the editor, two members, Temple and Shaw, described the CCF in Ontario as ailing seriously and concluded that neither the Regina Manifesto nor the Ontario membership was to blame. They then asked, "What of the leadership? Is it progressive? This question should be seriously considered by all clubs in view of the forthcoming Provincial Convention." They recommended a constitutional provision "preventing any leading executive position being held by the same member for more than two years . . . to insure new blood, new ideas to our movement" (Feb. 1938).

On March 5, Carrol Coburn defended the leaders in an editorial in the same paper. "The letter from Comrades Shaw and Temple," he wrote, ". . . is one which deserves the most serious consideration of all loyal CCF members. Undoubtedly there is something seriously wrong with our party in Ontario. A stagnant and apathetic membership is the unmistakable sign of decay. However, their remedy is one with which I cannot agree; nor will it, I believe, be acceptable to the great majority of our membership. . . .

"Is our membership here as enthusiastic and as well-informed as it must be if the CCF in Ontario is to develop into a strong, aggressive, working-class party? I am afraid the answer must be definitely no." To support this view, he cited the failure of the clubs to live up to their pledges, in contrast with the devotion of the top leaders. "To quote Karl Marx: 'The emancipation of the working class is the historic task of the workers themselves.' Leadership is not imposed from above. In a strong and vital movement it surges up in a sweeping flow from below. That flood, in the CCF today, has fallen to a miserable trickle. It is easy to condemn our leaders, to demand that they be replaced. But till we ourselves are prepared to bear the portion of the task, no leader can bear it for us. The fault is ours—and we alone can correct it."

In the next issue of the paper, March 12, a letter from Rev. Ben Spence concluded with the following proposal: "May I suggest therefore that one of the things the CCF needs is a more thoroughgoing democracy and less dictatorship, more guidance and less issuance of orders, more inspiration and less attempt at suppression, more freedom of action to the units [clubs] and less interference with their activities."

Two weeks later Coburn replied in a letter that the issue was and had been the United Front, which Shaw and Temple promptly denied in the next issue. The controversy grew steadily in bitterness and in the number of people who became involved; it included an editorial attacking the attackers, i.e., Temple, Shaw and the others who had sided with them.

The CCF's leaders were inclined to describe the Communist party as more of a pest than a menace to their own. But throughout the history of the CCF, the great majority in the party dreaded nothing more than the public's association of socialism with communism and of the CCF with the Communist party, a fear made all the greater by the latter's frequent and public appeals for close relations between the two parties. Although the CCF peevishly shunned each embrace of this embarrassing suitor, not all of its members were repelled, and every response produced alarm and disruption. Whether greater formal control over its branches would have reduced the number or seriousness of these occasions is open to question. But, in any case, the CCF's leadership grew increasingly convinced that "something had to be done" about them.[27]

The structure of a popular movement created many problems for an organization seeking power by the conventional means. In his Report as National Secretary in 1935, M. J. Coldwell wrote,

"My year's experience as Secretary-Treasurer leads me to believe that if we are to conduct our educational and political campaign efficiently, our affiliated bodies will have to cooperate more closely with the National Office. I realize, of course, that is to some extent due to the fact that we are a Federation rather than an organized party, and consequently our provincial organizations are to a very large degree self-contained and autonomous."

These remarks had been preceded by a lament about the lack of funds and the failure of the provincial bodies to contribute adequately.[28]

The chief problems, besides inadequate finances, were policy clashes in public, inconsistent practices and inefficiency in elections. The loose federal structure not only made the financing of the central apparatus haphazard but gave that body little power. The consequent local autonomy resulted in frequent embarrassment for the national organization, since the provincial sections felt free to go their separate ways, and for the latter as well because they encountered similar problems on the local level. Attempts by the senior bodies to impose a unified policy on their "erring" branches led to angry charges of dictatorial interference.

[27]See chap. v, p. 66.
[28]National Council, Minutes, Nov. 30, 1935.

These problems of maintaining unity plagued the movement through-out its first period and were largely responsible for the sequence of organizational change which followed. Indeed, much of the CCF's ad-ministrative history consisted of efforts to weld it into a single, cohesive organization nationally[29] and to strengthen the central controls within the provincial sections and even at the constituency level.

Thus, in so far as they had rejected the established political system, the CCF's founders had designed a structure that differed from the conventional ones. But, by accepting the fundamental rules of that system, they set the new movement on a course which brought that structure ever closer to these others.

INVOLVEMENT

Membership involvement requires a special mode of investigation. To discover an organization's official policies or structure, including its members' formal obligations to it, one need only consult its constitu-tion or the words of its official spokesmen. But these sources tell little about the members' actual feelings about the group. Although their formal obligations to it may be identical, one member may see the organization as the way to the millennium, deserving everything he can give it, while another may have to be reminded annually that he belongs, and still others may fall anywhere between these extremes. The significance of these orientations for any organization is obvious. But they are hard to perceive directly and must instead be inferred from the nature and extent of the members' participation in the group. Par-ticipation is an especially sensitive index of involvement in voluntary organizations because, as their name implies, it is free from external constraints, such as force or "necessity."

A new social movement usually revolves about groups which maintain their zeal despite the absence of public support. They combat discourage-

[29]In this respect, the CCF's history roughly paralleled that of the British Labour party. This process occurred much more quickly and easily in the CCF, but the latter did not have the Labour party's problem of welding the trade unions and socialist groups into a single body.

The original terms of union adopted by the two parties are strikingly similar; the CCF's founders were undoubtedly familiar with those of the Labour party and may have decided to adopt or adapt them. In both instances, the central organization was initially regarded as little more than the co-ordinating body of the semi-autonomous groups. There was a sharp difference, however, in the aims expressed by the two founding bodies. The CCF adopted a socialist objective, while the socialists on the Labour Representation Committee (out of which the Labour party grew) reluctantly settled for a much milder statement of aims as the price of the trade unions joining the committee.

ment by recalling that beliefs which appear radically new always meet strong resistance at first, even though they express the oldest and simplest truths. But since these truths embody a transcendent purpose, they will inevitably succeed. These kinds of convictions and the incentives which they generate have been called "sacred morale"[30] by Herbert Blumer.

The [sacred] goal represents the primary as well as the ultimate value in life; its achievement becomes a matter of irrevocable duty and of divine injunction . . . this type of morale is to be found most noticeably in the case of religious sects and movements. From the early Christian bands down to the contemporary Jehovah's Witnesses there have been innumerable instances of sectarian groups showing the most dogged persistence in the face of ridicule, punishment, hardship, deprivation, assault, and loss of life. This attachment to a sacred objective may be found also in the case of certain reform movements—more frequently in the case of revolutionary parties. . . .

Since the goal is sacred, people have a conviction of its supreme rectitude which renders them impervious to critical reflection upon its character or value. Since the goal is sensed as supremely perfect and accordingly in harmony with the true nature of the universe, people are convinced that its attainment is inevitable. Obstacles, delays, reversals, defeats and frustrations become merely the occasion for renewed effort just because ultimate success is bound to occur. Finally, there is the conviction of being intrusted with a sacred mission. Because of the supreme value of the goal, because of the divine sanction which it implies, the people attached to the goal feel a sacred responsibility for its realization. They have a cause. They feel themselves to be a select group, especially chosen to execute a transcendental mission. With such convictions and self-conceptions a group is likely to develop an amazing determination in its quest and a striking cohesion in its ranks.[31]

Outrage with the existing order, a vision of its indescribably perfect successor, certainty about how its inevitable arrival can be hastened, and the anguished feeling that almost no one is listening but the enemy —these are the ingredients which, when combined, engender in a man the rousing and buoyant self-image of rebel, prophet, and selfless, persevering servant of mankind. They transform his fellows into his "comrades,"[32] in feeling, not merely in name, and kindle within the group that warm sense of minority solidarity that is its main source of cohesion.

Not all of the original CCFers shared these feelings. Many apparently counted on rapid success, as a sharp decline in membership after the

[30]The terms "involvement" and "morale" are used as interchangeably as possible throughout this study.

[31]Blumer, "Morale," pp. 220–21.

[32]This form of address was very common in the CCF throughout the first period but fell rapidly into disuse thereafter except among left wing members.

1935 election shows. But, to the more committed, the election results were disappointing rather than disillusioning. What country had ever rushed to embrace socialism, they asked. Had not every successful movement endured years of almost total rejection in the beginning? Thus sustained in their faith and freed by their personal circumstances from other commitments, these pioneers gave themselves fully to their cause and saw in every gain, however small, a further sign of its inexorable advance.

For a few, indeed, the CCF was virtually all-encompassing. At one point, the Ontario Executive reported that "the full-time permanent staff at headquarters had consisted of [twelve members]. . . . The only charge for the services of these officers has been $15 a week for the Provincial Secretary, $6 a week for the assistant, and lunch and carfare for the stenographer."[33] Many others in the small band also found the movement so close to the centre of their lives that no clear distinction existed between politics, sociability, entertainment and even work. The CCF membership card was a low cost ticket of admission to all four. A former member of that group characterized its involvement most succinctly when she concluded her reminiscences with the remark, "For us the CCF was mother, father and the church."

INITIAL CHANGES

Towards the end of its initial phase, the party began to undergo major changes. The outbreak of war in September 1939 brought the first significant policy shift—reversal is more accurate—and probably the most important one in the CCF's history, the abandonment of pacifism. Pacifism had always been opposed by a substantial minority. In the war's first weeks, this issue divided the party seriously—many feared it would split—as J. S. Woodsworth, the National Leader, headed a strong pacifist minority. The debate on the war policy in the National Council, immediately preceding Canada's entry, was long and painful.[34] The difficulty in arriving at a compromise acceptable to both groups is clear in the selections below, which catch the CCF's changing attitude to the war in mid-passage.

A "Special Bulletin" was issued by the National Secretary on Sept. 12, 1939, explaining the issuance of the National Council's statement of war

[33]Report, 1936, p. 13.
[34]For more detailed accounts of these events see McNaught, *A Prophet in Politics* and MacInnis, *A Man to Remember*. Both are biographies of J. S. Woodsworth.

policy. Sent to National Council members, provincial officers, and the CCF press, it stated that Woodsworth remained president with the unquestioned support of every section of the movement: "The National Council statement nowhere expresses support of Canada's entry into the war. It was based on the assumption that Canada had been committed to a war policy by the government and then proceeded to outline the limits and conditions which should govern Canada's assistance to the allies."[35]

The following passage elaborates these views and difficulties:

The National Secretary gave an account of the National Council meeting of Sept. 6 and 7 and presented the statement on Canada and the present crisis.[36]

The Council, in his opinion, had made a mistake in not taking a definite stand in opposition to Canada's entry into the war, as asked by Mr. Woodsworth. The overwhelming majority of the delegates would, he believed, have voted against participation if a vote had been taken on that issue.

Over-simplification in analyzing the character of the war should be avoided. To brand the war as purely imperialist would imply that all the Socialists of Great Britain, France and Poland were completely wrong. It is significant that there was no split in the Socialist ranks in these countries as there had been in 1914. Our opposition to the war was not on the ground that we are Socialists, but that we are *Canadian* Socialists.

The most effective way of showing the Canadian people what our policy means is a well organized campaign against our expeditionary force, against profiteering and against infringements on civil liberties. In this fight, the points which differentiate our position from that of the other parties will become more evident than they can be made by any declaration.

The only correct way to interpret the National Council's Statement, [he] said, was that the council had taken Canada's being at war as a fact. There is no suggestion in it that the CCF approves of Canada's participation. It outlines the same policy as a neutral country might have adopted.[37]

Despite the ambiguity of these statements, what mattered in the long run was that the National Council had supported Canada's entry into the war and that, in Parliament, all the CCF's MPs, except J. S. Woodsworth, had voted in accordance with that decision. The full significance of the pacifist issue can be appreciated by comparing the CCF with the British Labour and the United States Socialist parties, both of which also found it a bone in their throats. The first two changed their pacifist leaders and policies[38] and soon won very large

[35]McNaught, *A Prophet in Politics*, p. 307n.
[36]Canada declared war on Sept. 10, one week after Great Britain and France.
[37]Provincial Council, Minutes, Sept. 17, 1939.
[38]The termination of Woodsworth's political activity in 1940, as a result of failing health, probably reduced the public's association of the CCF with pacifism and may have averted a crisis about the party's leadership akin to that which had led to George Lansbury's resignation as Leader of the British Labour party, in 1935, over the issue of pacifism.

followings, while the last retained its pacifist leader, Norman Thomas, and his policies, and rapidly lost almost its entire following.[39] Whatever other factors may have affected the contrasting fates of these parties, the abandonment of pacifism was unquestionably a major turning point for the CCF. In so doing, it removed the largest barrier to its association with the world and, for the first time, aligned itself with the overwhelming majority of Canadians against a common enemy.

In Ontario, failure to make headway raised serious doubts about that Section's basic strategy and structure. The passage below is one of the earliest foreshadowings of an approach to the public closer to that of a conventional party. In his report on the disappointing 1937 provincial election, E. B. Jolliffe, the Provincial Campaign Manager and later the Ontario Section's first Leader, recommended

that special efforts be made to combat the defeatism existing in many clubs . . . that our efforts should be directed to the building of a mass party led by socialists rather than to the maintenance of a small revolutionary party . . . that attacks on other progressive organizations should not be so open as they have been in the past. . . . [He also advocated] the importance of developing personalities around whom the campaign could be conducted . . . [and a simpler approach to the voters]. . . .[40]

At the next Convention, in 1938, two constitutional amendments repaired what the leaders had come to consider major flaws in the CCF's structure. The first, which was strongly contested, permitted trade unions to affiliate as entities.[41] The second, which stipulated that no provincial or federal candidate could have official status without Provincial Council endorsation, was designed to strengthen the central administration and avoid embarrassing incidents.

Three years later, another Convention tried to alter the club structure which was coming under mounting criticism as an ineffective electoral organization. The reports of the discussions which preceded this move indicate, however, that it was prompted as much by despair as by foresight.

J reported that the morale of the membership is not good at the present time and that council members should go out of their way to encourage and inspire the units [clubs]. The question of constituency organization as an alternative to club organization was raised. M said that party organization should parallel electoral organization and should be devised so as to embrace the largest number of supporters and sympathizers in addition to the active members. . . .

[39]See Bell, "Marxian Socialism [in the United States]," pp. 392–94.
[40]Provincial Council, Minutes, Nov. 6, 1937.
[41]The national organization had made similar provision some months before.

[The Provincial Secretary] said that the club structure is breaking down; that before it collapses completely another form of organization should be established; and that the only suitable basis of organization is the Constituency [Riding] Association.[42]

The next Provincial Convention, in April 1941, passed the following constitutional amendment requiring the formation of riding associations:

Members of the CCF in each riding shall, as soon as possible, bring into being a riding association which shall consist of all members of clubs and all members-at-large[43] in that riding. This association shall be responsible for the organization of the riding for election purposes and for propaganda in the riding as a whole. The association shall hold a minimum of 3 meetings a year and shall elect an executive to be responsible for the work of the association between meetings. Members-at-large shall have the same privileges as members of clubs in the riding association.[44]

Few constituencies formed these associations immediately, just as few unions had rushed to affiliate after being permitted to do so. However, when the next period began (several months later), constitutional provisions for both of these developments were in existence.

Its first period had provided the Ontario CCF with little cause for optimism. Despite a vigorous start, the movement was soon overrun and almost crushed by a host of troubles. In 1937, M. J. Coldwell, then National Secretary, had written about his organizational tour of Ontario to his assistant, David Lewis,

I have no doubt that you wonder from time to time how I am finding the situation in Ontario. Well, as I proceed, my chagrin increases. There is no effective organization anywhere. The Clubs are inefficient as a rule and quite unsuited for the conduct of a campaign. I have come to the conclusion that Ontario will have to be reorganized completely. I arrived here [Windsor] last evening, and addressed two small meetings, one of which they had forgotten to advertise. I followed right on the heels of Heaps [another MP], who didn't appear. . . .

To me Ontario seems to be in a frightful mess; much worse than I imagined and I feel that except for some contacts I have made my trip so far has been a terrible waste of time. Yet it's not a waste because I know now what I did not know before. . . .[45]

[42]Provincial Council, Minutes, Nov. 2, 1940; Provincial Executive, Minutes, Nov. 16, 1940.
[43]A term for members who belonged only to the central organization and not to a club.
[44]Provincial Convention, Report, 1941. The amendment did not call for the dissolution of the clubs because they were regarded as essential for many ridings, especially the huge ones of northern and western Ontario as well as many rural ones. It did, however, require the formation of riding associations in these areas too.
[45]Coldwell to Lewis, Sept. 25, 1937, from the Archives of the CCF National Office, Ottawa.

As the period drew to a close, four years later, conditions could hardly be said to have improved. The CCF was more unpopular than ever, judging by its shrinking public following and membership; money and allies were still non-existent, but internal strife remained abundant. The movement was, in brief, developing a resemblance to the classic radical sect whose voice barely carries beyond its own minute circle.

However, the national party continued to be the dominant force on the left, mainly because of its strength in the west. And, in the east, the movement's intense cultivation of individuals had recruited the youthful core of leaders which continued to direct it to the end. Among them were some who were becoming deeply involved in the trade unions and who eventually brought strong union support to the party. Finally, a major crisis had turned the CCF's policy in a wordly direction, and despair, perhaps, had driven its leaders to begin changing its organization from that of a movement to that of a party.

But, if it was to be a national party and not simply another western protest movement, the CCF had to show strength east of the prairies. Since Quebec and the Maritimes were hopeless, its fate hinged on Ontario.

v. Major Party: Ascent
1942-45

TOWARDS THE END OF 1941, the CCF ceased to be a lost cause. The dark period of the war was turning men's thoughts to a bright new social order. The Four Freedoms, the British Beveridge Plan, a comprehensive welfare scheme, and admiration for the Soviet Union were all in the air. Although the depression was over, its memory was still fresh, and people everywhere agreed, in language surprisingly like the CCF's, that the world must never return to its pre-war state.

The atmosphere was perfectly tailored to the CCF's appeal for a new society, and, beginning in late 1941, a succession of dramatic CCF triumphs confirmed the public's new mood and made the party's national ascendancy appear imminent and irresistible. It moved into the lead nationally for a brief moment in September 1943,[1] swept Saskatchewan the next June, won four of the eight federal by-elections which it contested between 1942 and 1945 and gained impressively in several provincial contests. In addition, its support in the armed services ran far ahead of the civilian public's, which augured well for the party's future and made ideal publicity in the present. The Conservatives, meanwhile, were preoccupied with changing their name and leaders in an effort to reverse their fortunes, and the popularity of Liberal Prime Minister Mackenzie King, who seemed mesmerized by the conscription issue, fell to an all-time low.

However, the most remarkable CCF advance occurred in Ontario. Its opening shot was Joseph Noseworthy's stunning upset of the national Conservative Leader, Arthur Meighen, in a Toronto by-election in February 1942[2]—the party's first federal victory in Ontario—and it

[1]According to the Gallup Poll. See App. A, Table XVIII.
[2]The Liberals did not contest the seat. A familiar story has it that King so

reached its climax in August 1943 with the greatest success in the CCF's entire history. The party entered the provincial campaign without a seat in the legislature and emerged with 34 (out of 90), only 4 less than the victorious Conservatives.[8]

The momentous events of the world and the party wrought substantial changes in the latter's composition and in the lives of its members. As the world and the party began to converge, two-way travel between them increased, and each made considerable inroad into the other. The public suddenly viewed the CCF—its pacifism gone, its trumpet calls to class warfare muted and its star in the ascendancy—with a new interest and sympathy and flocked to it in growing numbers from all walks of life. Industrial workers, many newly unionized, formed the largest single source of recruits, but many others came from groups hitherto virtually untapped by the CCF—farmers, French Canadians, professional people and even businessmen. The earlier members experienced a twofold change. Their worldly lot had improved in the general economic recovery, and they were rapidly becoming a distinct minority of "old timers" in a party that was much more representative of, and closely linked with, the surrounding society than ever before.

A significant change occurred in the CCF's leadership as well, as it was augmented by the growing body of MPs, MLAs, party administrators and senior officers of rapidly expanding unions. Among all of these representatives and officers were many of the former clergymen, teachers, welfare workers and lawyers who had previously been prominent voluntary leaders. Now, however, their gainful occupations were in the party, the legislatures and the unions. They had, in brief, become professional politicians and trade unionists, and the CCF had begun to acquire a corps of professional leaders, many of whose careers were tied more closely than ever to its electoral success. Moreover, as legislators and union officers, some were drawn frequently into the issues of the day and their numerous contacts with the associations and members of their communities and with their own "expert" advisers tended to "broaden" their viewpoint.

---

hated and feared Meighen that, in order to prevent his return to the House of Commons, he left a clear field for the CCF in York South. For a reference to this story see Hutchison, *The Incredible Canadian*, p. 301. Some CCFers support this story by stating that Liberals in Toronto were urged privately to support the CCF.

[8]The way for this advance had been opened by a long and bitter feud between two of the Liberals' leaders—the Prime Minister of Canada and the Premier of Ontario—which so weakened their provincial party that it has still not recovered its position.

IDEOLOGY

All of these developments led to significant changes in the CCF's thinking. The views of any organization invariably reflect its members' connections with the surrounding society, which is, of course, why some groups shield their extremely unorthodox convictions by physical withdrawal. While CCF ideology in the first period hardly approached that extreme, nevertheless the members did require some protection from a disbelieving world in order to hold radical views, a separation which their tight cliques had provided.

The extensive structural changes[4] which occurred in the CCF during this new period therefore affected its ideology in two very general ways. Stronger links with the world loosened ties within the party, a combination which inhibited the cultivation of unorthodox beliefs, while the decreasing autonomy of the CCF's branches, as the centre tightened its grip upon them, impeded the expression of such beliefs.

Specifically, the war, the ending of the depression and the CCF's success narrowed the ideological gulf between the party and the public. The war was the first and most important agent of this change. It united the country against an outside enemy, ended the depression and thereby demolished the appeal of class conflict. And the CCF, reciprocally, in abandoning first pacifism and then, progressively, its other reservations about an "all-out war effort," finally entered the main stream of popular opinion and was drawn steadily towards its central current.

The most official indications of this shift in viewpoint appear, as usual, in the policy statements of the national conventions. The two major documents issued during this period[5] marked the party's retreat on the two great issues, pacifism and social ownership, which had contributed most to its distinctiveness. The first statement linked these two issues, elaborating a policy which had moved steadily from pacifism to "conscription of wealth rather than manpower" to "no conscription of manpower without the conscription of wealth" and, finally, to "conscription of wealth as well as manpower." The second statement, described later by a senior officer as "the next comprehensive statement of CCF principles and policy after the [Regina] Manifesto,"[6] obviously modified the latter's stand on social ownership.

[4]See pp. 62–67 below.
[5]"For Victory and Reconstruction" and "Security with Victory," adopted by the seventh and eighth national conventions respectively, 1942 and 1944.
[6]Ken Bryden, Ontario Provincial Secretary, in the *CCF News*, Dec. 1956.

SOCIAL OWNERSHIP

The socialization and democratic control, under either public or co-operative ownership, of industries which are monopolistic in character, or which are being operated to the detriment of the Canadian people, in order to free the Canadian economy from the domination and restrictive practices of monopoly control and to make possible national planning for maximum production. . . .

The socialization of large-scale enterprise, however, does not mean taking over every private business. Where private business shows no signs of becoming a monopoly, operates efficiently under decent working conditions, and does not operate to the detriment of the Canadian people, it will be given every opportunity to function, to earn a fair rate of return and to make its contribution to the nation's wealth.

The right wing defended this stand on the usual grounds that it contained nothing that was not in the Regina Manifesto.[7] It actually seems less a reversal of policy than a decision to emphasize and elaborate the milder of the two approaches evident in the Manifesto. Indeed, it was precisely this emphasis and elaboration that marked the entire path from the Regina Manifesto to the Winnipeg Declaration.

Success helped to move the party along that path by altering its attitude to the public.[8] As it attained the status of a major party, the CCF became involved in issues which had not previously engaged it because they bore little apparent relation to socialism. In its new status, it felt compelled to consider them, especially since its views had become more important to the interested groups in the community. However, though the pressures and opportunities for the party to widen its appeal mounted, the full extent of this change was not immediately apparent because the spirit of the times encouraged the CCF to continue its crusade for a new social order.

Consequently, during its upsurge, the party was able to blend these two kinds of appeals—of a future socialist society and of specific, immediate reforms—into a *raison d'être* of sufficient breadth to attract many who were not committed to socialism while still keeping within bounds the fears of those who were. To the latter's remonstrations that no CCF government could succeed *until* the public understood socialism, the leaders and the majority replied, in a swelling chorus, that the best way of advancing the socialist cause was first to get elected. The achievements of a CCF government, they explained, would be the most

[7]For a detailed exposition of this argument, see the debate on the Winnipeg Declaration, chap. VII, pp. 95–96.

[8]Similar changes had occurred earlier in Saskatchewan as the CCF approached power there. See Lipset, *Agrarian Socialism*, chap. VII.

effective means of securing that understanding because they would dispel the public's unfounded fears and myths about socialism.

This significant shift in time perspective stemmed not only from the imminence of power. It also reflected the CCF's growing acceptance of the world, epitomized in the belief that it could attain its objective by merely curbing rather than "eradicating" capitalism, and that its task was therefore much less difficult than originally envisaged. That the objective itself was somehow changing was still, at this point, more a matter of feeling than of conscious recognition.

The most obvious manifestation of this change, in the party's regular activities, was a diversion of interest, at all levels, not so much from socialism in particular, as from ideological discussion and debate in general. One prominent leader, reviewing these events, commented, "By the time the war came, people [in the CCF] were tired of all this talking. We had got past the phase of only talking."

The war and full employment had undoubtedly left CCFers with much less to talk about. Unlike the clubs, the larger and more formal riding associations met monthly instead of weekly and relegated discussion of socialist theory and international affairs to the background, concentrating instead on organizational matters. "Socialist education" was reinterpreted in "practical" terms—the necessity of getting the socialist message across—and, in major party fashion, "doing" henceforth replaced "talking" as the CCF's leading activity.

STRUCTURE

With success and an accelerated time perspective, the CCF became as preoccupied with "organization" as the established parties were, and interpreted it, as they did, primarily in terms of winning votes rather than souls. A sweeping rearrangement of its structure followed.

The more lasting changes were the result of deliberate planning, but they were touched off by more spontaneous and conspicuous ones—

TABLE IV

CCF MEMBERSHIP IN ONTARIO, 1941–45
(Total in June 1945 = 100)

1941	8*
1942	17
1943	40*
1944	81
1945	100

*The 1941 and 1943 figures are for April and October respectively; the rest are for June.

the party's growth and prosperity (see Table IV). Its membership began to increase everywhere late in 1941; in Ontario, the expansion soon turned into an invasion, which continued without interruption until it reached the all-time peak of 20,000 in June 1945.

With members came funds (see Table V) in what some regarded as an irreversible sequence,[9] and their fees and donations brought unprecedented prosperity to the CCF.

· TABLE V

GROSS RECEIPTS OF THE ONTARIO CCF, 1935–45*
(Gross Receipts in 1945 = 100)

1935	13
1937	11
1940	8
1941	16
1942	45
1943	75
1944	96
1945	100

*Figures were not available for some years. For the complete record from 1940 on, see Figure 1, p. 110. (None of these figures includes election funds.)

As the Ontario CCF grew, prospered and came within sight of power, it set out to build an organization capable of accommodating and mobilizing this influx and of reaching out for still further support. In the process, it steadily replaced the spontaneous and haphazard structure of a movement with the formal and systematic one of a party.

In a recent discussion of these changes, a senior CCF officer of that period expressed the common view of his colleagues: "We had no organization worth talking about until around '42 or '43. That's when we began building a real organization." He was referring to the party's expansion and to what he termed its "centralization." These simultaneous processes of branching out into the society and of strengthening the central bodies will perhaps be more easily followed if we begin at the top and work down and out to the local branches and the party's allies.

One of the Ontario Section's earliest moves was the selection, in 1942, of its first Political Leader.[10] Until then, it had been headed by its administrative chief. The public and sometimes even the members

[9]See the last paragraph of the Finance Committee Report, p. 64 below.

[10]The British Labour party did not overcome its aversion to strong leadership at the top for over two decades. It chose its first official Leader, Ramsay MacDonald, in 1922, only two years before first taking office.

take very little notice when a party replaces its administrative head, but a change in political leaders is a completely different matter, a fact which tends to place considerable personal power in the latter's hands.[11]

The Provincial Council expanded steadily—from twenty-two in 1941 to thirty-seven in 1944—in an effort to make the leadership more representative both of the party and the community, and, particularly as factionalism diminished, it turned from ideological debate to problems of administration and recruitment. Specialized bodies to carry out these tasks were created—the standing committees reporting to the Provincial Executive, which had never exceeded a dozen in the first period, rose to nineteen in 1943. Among them were a Trade Union Committee and later a Veterans Committee. At the 1943 Convention, plans for a great expansion of the professional administrative staff were announced. In its report the Finance Committee presented the rationale for this expansion together with a greatly increased budget for the coming year.

"Now is the winter of our discontent made glorious summer."
I know we are all pleased with the fine results we have obtained in the west. We are also getting fine support in the Maritimes. This is all very hopeful. But all eyes from East and West are focussed on Ontario. Because it is known and might serve some useful purpose to remind ourselves that not until we weld the strongest link right here in this province will the CCF rise to power in Canada.

Events will not wait. Our chance is NOW. We must take advantage NOW of the tremendous possibilities staring us in the face. It is necessary NOW to make that extra effort, spend that extra dollar, which will ensure success.

It is with this objective in view that the Finance Committee asks you to make possible the inclusion in our working programme of a Trade Union Director, a Rural Organizer and a Publicity Director.

1. *A trade union organizer* to further expand and to encourage the very fine co-operation that we are now obtaining from the trade union movement. The trade union movement stands today as our right fist aimed at the heart of the government. But our other fist, the farm movement, is still tied behind our backs. Therefore we also need

2. *A Rural Organizer* to close the vulnerable gap on our other flank. I have every confidence that if we tackle the organization of rural areas with the same determination that we set out to engage the confidence of the trade unions, we will achieve equally wholesome results.

3. We need a *Publicity Director* . . . The Financial Report has indicated how this added personnel can be paid for. What it amounts to is this: More personnel for more organization and publicity: more organization and publicity will add more membership; more membership will provide more money; and more money will pay for more personnel.

[11]For a detailed analysis of how that power accumulates, see Michels, *Political Parties.*

Exactly how soon and how thoroughly these plans materialized is not clear. But they do show the party's desire to capitalize on its new solvency by developing a professional and specialized administrative staff.

Besides growing larger and more professional, the CCF's top governing bodies acquired greater powers, both actual and constitutional. New constitutions and constitutional amendments legitimized the reorganization.[12] Among other changes, they standardized election procedures in various minor ways that gave the central administrative bodies greater control over the conduct of campaigns. Another provision, which permitted the Provincial Council to refuse anyone CCF membership "at its discretion," seems to have had Communist "infiltration" especially in mind. During this period too, many of the procedures were inaugurated which indirectly strengthened the "administration" at the conventions.[13]

Major changes occurred on the local level too as the Ontario CCF hastened to remodel its basic structure. Dissatisfaction with the clubs had led to an earlier attempt to set up riding associations,[14] but the problems of making the large new membership feel welcome and comfortable accelerated the change.

The difficulties arose both from the nature and number of the new "comrades," a term which many of them considered, at best, incongruous. Some had been well-known Liberals and even Conservatives; many others had been considered quite apolitical, and still others had been thought insufficiently resolute or radical. As these hosts of strangers thronged aboard the CCF bandwagon, many "old timers" grew increasingly suspicious and alarmed. For the latter, as is so often the case, success was a mixed blessing. While it vindicated their faith, it also brought unavoidable sadness. Their devotion and "sacrifices," they knew, had kept the CCF alive in the barren thirties. Now, with the goal finally in sight, *their* party was being taken over by people who had not shared these sacrifices and whose motives and beliefs were often suspect. Very few of the older members, except perhaps the leaders, did not experience some of these sentiments.[15] Understandably therefore

[12]The Ontario Section and the national organization adopted new constitutions in 1944 and 1946 respectively.

[13]For a description of these procedures, see chap. III, pp. 27–30.

[14]See chap. IV, pp. 55–56.

[15]The shunting aside of many "pioneers" to at best a symbolic status just as the main fruits of success become available seems to occur in many new organizations. However, their resentment usually has other roots which Michels explains well: "Those who have been long in possession—and this applies just

their ranks sometimes stiffened against the heavy reinforcements. A top leader, in an unexcelled position to know this situation, described it many years later.

"The clubs were very often ingrown little groups. Many of them as well as many in the CCF clearly did not welcome newcomers. There was a widespread fear that the party might come to power on the backs of people who didn't understand socialism and weren't sympathetic to it. . . .

"There were also many members-at-large who didn't want to associate themselves with certain clubs [in their ridings], and you couldn't blame them."

Other leaders dismissed the "old timers" as "talkers" and enthused about the energy of the newcomers. In any case, the cliquishness which had sustained a small and feeble organization came to be seen as a handicap to one that was large and vigorous. By merging the clubs into riding associations, the party's leaders hoped to lower the impenetrable barriers that had arisen from the long and intimate association of small groups.

Concern about "discipline" also seems to have spurred this change. In reply to a question about the reorganization into riding associations, the officer who was quoted earlier[16] said, "It had to be done in order to have any kind of a party. It was necessary to be able to do something if some club sent a donation or a speaker to the League for Peace and Democracy."[17] The larger riding associations, it was felt, would be less vulnerable to Communist overtures than the clubs.

The party's landslide victory in Saskatchewan was taken as the final proof, if any were needed, of the value of riding and poll organization. Ever after, the CCF sought to emulate the structure of its Saskatchewan Section and, incidentally, that of the "old parties," which the latter resembled.

Thus, the centralization which occurred at the national and provincial levels was extended to the local branches as the clubs gave way to riding associations, which were larger, less personal, less likely to take deviant paths and more congruent with Canada's parliamentary system.

A central feature of the CCF's growth was its reaching out for support to other organizations and leaders in the community. An early

as much to spiritual and psychical possession as to material—are proud of their past, and are therefore inclined to look down upon those whose ownership is of more recent date." Michels, *Political Parties*, p. 168.

[16]See chap. IV, p. 50.

[17]A Communist front organization previously known as the League against War and Fascism.

indication, perhaps no more than a straw in the wind, of this process and of the widening gap between the leaders and the rest was reported by a former leader who was close to, but not at, the top in those years. In recent conversation, she recalled that

"The first sign of the change, though I didn't realize it at the time, was in Jolliffe's distribution of tickets to the opening of the Legislature in '43 [after the great CCF success in Ontario]. I and others like me were bypassed in favour of people who were important, potentially sympathetic but not yet committed."

The strongest support came from the trade unions, especially from several of the new, mushrooming unions in the Congress of Industrial Organizations (CIO), many of whose officers were CCF leaders or sympathizers. The leadership nuclei of some of these unions had been recruited from the CCF, in the 1930's, largely on the basis of personal and ideological affinities. This system of interlocking directorates became the party's gateway to a far-reaching web of connections, first in the Canadian Congress of Labour (CCL) and later in the merged union body. In 1943, this group led the way as the CCL officially endorsed the CCF as labour's "political arm" in the following resolution:

Whereas, in the opinion of this Congress the policy and programme of the Co-operative Commonwealth Federation more adequately expresses the viewpoint of organized labour than any other party:
Be it therefore resolved, That this Convention of the Canadian Congress of Labour endorse the Co-operative Commonwealth Federation as the political arm of labour in Canada, and recommend to all affiliated and chartered unions that they affiliate with the Co-operative Commonwealth Federation.[18]

Closer ties with the unions affected the party's structure significantly. They established an additional centre of gravity in CCF affairs, one that grew steadily in influence, culminating in the formation of the New Democratic party.

INVOLVEMENT

By changing the public image of the CCF from crackpot to bell-wether, the events of the early 1940's helped to alter its members' incentives as well as its viewpoint and structure. They attracted a large body of new adherents who were more repelled by anything that smacked of sectarianism than by political parties *per se*. Instead, they saw the latter as the appropriate instruments for achieving specific and immediate changes and as sources of perhaps slightly daring but, on

[18]Canadian Congress of Labour, Proceedings of Fourth Annual Convention, Sept. 13–17, 1943.

the whole, quite conventional political careers—in either case, worth while only in so far as they were effective in the existing world.

Immediate victory was therefore more urgent to these newcomers than it had been to some of the "old timers." The latter's reactions to success, it has been suggested previously, were more complicated. The growing rapport between the party and the world reduced the isolation which had held the earlier membership closely together and enabled the party to survive the severe climate from 1936 to 1942. But when the world suddenly turned warm and inviting, it played havoc with the old incentives. The numbers of new adherents robbed the "old timers'" vision of its uniqueness and simultaneously transformed the intimate band of "comrades" into an impersonal army. In addition, the ebbing of the CCF's sense of outrage and of its utopian hopes dampened their evangelical fervour by promising milder retribution to the guilty and less than complete salvation to the deserving. The change in out-look thereby undermined the rebellious and prophetic aspects of the members' self-images by threatening to turn rebels into reformers and prophets into politicians. But if these numbers of new adherents routed the old sectarian incentives, they brought, at least for a time, strong wordly ones as replacements.

What held many of the "old timers" was, of course, the vindication of their faith and, after so long a struggle, the intoxicating prospect of victory. Intense excitement gripped the entire party, kindling hope and enthusiasm everywhere. Even where victory still seemed remote, CCFers rejoiced in the party's overall success, and the countless stories of how unyielding perseverance had won so many "hopeless" ridings added significance to their own modest gains, incentive to their efforts and further members to their ranks.

All of these changes were part of the larger process in which the visions of that other social order—quite remote but quite perfect—became obscured as the CCF drew closer to the existing one. With the fading of that dream of perfection went some of the hopes and loyalties of those who would settle for nothing less.[19] But as the main body neared the existing world, it detected opportunities for achievement, for itself and mankind, hitherto scarcely dreamt of, and the hope of imminent victory became the mainspring of involvement in the CCF, as it was in the "old parties."

Nevertheless, just because the CCF appeared on the road to victory,

[19]How many left the CCF at this time is unascertainable because of the absence of the membership card files for the years before 1945.

the changes that were occurring in the types of involvement are especially difficult to document. Reversal is a more sensitive gauge of the commitment of members to an organization than is success. Defeat leads them to question how deeply they are committed to this specific body as *the* means of achieving their aims, of whatever nature, and how important these objectives are compared to others. Every major CCF setback produced answers to these questions: many members left; many became less active; still others remained deeply involved.

Success obscures these differences because, by increasing the incentives to participate, it decreases the possibility of discriminating among them. Thus, in the CCF, only the two extremes—those who hoped and those who dreaded that victory would mean the end of socialism—saw any reason to distinguish between these two objectives. The great majority regarded them as inseparable. More important, it did not have to think about whether it was more interested in a socialist society than in immediate reforms or in its own careers than in the welfare of its fellow men. Victory, by promising to fulfil all of these aims, eliminated the necessity of choosing among them.

Thus, the CCF boom held out to its adherents the stirring prospects of remodelling their society in accordance with their ideals and of the personal rewards that go with being on the winning side. Both types of incentive—they are seldom separable, especially in prospering organizations—attracted many newcomers and encouraged those survivors of the earlier period who had acquired demanding new pusuits —in the trade unions, for example—to keep the party and political careers very high on their personal lists of priorities.

However, since success not only altered involvement in the CCF but also obscured that fact, the full extent of the change did not become apparent until after the party's reversals. Then, the great exodus of members and the retreat of many more into inactivity demonstrated that, between 1942 and 1945, expectations of imminent success had replaced the earlier sectarian incentives as the dominant type in the CCF. Documentation of that change, however, must await the subsequent periods, which revealed it.

In becoming the dominant type, these incentives contributed both to the CCF's reorganization and reorientation. They stimulated the building of an effective electoral machine and encouraged the party to modify its viewpoint and to become absorbed in worldly issues in order to broaden its appeal. In addition, the decline in personal involvement among the members and in the distinctiveness of their self-images gave considerable

impetus to the process whereby formal arrangements increasingly replaced personal relations and strong feelings as the CCF's means of
cohesion and mobilization at all levels.

Sweeping internal changes, many of which continued thereafter, originated during the CCF's momentous rise. Broadly, they were: in
ideology, a diminishing hostility to the social order, modification in the
proposals to change it, and a shift of time perspective towards the
present; in *structure*, an enormous increase in size and prosperity, a
more formal and uniform organization, a larger, more specialized and
more professional leadership, a flow of power from the branches to the
centre, the establishment of firmer roots in the community, and a less
cohesive informal organization; in *motivation*, a change from sectarian
to more worldy incentives, centring on a greater desire for immediate
victory. Briefly, they add up to a shift from the character of a political
movement towards that of a conventional party.

VI. Major Party: Decline
1945-49

THE WATERSHED IN THE CCF'S HISTORY occurred within a month of the end of the war in Europe. The country had enjoyed five years of prosperity; welfare legislation had begun to appear just in time for the 1945 federal election, and the CCF's remarkable gains had provoked its foes to counter-attack with unprecedented perseverance and ferocity.[1]

The reversals which were so devastating to the CCF occurred first in the Ontario provincial election, June 4, 1945, and, one week later, in the federal election. In the first contest, the CCF's representation in the Ontario legislature was cut from thirty-four to eight and its share of the vote fell from 32 per cent to 22 per cent. The results of the federal balloting were even more disappointing; the CCF won only twenty-eight seats in the House of Commons (out of a total of 245) and only 16 per cent of the votes.[2]

Nevertheless, the party continued to show strength both nationally and in Ontario during this period. It gained four federal seats in by-elections between 1945 and 1949 and, in Ontario, it made an impressive comeback in the 1948 provincial election, winning twenty-one seats and 27 per cent of the votes, and regained the status of official Opposition.

[1]The signal for the most sustained and massive of these assaults was a speech by Harold Winch, CCF Leader in British Columbia, in which he explained that a duly elected CCF government might encounter violent resistance which it had the right and indeed the duty to crush by force. This was, of course, the traditional view of the left wing faction. What made the speech so noteworthy was that it was delivered at the height of the party's popularity by a prominent leader and that its reference to force, which the party's leaders defended in public but deplored in private, was widely cited as evidence of the CCF's similarity to the Communist and National Socialist parties.

[2]The capture of second place by the Conservatives with sixty-seven seats and 28 per cent of the vote shows the extent of the CCF's defeat.

IDEOLOGY

Throughout this period the CCF continued to behave and to be treated as a major party. That position or at least self-image determined its strategy in the next federal campaign (1949), although by then its immediate aim had receded to becoming the official Opposition.

Members of the Executive agreed that the general strategy of the CCF campaign should be to emphasize throughout the country that the Progressive Conservative Party is losing rather than gaining ground; that there is every likelihood that George Drew [the Conservative Leader] will go back with a smaller number of seats than he had in the last parliament; that the CCF will gain at the expense of the Conservatives; that therefore the real fight is between the CCF and the Liberals.

It seemed clear that the Liberals will try to play up a Conservative threat in order to frighten many who would otherwise vote CCF into voting Liberal in order to keep out the Tories. The above should, therefore, be brought forcefully to the attention of the Canadian people, so that they may become convinced that there is no Conservative threat, as far as their coming into power is concerned, and that therefore the sensible thing for all progressive people to do is to make sure that the CCF goes back to parliament with as large a contingent as possible, and becomes at least the Official Opposition.[3]

However, more important than the voices of its inner councils was the unprecedented tone in which the party now addressed the public. Until 1945, its fundamental appeal had always been optimistic. Before the war, it had offered a utopian alternative to the existing hardship. Wartime prosperity had confirmed its belief in central planning and had provided it with a new message of hope—through planning, Canada could achieve full employment and prosperity in peacetime, as it had in wartime.

Continued prosperity after the war forced the CCF for the first time into a defensive and pessimistic position in which it warned incessantly of an impending depression. The failure of that depression to materialize was attributed successively to the wartime shortage of civilian goods, to the intensifying cold war and, finally, to the war in Korea. Whatever the merit of these arguments, they changed the CCF's voice from one of hope into one of gloom.

Besides finding little that was cheerful to say to the public, CCFers were having trouble finding anything of much interest to say to each other, unmistakable evidence that their general viewpoint was not very different from their rivals'. The party's discussions of "education" best

[3]CCF National Executive, Minutes, April 30, 1949.

revealed this decline in ideological distinctiveness. The following passages are typical:

> K said that Riding Associations and units were discussing business matters to the exclusion of policy. . . . S suggested that the Education Committee send out a monthly topic for discussion at CCF meetings.

> There is a great shortage of both the leadership and the material necessary to maintain interesting club meetings in most places. Some attractively prepared topic material which could be studied by some one person, who could then give a talk on this subject to his club might help to provide a solution for this problem.[4]

This state of affairs was hardly confined to Ontario. A report on education to the National Council complained of a "lag" in CCF educational activities nationally; "only 3 of the 10 provinces have active education committees," it noted, and it quoted a Saskatchewan leader as saying, "our CCF schools used to emphasize CCF policy, principles and socialist philosophy. In the last couple of years we have turned them into organization conferences."[5]

The decline in ideological distinctiveness went hand in hand with the shift in emphasis from "talking" to "doing," as the passages below indicate. They express widely held official views about membership education.

> Faced as we are with a crying need for greater variety in CCF activities, it is important to convince our people that almost any activity can be made an educational activity. At one end of the range of educational activities there are leaflet distributions and radio broadcasts to meet the mass education need; at the other end, study groups and weekend schools to provide the more detailed study required for leadership training. But between the extremes lies a whole range of activities whose educational possibilities are usually missed. Social activities are educational activities. Fund raising can be made an educational activity. A scrutineer class can be not only an opportunity to learn the duties of a scrutineer but also an opportunity to emphasize the whole socialist philosophy as revealed in CCF organization and conduct of an election. And so on.

> Three guiding principles should be borne in mind at all times;
> *First*, education work is not restricted to the more formal study of socialist principles and CCF policy. Rather, anything which will make CCF groups more interested and active legitimately falls within the scope of education work, for the great majority of people can and will learn chiefly through doing things.

[4]Provincial Executive, Minutes, March 25, 1946; Organizer's Report, Records of Organization Committee, 1951.
[5]National Council, Minutes, Oct. 1, 1949.

Second, it follows therefore that education work should be integrated, in varying degrees, of course, with all CCF activities. It is the leaven in the loaf of CCF activities as a whole.

Third, it also follows that emphasis should be placed on education techniques as much as content, for a larger proportion of CCF members must learn how to do the hundred and one jobs required to build and administer a democratic organization.[6]

However, the gap between what officialdom believed could be stimulating and what the members found interesting had become very large and remained so to the very end.

Official policy also continued its gradual movement along its familiar path. In the next major policy statement,[7] the 1948 National Convention took the following stand on social ownership:

... the CCF believes that some parts of the economy must be brought under public ownership. Some are more suited for cooperative ownership. . . . Finally, there are large areas which can best be left to private enterprise.

The Role of Private Enterprise

The application of these measures of socialization will considerably extend the area of public business under social and co-operative ownership. But it will also leave a large section of business in private hands. In order to achieve effective production and distribution in both the public and in the private sectors of the economy *a CCF government will help and encourage private business to fulfill its legitimate functions.*

Experience has shown that where public business flourishes, private business thrives also. The private trader or industrialist, freed from the domination of industrial and financial monopolies, will have a better chance to exercise his enterprise and initiative to earn a fair rate of return and to make his contribution to the nation's wealth. [*italics added*]

This statement, like its predecessor, contained no startling innovations. Nevertheless, it moved in the same direction from the 1944 statement as the latter had from the Regina Manifesto. One sign of the change was the increasing use of the term "private enterprise" instead of "capitalism." However, the most significant aspect was the steady shift from virtual prohibition of capitalism, in 1933, to an elaboration, still in negative terms, of the conditions under which it would be permitted to continue, in 1944, to a positive readiness to "help and encourage private business to fulfill its legitimate functions," in 1948.

[6]National Council, Minutes, Oct. 1, 1949, Jan. 3, 1950.

[7]The last previous one had appeared in 1944. The title of the new statement, "Security For All," possibly foreshadowed the CCF's new role throughout the 1950's as champion of the underdog rather than of the great majority. Although "Security For All" was unusually explicit about which industries the party proposed to nationalize, the subject of social ownership continued its steady retreat into the inner pages of these documents.

STRUCTURE

Once again, the great change in the CCF's fortunes affected its organization more visibly than it did its doctrines. Immediately after the débâcle of June 1945, membership figures plummeted everywhere; in Ontario, they were almost halved in two years. The mass exodus was arrested temporarily in 1948, and in some provinces sharply reversed,[8] but it did not really end until 1951. After that, membership figures remained comparatively stable.

In Ontario, as elsewhere, the CCF's response to the double defeat of 1945 was far from uniform. In fact, it may be compared to that of a large tree to a hurricane. The entire structure shook and swayed, but the trunk and the central branches remained intact. The peripheral branches lost the most fruit and many of them were broken off or badly damaged.

The trunk and central branches of the party in Ontario (and beyond) were in Toronto and Ottawa. The former contained more CCF leaders and members than any other Canadian community. It housed the party's provincial office and the national or regional headquarters of many large trade unions, while Ottawa, though poor CCF territory, was the locale of its national office, of its members of Parliament and of the Canadian Labour Congress headquarters. These bodies provided the groups of party functionaries and allied union officers who formed the CCF's most solid nuclei, and, consequently, the party weathered the storm that began in 1945 most successfully in these two centres. But in the many areas where these informal nuclei did not exist, the local organizations collapsed or hovered on the verge of disintegration.

Table VI suggests that, as in the difficult period from 1936 to 1942, the CCF owed its survival after 1945 largely to the personal cohesion of its top leadership. For example, the party's organization fared much better in Ottawa, where these groups of leaders were more numerous, than it did in Hamilton, Oshawa and Windsor, three heavily unionized cities where CCF popular support was always much greater. Indeed, it fared no better in these industrial centres than in the province as a whole.

Most disastrous were the losses throughout northern Ontario, both in absolute numbers and because the entire area had been extremely promising. Enthusiasm for the CCF, as indicated by membership, had hit its peak in the north a year ahead of the rest of the province. A party leader remarked, "In '43 we were as strong up there as in Saskatchewan. Every railroad town was a CCF stronghold." So great were these losses

[8]Notably in Saskatchewan, when the CCF Government was first re-elected.

TABLE VI

CCF MEMBERSHIP IN ONTARIO, 1944–49
(Membership in June 1945 in each area = 100)

	1944	1945	1946	1947	1948	1949
Ontario	81	100	72	57	56	55
Toronto	72	100	123	109	102	81
Ottawa	65	100	73	74	75	71
Hamilton	80	100	54	51	50	44
Windsor	48	100	48	52	39	45
Oshawa	49	100	53	59	91§	95§
Northern Ontario	113	100	53	35	45	54
Eastern Ontario*	73	100	43	27	19	27
Central Ontario†	66	100	52	42	44	37
Western Ontario‡	79	100	79	53	46	50

*Exclusive of Ottawa.
†Exclusive of Toronto, Hamilton and Oshawa.
‡Exclusive of Windsor.
§The organizational activity accompanying the CCF's victorious by-election campaign (June 1948) in this riding probably accounts for this seemingly inconsistent figure.

that the eight northern ridings,[9] which contained 36 per cent of the Ontario membership in 1944, had only 16 per cent in 1947. In that interval, membership in one riding shrank from 1,506 to 318 and in another from 1,094 to 208. The CCF was especially concerned about its organization in the north, but the reports of faltering and prostrate local organizations in that area were typical of those that flowed in from all parts of the province.

A report from the Provincial Organizer in [an important northern riding] stated that "there is not a single functioning club in the whole riding . . . nor is there any functioning riding organization." . . . even ridings like R, N, and C, all of which elected members in 1943, have no functioning riding organization today.[10]

TABLE VII

GROSS RECEIPTS OF THE ONTARIO CCF, 1945–49

1945	100
1946	69
1947	101
1948	79
1949	65

As membership diminished, so did funds (see Table VII), because the fees and individual contributions of the members were the party's main source of revenue. Since the CCF's financial commitments were

[9]Ontario had eighty-two federal ridings during that period.
[10]Organizing Committee, Minutes, Nov. 12 and 15, 1947.

based on an anticipated rise in membership, the abrupt drop which occurred instead plunged it deep into debt. Furthermore, the efforts simply to maintain its position required more money than ever, but membership continued to shrink. Nor could the party adjust its finances to this situation easily. To budget for an anticipated loss of membership and reduced expenditures constitutes an obvious admission of expected failure, which any organization, but especially a political party, is very reluctant to make. Consequently, the initial collapse and the continued pressure to plan for expansion prolonged and aggravated the CCF's financial crisis for some years.

The party appealed frantically to its members and friends for help. A trade union donation accounted for 14 per cent of its revenue in 1947 and, in part, for its surprisingly strong financial position in that year. But the insatiable and unco-ordinated demands for money provoked considerable irritation and even some organized, open protests within the CCF's own ranks. One group of important ridings sent the following resolution to the Provincial Council:

> Whereas at the present time many of our members do not understand the reason for the constant appeal for funds, and whereas these members contribute to the CCF with their fees and dues, and by donations at election time. . . .
>
> And whereas the appeal for money through the mail leaves them with a feeling of resentment and disgust and with a tendency to cancel their membership in the CCF with the consequent loss for the movement both in funds and goodwill.
>
> Be it therefore resolved that we the representatives of Zone 9 duly assembled register our protest against such methods as the recent appeal through the mail and request that in future *ALL* financial appeals be made through the constituency associations or by general appeal in the CCF News and be it further resolved that one copy of this resolution be sent to the Provincial Council and one copy be sent to the Chairman of the Finance Committee.[11]

Not surprisingly, the party's many difficulties eventually led to murmurs against its provincial leadership.

> The CCF Caucus in the Ontario Legislature wrote to the Provincial Executive criticizing some [unnamed] members of the Provincial Council for "participating in a campaign for a change in the provincial leadership, and as part of that campaign had sent letters to CCF members in our ridings."
>
> The Caucus felt that the Council members responsible should have discussed their feelings and intentions in Council and that such letters are indiscreet because they "may get beyond the people to whom they are written."[12]

[11]Finance Committee, Minutes, Jan. 24, 1946.
[12]Provincial Council, Minutes, Oct. 30, 1947.

The Ontario CCF's last major encounter with the Communist party occurred during this period. As usual, it resulted from the latter's tactic of seeking co-operation with the CCF and the willingness of the CCF's left wing to comply. The controversy led to the expulsion from the party, in 1948, of one of its representatives in the Ontario legislature and the collapse of CCF strength in his riding, formerly one of its strongest in Ontario.[13]

Although controversies of this kind did not always involve great numbers of CCFers, they invariably presented the party with problems of considerable delicacy. The following letter, written by the National Secretary to his counterpart in Ontario, explains these difficulties fully and frankly:

Feb. 12, 1948.

Will you please take the following matter up with your provincial executive. . . . We had considerable discussion of it in Caucus yesterday morning, and finally decided to obtain the opinion and advice of your executive.

The problem which I wish to put before you arises out of the numerous invitations which we receive in Ottawa for CCF MP's to speak at cost-of-living rallies under the auspices of committees which seem clearly to be in some way sponsored or controlled by Communists, and even more clearly to be part of the LPP[14] campaign for the price-control petition. The matter came to a head as a result of X's experience [X was a CCF MP] last Friday, and of persistent requests from Minetown [another important riding] for a speaker. . . .

The general impression which X got from the meeting was that it was not ours in tone or purpose. I should add that he was very glad he was there, and felt that a CCF MP should have been there, but he was equally glad that it had proved impossible for Mr. Coldwell [the CCF National Leader] to go. . . .

Minetown [asked for one of several speakers], and I was able to wire them truthfully that none of these three is available. . . . However, I am likely to get a request for some of the other MP's. In any case, I am pretty certain that my delays in wiring, and consecutive negative replies, will have told the local people that we are not anxious to send anyone to their rally. Where do we go from here? How do I finally deal with [their] request? And what shall we do with similar requests which are almost bound to come with the new LPP line?

Most of the MP's are very dubious about the value of their rushing out to meetings under such auspices. There is always the likelihood that the meetings will be much more valuable to the LPP than to us. There is always the possibility that a CCF MP will find himself on the platform surrounded by people whose presence could be exploited by both the Communists and the other opponents of the CCF. In short, the LPP strategy is obviously to

[13]This was one of the peripheral battles in the long and bitter struggle for control of the Communist-led Mine, Mill and Smelter Workers Union.

[14]LPP stands for Labour Progressive party, the name under which the Communist party, outlawed at the beginning of the war, reappeared in 1943.

accept CCF speakers at meetings which they stimulate, but which are ostensibly under the direction of innocent people.

On the other hand, there is the problem of the reaction of the unions, and particularly the rank and file union members. For example . . . S insisted that the committee and its actions are bona fide and that the CCF should co-operate with it since it is their rally to support the CCF stand on price controls in Parliament. What I am personally afraid of is that precipitous refusals to co-operate in such circumstances might serve to drive people like S and others into the arms of the LPP, who would not be slow to exploit the situation.

[One CCF MP] suggested that we ought to lay down the rule that CCF MP's will address meetings only when they are sponsored either by bona fide unions, or by CCF organizations. This may be a way out, although I, personally, cannot quite see it. Obviously the U.E.[15] is a bona fide union, and yet we would not wish to speak under their auspices. Equally obviously, a YMCA group belongs in neither category, and yet we would be ready to accept an invitation from them. Furthermore, there may easily be occasions where local CCF organizations might wish to organize meetings under neutral auspices. In short, it seems to me that the solution suggested may not work.

Just [now] a long distance call came in from T of Minetown riding. He pleaded that we send one of our MP's. He suggested that if we did not, there is the danger that they may invite [an LPP MLA]. He insisted that the union has a firm grip on the committee involved, although he admitted that Mrs. C, Chairman of the Committee, is LPP. It was clear from his conversation that if we failed to send one of our MP's in, people like him and S would be very hurt, and that their regard for the CCF would undoubtedly suffer. I imagine that their reaction would be the same as that of many similar members in the union. Even though I appreciate that some of these people often lend their support to the wrong group inside the union and are pretty gullible, I also appreciate that it would be silly to slap such people in the face, since basically they are good union supporters of the CCF. I don't know what we shall decide with regard to Minetown. . . . But whatever our decision in this instance, the problem will still remain, and some general policy must be evolved.

May I therefore ask that your executive give this consideration. We will probably also discuss it at the national executive meeting the following day, to which B could bring a report of your discussion.

P.S. I had, for various reasons, to take the responsibility of making a decision myself re Minetown. After discussing the matter with several MP's, I have informed Minetown that X, MP, will be their speaker.[16]

Two weeks later the National Secretary answered these queries in a policy directive to all the provincial sections:

Feb. 27, 1948.

To CCF Provincial Secretaries:

After its meeting of February 15, the National Executive discussed the organizational problems presented by the new LPP line in Canada. The

---

[15]United Electrical Workers.   [16]Provincial Council, Records, 1948.

Executive instructed me to write the provincial offices and request that they pay careful attention to this matter.

Already we have had instances of the kind of local problem with which CCF organizations were faced in the '30's, but which were on the whole absent during the course of the war. The communist-controlled consumer organizations, meetings and rallies ostensibly called by trade unions (usually under communist control) seek to draw CCF members into activity with the communists. It is also clear that the communists have begun a policy of attempting to infiltrate CCF organizations, and one must expect this policy to be applied with increasing determination. . . . The fact that the National Executive and several provincial executives have already had to give hours of valuable time to a discussion of this problem suggests that we may again be faced with the kind of thing from which our movement suffered some years ago, namely, the waste of time and energy fighting communist issues, instead of building our movement.

The National Executive was unanimous in its belief that the only way to avoid possible serious trouble later is to tackle the communist problem vigorously and immediately. It endorsed the statement issued by our National Leader . . . the day immediately after Tim Buck's [the LPP Leader's] "speech of love," and it expressed satisfaction that this statement had been issued so promptly and so clearly. We believe and suggest that every provincial executive should alert all the CCF members and local organizations in the province on this issue. They should be asked to examine carefully invitations to general, various nondescript committees, and to avoid becoming a front for the LPP. They should be warned to be a little more careful about the admission of members whose loyalty to the CCF may be in question. They should be strongly urged to take an active part themselves in issues of the day, so that the local CCF may give the necessary leadership, instead of becoming the tail of some activity organized and led by others. . . .

In every case, the National Executive believes, the CCF provincial bodies as well as local ones should make clear the established policy of the CCF to have nothing to do with the communists, to make no electoral arrangements whatever with them, and to refuse to recognize their official support, whatever individual communists or fellow-travellers may wish to do at the time of an election. . . .[17]

Within half a year of these events the Communist coup in Czechoslovakia took place, inaugurating the genuine cold war and thereby ending the Communist party's serious threat to the CCF.

The preceding chronicle of frustration and despair is, of course, but one side of the story. The party did not remain passive while large segments of its organization were crumbling. Instead, throughout this period, it made many efforts to arrest the process.

In August 1945, it decided to hold its first province-wide membership drive in the following spring "to secure renewals in the various ridings

[17]*Ibid.*

with the idea of holding our present membership in Ontario."[18] The drive was extremely successful in Toronto, where it brought the membership to an all-time high in 1946 (see Table VI). (Although that peak was not maintained, even so, in 1948, CCF membership in Toronto still held at the 1945 level.) Almost everywhere else, especially in the north, the initial results were disappointing. However, annual membership drives became a permanent and vital aspect of CCF organization in many parts of the province.

Another early effort at consolidation was an expansion of the Provincial Council from thirty-seven members to fifty through the zone plan. All ridings were grouped into zones, each of which was to elect a member to the Provincial Council. The object of this expansion was to make the Council more representative and to facilitate contact between the top leadership and the far-flung rank and file through the local leaders.[19] Another aim was undoubtedly to draw the latter more deeply into the CCF's affairs and thereby to strengthen its local leadership and organizations, which, the top leaders felt, were its main weakness.

Among the most important changes was in the method of raising money. The Ontario CCF's initial response to the post-1945 financial crisis had been desperate and confused, with the results noted earlier,[20] but, before long, order began to emerge. Appeals for money were coordinated, as the party adopted a new approach to the problem of finances, one which it justified in the following general terms: " . . . membership is the heart of the problem of finance . . . our members must realize that the membership fee is only a bond of identity which covers the service charge only on that membership."[21]

On this principle, in late 1945, the Ontario CCF decided to inaugurate a system of graduated membership fees[22] which would be collected

[18]Provincial Council, Minutes, Aug. 25, 1945.

[19]This suggests that the distance between a party's top leaders and their followers is usually determined by its electoral fortunes.

[20]See p. 77 above.

[21]Finance Committee, Report to Provincial Executive, April 2 and 8, 1946.

[22]This plan originally set up two main categories of membership: Regular and Sustaining. Regular membership cost $2 a year; it was raised to $3 in 1946 and to $5 in 1960. Sustaining membership was initially set at a minimum of $25 per year. Within two years, that rate was reduced to $10, where it remained. However, in 1951, a third membership category, the Five Hundred Club, was created for those who contributed $60 or more annually. (The name of that category expressed the party's hope of finding 500 members who would join it.)

All membership fees were for one year, and Sustaining and Five Hundred Club members were not entitled to any special privileges. Many members in all categories made donations together with their fees, apart from special election contributions and the like. The membership category to which one belonged was a

as part of an annual financial campaign. The new system was highly successful and, throughout the 1950's, Sustaining and Five Hundred Club membership fees constituted the Ontario Section's largest single source of revenue and enabled it to become a financial mainstay of the national organization. The latter encountered serious financial difficulties of its own. In 1946, it proposed and the provincial sections accepted, a one dollar national fee per member to replace the haphazard system of provincial quotas which had hitherto been its main source of revenue. The payment of the national membership fee constituted the first direct financial link between the individual member and the national body.

INVOLVEMENT

The most drastic change which the double defeat of June 1945 inflicted on the CCF was in morale. During the preceding years, the members' involvement had come to rest heavily on the prospect of early victory. Therefore, when these resounding defeats removed that prospect, morale slumped accordingly. The effects were especially devastating in the weaker areas, where hope of victory in the foreseeable future all but disappeared.

The most conspicuous evidence of this relation between involvement and expectations of imminent success is the sharp drop in membership immediately after June 1945 (see Table VI). But these figures, so visible as an index, do not reveal another significant consequence of sinking hopes—the sharp reduction of involvement among many who remained. The CCF's records, particularly the reports of the organizers, document that reaction thoroughly. The two passages below appraise respectively the problems of the party in Ontario and in the country as a whole.

Conclusions. None of the ridings I visited either before or after the election are among what we might call our better ridings. At the same time several are in what could be referred to as the medium group and are probably areas which we will have to win before we can claim a majority in Ontario. One thing that struck me was that, though in most of these ridings we have a nucleus of hard workers of varying degrees of competence, few of these workers have any idea of how to carry on a dynamic CCF campaign. I suspect that their shortcomings are most apparent in between elections when, I imagine, CCF activities in their particular ridings go dead except

---

matter of one's own choice, subject, of course, to the informal pressure which the system was intended to produce. For example, many officials in at least one allied union joined the Five Hundred Club through a check-off system which the union administered.

for a few club meetings attended only by the faithful. The lack of effective action at election time is the inevitable result of sterility in between elections.

There are thousands of people across this country who have drifted out of the CCF because of our organizational incompetence—a growing belief on their part that organizationally we are not a going concern. There is nothing which has such a disastrous effect on the morale of a local group, particularly its leadership, as to watch memberships drop from 100 to 50, then 25, and even 10. That has happened in scores of ridings during the past few years.[23]

The following report explains why these difficulties were most pronounced in the party's weakest branches:

Though we think there is growing support for the CCF in S [riding], the present candidate and election prospects are poor. The difficulty is that the local people have slugged through several elections now and feel that they know their limitations. They don't think they can swing the riding. We worked hard to persuade them that winning the riding was not the only reason why we should run a CCF candidate. . . .[24]

Defections and apathy appeared to be more extensive in areas of this kind and among the more prominent people who had entered the party during its exciting upsurge. Some members declared the party well rid of opportunists and talked about a valuable winnowing process. But most CCF leaders did not agree. In an interview, one of those at the very top did not attribute that exodus to insincerity.

You were asking about the old core of socialist members. Well, they were never very effective. The success in 1943 was much more the work of the newcomers. Many of those new people had never really been interested in politics, but they were fed up with the old parties. They were harder to hold, though, partly because they were usually people with many other interests.

Another top leader expressed a similar view: "People like a winner. It attracts interest. I don't mean that these people [who left] weren't completely sincere, but. . . ."

The magnitude of these and of subsequent defeats not only discouraged the members but also led the public increasingly to conclude that the CCF had "no chance" and that a ballot cast for its candidate would be wasted. Thus with public interest receding and with their own shrunken membership more discouraged, many riding associations, if they carried on at all, did so with correspondingly less enthusiasm. The result was usually a weaker campaign and candidate in the next election and therefore an even more devastating defeat.

[23]Organizer's Report to Provincial Secretary, Sept. 10, 1949; Organization Report to National Council, March 1–2, 1952.
[24]Organizer's Report, summer 1951.

Just as the CCF's successes at the beginning of the decade had set in motion a process in which victory, hope and popular interest had all grown by nourishing each other, so the setbacks in 1945 reversed that process and initiated a similar relation among defeat, discouragement and loss of public interest. Nevertheless, the party did respond with immediate and sustained efforts to consolidate its position, and, during the next decade, the fact became increasingly apparent that while these reversals had damaged the CCF severely, they had not smashed it. These two trends—a gradual downward spiral and growing efforts to reverse it, both of which began in June 1945—mark the party's main course throughout its final phase.

VII. Minor Party
1950-61

THE 1950's WERE, on the whole, a peaceful and prosperous time for Canada. Their great enemy, Canadians agreed, lay abroad, and few issues divided them passionately at home. Earnings and employment were high, and where economic misfortune did strike, its victims often received some protection from the welfare measures which had begun to appear towards the end of the war and continued thereafter.

Most CCFers, of course, continued to share in the general prosperity. Many were becoming deeply involved in their careers and families, which had begun to sprout during the war or immediately after; the prosperous post-war climate permitted these careers to establish firm roots in many directions, often in the trade union world. Finally, although the effects of this development must be pure conjecture, the party's stalwarts had grown two decades older.

The new period was, however, less prosperous for the party. The latter's final phase may be said to date from the federal election of 1949, which reduced its representation in Ottawa from thirty-two[1] to thirteen and its share of the vote from 16 per cent to 13 per cent. These results certified that the CCF's 1945 defeat had not been an accident and dismissed its last claim to major party status.

By the next federal election, in 1953, a succession of defeats, including one in Ontario in 1951, had clearly established the CCF's minor party standing. Its acceptance of this position was reflected in the remarks of its National Leader: in the 1945 campaign he had been introduced by enthusiastic chairmen as "the next Prime Minister of Canada" but in 1953, at what was intended to be an inspirational meeting of election workers, he limited his forecast of CCF success to repeating, "We're going to have a very good group in the next house."

[1]By-election victories had increased it by four since 1945.

By the 1957 federal campaign, the party's problem was to retain third place against the challenge of Social Credit. Finally, in the Conservative sweep of 1958, the CCF's representation in Ottawa fell from twenty-five to eight, including the loss of most of its top leaders, despite a mere one per cent slip in its popular vote.

In Ontario's provincial elections, despite the remarkable comeback in 1948, the pattern was essentially similar. The next contest, in 1951, sliced the party's representation in Queen's Park[2] from twenty-one to two and its portion of the vote from 27 per cent to 19 per cent. More significantly, the Liberals dislodged the CCF permanently from second place. Although the CCF gained one seat in 1955 and two more in 1959, it kept falling farther behind the Liberals. Thus, early in the final period, the CCF had been reduced to a minor party both nationally and in Ontario.

IDEOLOGY

As long as it was a major party, the CCF was able to campaign in the customary manner of these parties—by emphasizing what it would do about the issues of the day when *it* got into office. Pronouncements about socialism did not cease but they were muffled by the constant din of the battle for power. When the CCF was forced out of the main contest and could no longer campaign on its intentions when in office, the question of its *raison d'être* again became prominent, and the party returned to the theme of "capitalism and depressions."

For some years after the war, it will be recalled, the CCF had insisted that capitalism owed its apparent success entirely to "artificial" stimulants. When they disappeared, a major depression or, in the ominous terms of the left wing, a new artificial stimulant would be inevitable. In this return to the theme of depressions, the CCF was no longer protesting present suffering; it was recalling a receding past and predicting a disastrous future which failed to materialize. Meanwhile, its public support was slipping slowly but steadily away.

With growing conviction, the CCF drew two main lessons from these repeated rebuffs and the nation's continued prosperity. First, it concluded that its consistently gloomy prophecies were alienating the public. The disadvantages of this approach were discussed openly at a special National Council session on basic strategy.[3]

the National Executive, in planning the council meeeting, had planned . . . that most . . . of the time might be devoted to a re-appraisal of the application

[2]The Ontario legislature.
[3]The quotations are from National Council, Minutes, Jan. 13–15, 1956.

of our CCF philosophy and program today. Everywhere, except in the province of Saskatchewan, there has been a serious decline in CCF support since the end of the war; it has been particularly sharp in rural areas and among the middle classes. The National Council, comprising as it does the leadership of the movement, has a direct responsibility in endeavouring to discover whether the proper application of a democratic socialist philosophy and programme to the present economic and political conditions in Canada is being made.

In his address to the meeting, the National Leader, M. J. Coldwell, remarked,

During the second world war the CCF shared the view universally held, that early in the postwar period the world would face another and perhaps even greater and more widespread depression than that of the thirties. . . . I do not believe this to be any longer a valid assumption which should govern our policies and plans for the next five years.

In a "summary of the chief points raised during the [Council's] discussion," a subcommittee stated as the first recommendation that

The immediate CCF appeal should not be based, as it has for the past 15 years or more, on the anticipation of a depression or major recession. Whether such a depression comes or not, the public has heard us say this so long and so often that they no longer listen to appeals based on this premise.

The discussion reveals the CCF's search for a new direction both in doctrine and in approach to the public. With respect to the latter, the party relegated to the background the "negative" approach of an inevitable depression and concentrated instead on a "positive" emphasis on specific reforms to alleviate the existing "injustices of capitalism."[4] Throughout the 1950's the CCF concentrated so heavily on the issues of increased old age pensions and, above all, of a national health plan that an unwary outsider might have concluded that they constituted the party's central reason for existence. They were, in reality, expressions of the new strategy of intensive championship of specific reforms.

However, except in Saskatchewan, it was the "old parties," and not the CCF, who implemented welfare measures and thereby endangered

[4]The 1958 federal election, however, was fought at the height of a recession. At a city-wide election meeting in Toronto, speaker after speaker of the CCF's top echelons thundered denunciations of "capitalism," in a style unheard for many years, to an audience that was surprisingly large and electrifyingly receptive. Although the appeal of the "old time religion" was so great on both sides, when the smoke of battle cleared on election night, the field was littered with the casualties of all of the parties save the Conservative. Among them were the CCF's two top leaders and all but one of its once mighty contingent from Saskatchewan.

the latter's distinctiveness and sense of purpose. The CCF responded to the threat partly by pointing to its bedrock beliefs but increasingly in the traditional manner employed by the "old parties" when major ideological issues seem absent—by charging its rivals with incompetence and insincerity.[5] The following effort to differentiate itself on the grounds of both competence and sincerity is a case in point:

The old parties are finally committed to hospital insurance, for delivery in 1959, as the first installment on national health insurance. But after 38 years of talking about it, provision of full health coverage is now postponed indefinitely. . . .

This development provides an eloquent comment on one of the recurring themes at election time: don't waste your vote by giving it to a CCF candidate, for they haven't a chance.

Obviously, in the light of our experience in this long battle for a modern health program, the people who have been losing their votes consistently since 1919 are those who voted for Liberals and Conservatives in the vain hope that these parties would fulfil their promises.

For the great majority of people in Canada who want full health coverage, the certain way to lose their vote in this election is to cast it for the old parties whose sorry record speaks for itself. On JUNE 10, if the people of Canada vote for the things they believe in, they will vote CCF. Observers of the House of Commons have stated many times, notably during the session just concluded, that man-for-man, the CCF group is the most effective one in the House. They are effective because they are fighting for things they believe in—and not merely with an eye to the ballot box.[6]

With its weakened position and its new concentration on specific reforms, the CCF set out to explain to its members and to the public the contribution made by a minor, reform party. At meeting after meeting, in every federal campaign of the 1950's, its speakers tirelessly revived a tale of thirty years earlier—how J. S. Woodsworth had wrested old age pensions from Mackenzie King, as the price of support, when he and a colleague had held the balance of power in the House of Commons in 1926. The point of the story was more than nostalgic; it was to assure wavering supporters that CCF votes would not be "wasted," even if there was no hope of a major victory. By holding the balance of power, it reminded them, a party would be in an excellent position to obtain concessions.

[5]In the 1950's, the CCF denounced them primarily on the conventional grounds of highway and natural gas scandals, lack of respect for Parliament, smug complacency and the like. In addition, many CCFers now saw their opponents in shades of grey instead of the earlier solid black, a view which the latter reciprocated, all the more readily perhaps because of the CCF's weakness.

[6]Donald C. MacDonald (CCF Leader in Ontario), "The Meaning of a Vote," front page article, CCF News, May 1957.

Besides using the balance of power argument, the CCF appealed for public support on complementary grounds:

> The [Election] committee has reviewed the full federal election program and has tentatively selected some points . . . to feature in the campaign. The Committee believes that the central idea to be stressed in the campaign is that the CCF though numerically weak in parliament has already accomplished a great deal for the people of Canada from old age pensions on and that increased CCF representation will mean even greater benefits for the people.[7]

The passage above expresses the party's prevailing self-justification throughout the last period. It took every opportunity to inform the public and remind its followers of its indispensable role in securing welfare legislation. The following represents a moderate version of these claims:

> I don't suggest that we have been responsible for every more or less decent piece of social legislation on the Statute Books. . . . But I am suggesting that most of those laws that are to any extent worthwhile would have been even longer in coming if it weren't for the prodding and growing strength of our movement.[8]

The CCF believed that it had aroused sufficient popular support for these reform measures to force the "old parties" to make at least gestures at welfare legislation, if only to check CCF popularity. The National Leader, M. J. Coldwell, expressed such a view in mild and humorous vein at a meeting in the 1953 campaign.

> We have been responsible for all the good legislation passed in Canada. . . . Mackenzie King admitted that to me himself on one of his fishing expeditions. He was telling me that the Liberal party was where I belong. (Expressions of amusement on the face of the speaker and the audience.) I told him that could never be. "Well," he said, "you prepare the ground for the social legislation which we can then pass." "And also take the credit for," I replied.

A more typical CCF comment on this subject is the following:

> There was an article in the papers recently by a woman who works for one of the big cake-mix companies. She said women just won't follow the directions on the package. They dump the stuff in a bowl and mix in whatever proportions strike them as right. Then they stick the mess in the oven, expecting a perfect cake to come out—and blame the manufacturer when it's a failure.

[7]Provincial Executive, Minutes, May 23, 1953.
[8]David Lewis, National Chairman, in an address to the National Convention, 1956.

This is exactly like the Old Parties' treatment of CCF ideas—except that most women buy their cake-mix and the Old Parties steal our ideas. . . .

Let us never imagine that we are doing our full job by rousing the imagination of Canadian citizens. Nor are we doing our full job by badgering Liberal and Conservative governments for reforms and improvements. The only way we can do our full job is by electing a CCF government to carry out fully and conscientiously the will of the people, without watering down every measure to suit pressure groups.[9]

Although its *raison d'être* increasingly became to force its rivals to adopt welfare measures, the CCF continued to denounce them when they did, charging that since these "thefts" from its platform were motivated solely by expediency rather than conviction, the "old parties" could not enact them effectively and enthusiastically. The CCF could, because these measures expressed its basic philosophy, to which the whole party unreservedly subscribed.

These contrasting portraits, which the CCF painted of itself and its rivals, summarize its arguments about its distinctiveness, its *raison d'être* and why it deserved the strongest support. Neither the CCF's claims of responsibility for Canada's welfare legislation nor its accusations of theft against the "old parties" were at all new; nor were they limited to CCF spokesmen. But in its last decade the party came to rest its claim for support more heavily on these arguments.

It would be wrong to conclude that the CCF altered its approach simply out of the belief that the previous one was inexpedient. Beneath that belief another and more significant one had been growing, as CCFers, together with socialists the world over, began to wonder, at first privately and then more and more openly, whether cataclysmic breakdowns of the capitalist system really were inevitable—in short, whether capitalism, for all its obvious "injustices," might not work, and whether the socialism of their original faith wasn't as much a panacea as a cure.[10] A speech delivered in 1955 by the party's National Chairman, one of its most influential leaders, perhaps best expressed this change of viewpoint.

In view of my official position as National Chairman of the CCF, I should emphasize immediately that what I say here this evening represents my own thoughts and opinions and is not necessarily official party policy. I am confident, from my knowledge of the CCF and its personnel, that most of the opinions I shall express are shared by a majority of our members and by a majority of the National Executive and Council. But, in fairness, it should

[9]Peg Stewart (President of Ontario CCF), "Female Type," guest front page editorial, *CCF News*, Oct. 1956.

[10]Because the Saskatchewan Government was the pride of the whole party, its peaceful and, indeed apparently cordial coexistence with "private enterprise" had inevitably made a strong impression on the CCF's outlook.

be understood that my remarks have not even been seen, let alone approved, by any of my colleagues on the National Executive or Council and that they are, therefore, made on my own personal responsibility. . . . .

Perhaps first among socialist controversies is the question of the extent to which the tool of public ownership can or should be used by socialists in modern society. The disagreement on this issue really dates back to the very first discussions of socialism, but it has become sharpened and more acute in the last quarter of a century . . . for several reasons which derive from the experience which societies have had in the past twenty-five or so years.

Until fairly recently it had been accepted by most socialists as axiomatic that nationalization of industry would automatically bring with it greater social and political freedom and a release from the obstacles to the widest liberty which private economic power produces. Place the ownership of the economy in the hands of the people through their government, the argument ran, and you will automatically remove the evil influence and power of private corporations and simultaneously give the workers unheard-of freedom. It was also accepted by many socialists as axiomatic that a country in which private capitalism has been abolished will automatically and necessarily be a country of peace, a country which will have no reason to want aggression against or domination over other lands.

PUBLIC OWNERSHIP NO PANACEA

The developments in the Soviet Union, in particular, and in other communist states as well, have completely shattered both these assumptions and have shown them to have been and to be entirely false. In the communist societies all wealth, or almost all wealth, has been taken over by the state. But, instead of greater freedom, there is actually no freedom at all. The power of the private corporation has been replaced by the totalitarian power of the communist party and state over the lives of the workers, farmers and every other section of the community. Far from releasing the wells of liberty, the concentration of economic and political power in the communist state has poisoned them altogether. That experience is conclusive evidence that public ownership alone does not guarantee freedom; that political and social freedom—the foundation-stone of any desirable society—is not dependent only on the form of ownership in the economy.

Similarly, we have learned from the actions of the Soviet Union since the end of the war and from the military structure of communist society as a whole, that there are pressures toward aggression and war other than economic ones and that the lust for power and the zeal of fanaticism are at least as powerful forces endangering peace as economic competition and conflicts.

In short, the comfortable generalizations of the early socialists have been proven by history to be false, or only partially valid, although they were genuinely and well meant. Socialists can, therefore, no longer regard nationalization as an automatic panacea for all ills, but must regard it merely as one tool that is available in appropriate circumstances for the furtherance of socialist ends. . . .

NEVER TOTAL NATIONALIZATION

It follows from what has been said that the democratic socialist today should continue to reject any suggestion of total nationalization. In fact, of course, he has always rejected it and has always emphasized that he is concerned with public ownership only of the key economic levers of society. Nevertheless, the idea is still abroad that socialists intend eventually, if not now, to socialize everything. I, as one socialist, have no such intention, and it is my firm belief that neither the CCF in Canada, nor its sister parties in Great Britain and all other free countries, has such an intention or ever had. Public ownership in a democratic society and under a democratic socialist government will never cover more than a part of the economy and only that part the public ownership of which is essential for the welfare of the people. The time is long overdue when this should be frankly stated without qualification and without apology.[11]

Thus, two main ideas were crystallizing among the party's leaders— that its traditional viewpoint was, at best, "only partially valid" and certainly was unpopular. They therefore demanded not only the change in strategy described earlier[12] but also a reformulation—"rethinking" was the usual word—of the CCF's basic policies. The result was the adoption by the 1956 National Convention of the Winnipeg Declaration, the most official and, as it happened, most publicized statement of the CCF's increasingly "moderate" ideology.

The desire to formulate a new set of principles which would bring the Regina Manifesto "up to date" can be traced much farther back. However, replacing or even revising the Regina Manifesto was a delicate matter. Over the years it had acquired an aura of sanctity as *the* expression of the principles of the founding fathers who, here as elsewhere, had grown in stature with the passage of time. Furthermore, the left wing had long since taken this hallowed ground as its main line of defence against the CCF's "drift to the right." From it they could best champion the venerable socialist maxim, now rarely heard, "From each according to his ability; to each according to his need." But, by basing its stand on the inviolability of the Regina Manifesto, the left wing increased the ambivalence of the other faction and especially of its leaders towards that document, as the following passage indicates:

The Eleventh National Convention of the CCF reaffirmed its faith in the underlying basic principles set out in the Regina Manifesto and instructed the National Council to prepare for submission to the 1952 convention "a statement of the application of democratic socialist principles for Canada and the world today. . . ." Some delegates expressed fear lest any rewriting of the Regina Manifesto should result in a "watering down" of its basic principles. "So long as the Regina Manifesto stands, we are safe," veteran Ernie Winch, MLA from B.C. declared. "I respect the venerable Regina statement," said David Lewis, "but it is not a sacrosanct Bible in every word and comma. . . ."

[11]Lewis, *A Socialist Takes Stock*, pp. 3–9.
[12]See above, pp. 86–90.

"As an expression of democratic socialism, the Regina Manifesto is just as effective today as in 1933", said Prof. Frank Scott, retiring [national] chairman, who helped write the document. "But . . . a re-interpretation of its principles is overdue."
By a big majority vote, the convention concurred.[13]

When the new statement did appear, six years later, as the Winnipeg Declaration, it aroused a furore, as the nation's press and periodicals, friends and foes of the CCF alike, unanimously agreed that it constituted a significant shift to the right. On the nagging question of social owner-ship, the most vital part of the document, it stated in the section headed "Social Planning for a Just Society":

In the co-operative commonwealth there will be an important role for public, private and co-operative enterprise working together in the people's interest.
The CCF has always recognized public ownership as the most effective means of breaking the stranglehold of private monopolies on the life of the nation and of facilitating the social planning necessary for economic security and advance. The CCF will, therefore, extend public ownership wherever it is necessary for the achievement of these objectives.
At the same time, the CCF also recognizes that in many fields there will be need for private enterprise which can make a useful contribution to the development of our economy.[14] The co-operative commonwealth will, there-fore, provide appropriate opportunities for private business as well as pub-licly-owned industry. . . .

Since this stand was identical to that in "Security for All" (1948), the attention which it received may seem surprising. It stemmed in part from the lingering public (and newspaper) image of the CCF as com-mitted to all-out socialism, but it also reflected the party's decision to enunciate its revised beliefs in the most open, official and binding way possible by issuing them in a statement of "basic principles" rather than, as heretofore, in election platforms.

As significant as anything which the Winnipeg Declaration said was what CCFers said about it to each other. Their debate revealed the ground upon which the party's last internal ideological battle was fought and its difficulties in arriving at a satisfactory ideology. The left wing naturally attacked the Declaration as a "watering down" of socialism.

There seems to be a widespread impression that the Winnipeg Declaration is the result of some deep "re-thinking" on the part of the CCF. Other socialist parties, we are told, have brought their programs up to date and it

[13]*CCF News*, Aug. 31, 1950.
[14]This sentence, combined with the title of the preceding section, "Capitalism Basically Immoral," neatly expresses the party's continued ambivalence on this subject. For the whole text of the Winnipeg Declaration, see App. B.

is time for us to do likewise. But a comparison of their efforts with ours shows that it is not "re-thinking" but the lack of it that characterizes the Declaration.

In Britain . . . the nationalization program has by no means been abandoned. The CCF, on the other hand, has de-emphasized public ownership by its conspicuous failure to specify exactly what its intentions are. This is not re-thinking, unless the word is just a euphemism for watering down the program. . . .[15]

The Gaitskell forces say less nationalization, but they have nothing else to offer in its place, no other means to sharing and brotherhood. When I see symptoms of the same thing here in Canada, I cannot help questioning.

Socialism to me is not a search for economic devices to make capitalism work. It is my religion, my very soul.[16]

In discussions with my socialist friends, I have detected disillusion and even disgust with recent events in Winnipeg. Much of this feeling is due to misconceptions which I think can be cleared up in this column.

Misconception No. 1—*The Winnipeg Declaration is a new divergence from the socialist notion that public ownership can contribute to a more just society.* A close study of the document reveals the falseness of this. There are no new ideas in it at all: it is a clear exposition of liberal democracy of the Bentham, Locke and Mill school.

No. 2—*There will be widespread objection to the Declaration.* Not so; it is perfectly acceptable to me, to you, to Uncle Louis and Col. Drew; indeed all Canadians who abhor sin.

No. 3—*This is a bit of expediency to woo labour.* Again if one examines the document very closely one can find only a slight reference to trade unions which in effect declares that we are in favour of such organizations.

No. 4—*The CCF is officially non-socialist.* One of the persistent cliches of the radical movement is that the capitalist press is always wrong. The Financial Post, the Telegram and all the other capitalist organs say the CCF is no longer socialist, therefore it is socialist!

No. 5—*The declaration was sprung upon the delegates without advance notice.* This is absurd of course. The National Council had its final draft ready the night before. That is almost twelve hours, surely plenty of notice.

No. 6—*The convention used a form of closure on the amendment offered by the delegate from Spadina.* This is a most wicked notion. The Chair announced he would accept two speakers, one for, and one against. Bob Kenzie spoke for his amendment and George Grube moved to table. That was ample discussion for a subject as unimportant as public ownership at a socialist convention.

No. 7—*The CCF has become monolithic in its drafting of policy; all policy declarations are presented from above.* This misconception is easily dissipated when one realizes that *some* of the resolutions came from the ridings.

[15]Bob Kenzie, "To Fight Materialism," letter to the Editor, *CCF News*, Jan. 1957.
[16]Fred Richardson, "Soul of Socialism," front page article, *CCF News*, Dec. 1956.

But need I go on? It is obvious that all who claim to be disappointed are woolly-headed newcomers or die-hard, doctrinaire, static, fundamentalist, non-conformers who should be drummed out of The Party forthwith.[17]

The dominant right wing replied to these charges by stating that the Winnipeg Declaration was a "modernization" and "clarification" of the Regina Manifesto rather than a significant departure from its principles. This view was expressed by the Declaration's two defenders, both top Ontario leaders, in the debate reported here and in the article, which follows it, by another prominent leader. (The debate took place in a riding association in which the left wing was unusually strong.)

The CCF's Winnipeg Declaration came in for some rather rough handling at a meeting of the Spadina Riding Association, when four panelists and an alert audience gave it a close and critical look.

Although criticism ranged from gentle wrist-slapping to robust kicks in the nether anatomical regions, a surprising degree of agreement emerged. Spencer Cheshire and Robert Kenzie, centre of the "public-ownership-clause" controversy in Winnipeg, beside the earlier 1933 Regina Manifesto, called the Winnipeg Declaration, "the whimperings of a child as compared to the robust shouting of an adult," and felt it, "the Winnipeg statement", put the CCF in "an hypocritical position" with regard to private enterprise.

On the other hand, George Grube and Ken Bryden, defenders of the Declaration, insisted it was no new departure in fundamental assumptions. "Absolute nonsense," proclaimed Ken Bryden of the charge that the CCF attitude to private enterprise had undergone a radical change. "Security with Victory," the 1944 program, and "Security for All," the 1948 program, came out a good deal more strongly on the subject, he declared. The newspapers, he stated, had "contrived" to confirm predictions of a CCF swing to the right by interpreting proceedings to bear themselves out in their roles as self-appointed prophets. The Regina Manifesto was drawn up "in the pit of the depression", and he favored a re-statement of principles every two or three years since "re-thinking" of its fundamental premises was absolutely essential for a Socialist party.

Kenzie took immediate issue with the view that there had been no real change. He quoted R. H. S. Crossman, British Labor M.P. who had been in Canada during the summer, as stating that the CCF was now unwilling to "scare investors off" by threats of projected large-scale nationalization . . . waving a copy of the Winnipeg Declaration, [Kenzie] called it "the same old poker game . . . its philosophy of equality of opportunity is not Socialist opportunity . . . it makes us all contestants in a race for personal gain. Competition is the rule, not co-operation."

Winnipeg had come out in favor of public ownership "where necessary," but had conspicuously failed to suggest proposed vital areas. On this point there appeared to be broad agreement. Ken Bryden pointed out that the CCF National Council was at work on an election platform which would

[17]Boris Mather, " 'Defence' of the Declaration," letter to the Editor, *CCF News*, Sept. 1956.

incorporate the resolutions for the 1956 convention, but agreed that divorcing principles from platform had been an error in judgment. George Grube agreed that National Council "had no business bringing the document three days before the convention" but roundly rejected other criticism of the Declaration. "You cannot socialize everything," he said. "Destroying all private initiative is communism. No democratic socialist ever held such a doctrine."

. . . Extreme critics of private enterprise failed to recognize that there were large sections of private enterprise where genuine competition exists. "It's stupid to say otherwise," he stated bluntly, pounding the table for emphasis. Equality of opportunity is the meaning of democracy, it does not mean that "one man sweats his guts out and is rewarded equally with the loafer."

Bryden was equally emphatic on this point. "Equality of opportunity is concerned with matters such as education and health", he insisted. "I repudiate 100 percent the suggestion that it is a spur to economic advantage."

The question of public ownership seemed to hang over the meeting like a giant unseen question mark and came up repeatedly. . . . Most of the audience questions were thinly veiled statements of opinion. Larry Bennett of the Steelworkers Union asked if the CCF is providing a program that differentiates it sufficiently from the old-line parties. "There has been a loss of integrity," he declared.

"Is the CCF the party of the working classes?" asked Boris Mather, CCF Spadina candidate in the last provincial election. "There is no mention of it in the Declaration." The CCF is a federation of labor, farm and co-operative organizations, replied Ken Bryden, and he would still describe it that way.

Another member of the audience characterized the Declaration as a kind of political supermarket . . . "anybody can buy anything he wants in it." Mrs. F. Easser declared herself reluctant to discuss the CCF program with prospective voters on the basis of the present Winnipeg Declaration; it was "too vague and ambiguous".

Another person asked what the CCF was doing to prepare itself for the organization of a "co-operative" society when it assumed office. Spencer Cheshire deplored general lack of participation by CCF members in co-operative movements, but other panelists re-affirmed their own faith in the "co-operative way of life", agreed that the Winnipeg Declaration, whatever its merits or faults, "can be credited with one clear achievement. . . . It has set CCFers to thinking harder about their party's program and general philosophy than anything since the Regina Manifesto." And nobody was arguing against the value of that.[18]

The Winnipeg Declaration is, like its predecessor, the Regina Manifesto, a thoroughly liberal document. To those who associate liberalism with the Liberal Party of Canada this statement may come as a displeasing shock. But the Liberal Party which banishes to the Senate any of its more active members who display liberal tendencies has long since abandoned Liberalism. And the CCF may well be proud that it has become in Canada the effective inheritor of the liberal tradition.

For the liberal tradition represented, in spite of its blindness to the fact that

[18]George Shane, "Pros and Cons," *CCF News*, Dec. 1956.

economic .equality was the only sound foundation for true freedom, very great and essential gains in human development, gains that have to be defended in every generation. . . .

Let those of us who are active in the CCF make it clear to all who believe in the liberal tradition and in a living and vigorous democracy that the CCF is their party.[19]

The left wing's stand expressed its constant opposition to the party's "rightward" movement. Like the minority factions of the Republican and British Labour parties, it accused the leaders of "me-tooism" and alleged that the CCF had lost considerable support because it had become too similar ideologically to its rivals. The left wing advocated instead a return to the kind of unmistakably socialist appeal of the early 1930's. Such a stand, it declared, would have two great advantages. Not only would the CCF's distinctive identity be preserved but the party would be in a much better position to seek power and to deal with the prevailing problems when the next depression inevitably arrived. Unlike the right's, the left wing's certainty that major depressions are unavoidable under capitalism had not weakened. It elaborated these views in a Provincial Council post-mortem on the 1955 Ontario election.

A said that in 1951 he had received 7,800 votes and had lost. Yet in 1955 the Conservative candidate won with 7,600 votes. Why did so many people not consider it was worth their trouble to vote? They were disgusted with the Tories but apparently they were not prepared to accept the CCF or the Liberals. In his canvassing he had a good response but, in spite of this, there had not been enough enthusiasm to bring the people to the polls on election day. In order to generate this enthusiasm we must return to the fundamental economic proposition that capitalism and the profit system do not solve the problems of modern society. It is important that we should also stress specific proposals such as public housing and health insurance, but in themselves these are not enough. It is necessary to show that there is a real difference between the CCF and the Liberals. Such an approach would probably not have made any significant difference in terms of seats in this particular election, but if we had followed it, we would have laid a better foundation for future elections. *Organization is important but we cannot evade the need for basic education.*[20]

This viewpoint and its spokesmen lost influence throughout the final period. Prosperity was perhaps the main reason, but another was the virtual collapse of the Communists' influence as a result of the prolonged cold war and their confusion during the "de-Stalinization" programme.

[19]F. A. Brewin, "Not 'Liberal' but Liberal," front page article, *CCF News,* Nov. 1956.
[20]Provincial Council, Minutes, June 25–26, 1955 (italics added).

The process by which the Communist party affected CCF doctrines appears complex. If the former were simply a more extreme "left wing" group than the CCF, one could explain the effect by elementary mechanical principles—if the pull on the CCF from the left weakened, the one from the opposite direction would be that much harder to resist. Despite the apparent naïveté of this model and the many CCFers who agreed with Guy Mollet's celebrated observation that Communism is not left, but east, this mechanical analogy is surprisingly useful. What makes it so was that many CCF left wingers, however much they disapproved of the Communists, did regard them as "left" of the CCF. Even those who did not hold this view tended to believe that "the workers" did, and it was "the workers'" reaction to the CCF that concerned them most. Consequently they opposed every CCF move to the "right" not only on ideological but also tactical grounds—that it would alienate many sympathizers and "drive" them to the Communists. In addition, like those who advocate aid for certain countries to forestall Soviet inroads, they demanded that the CCF take "positive action" to prevent Communist gains at its expense.

In earlier periods, CCF strategy had sometimes unintentionally reinforced the left wing's position. For instance, the party continually denounced two former Ontario premiers, Mitchell Hepburn and George Drew, as dangerous, would-be dictators. Such prominent and menacing "villains" were, of course, a first rate asset to the party. But the more successful the CCF's denunciation was, the harder it became, especially for its left wing, to resist the Communist party's blandishments that the CCF unite with it "in an all-out effort of all progressive elements to overthrow the forces of reaction."

Fear that the Communists might make inroads into the party's following usually strengthened the hand of the CCF's left wing. The steady Communist decline therefore helps to explain this wing's weakness in the 1950's and the consequent abatement of major factional disputes in the party as a whole. The feeble opposition at the 1956 National Convention to the adoption of the Winnipeg Declaration effectively demonstrated the final balance of power in the CCF. Thus, indirectly, the Communist party had exerted an influence on the CCF. With that influence virtually removed, the party was freer to move with the current.

A seemingly trivial incident at the 1953 Provincial Convention showed how far it had moved. A left wing delegate arose and, pointing to the large signs on the walls of the convention chamber,

Democracy Lives in the CCF
It's "People First" with the CCF
The CCF Puts the Punch in Parliament
TRUTH and JUSTICE Guide the CCF
The CCF is *Yours*
Today and Tomorrow Belong to the CCF
The CCF is the People
The CCF Leads the Way

he caustically asked the convention, "I wonder if there's any slogan on the wall here that couldn't be adopted by any of the other parties?"

William Kornhauser's study of American liberals and radicals illuminates the hazards that beset these political groups.[21] The chief threat to the radical organization is that its uncompromising rejection of the social order may isolate it from its audience through derision, fear and even repression. Liberal groups, on the other hand, may lose their distinctive identity and sense of purpose if they fail to differentiate themselves clearly from the other parties. This danger has been particularly acute for American liberal organizations because the Democratic party has been so potent a rallying force for liberals and even socialists since 1932. The absence of such a force in Canada during that period permitted the CCF to attract a much greater range of support than any American equivalent. Except for the Communists and some insignificant Trotskyite splinter groups, the CCF thoroughly dominated "left of centre" politics.

Even so, the CCF found it difficult to steer a safe course between the twin shoals of isolation and loss of identity. Until 1942 its comparative radicalism isolated it from the main stream of Canadian politics, as its consistent failures demonstrate, while its greatest danger thereafter was the absence of a sharp distinction from the other parties, as the above incident illustrates. The remarks of the Provincial Leader in reporting on the 1951 election indicate that the party was on the defensive about its distinctiveness by that date: "[He] said that it was sheer nonsense to say that the political platforms of the Conservatives and the Liberals are similar to ours. If the contents of the speeches and radio broadcasts of the three leaders were analyzed that would be clearly seen."[22]

Before we complete the CCF's ideological journey, we must recall that it was by no means a one-way movement. The following remarks are reasonably accurate, although they tell only half the story.

[21]Kornhauser, "Organizational Loyalty."
[22]Provincial Council, Minutes, Jan. 12, 1952.

This winter a newspaper man said to me, "But you must admit the CCF has moved closer to the Old Parties." I replied, "No sir. The Old Parties have moved closer to the CCF."

That is the literal truth. The old parties have decided that "the welfare State" is respectable now—they've taken it to their bosoms. But only because the CCF has awakened the people of Canada to their needs.[23]

Whatever the cause, in the 1950's the CCF's main rivals did favour many welfare measures and were friendly towards the trade unions, although, in both instances, with greater reservation. All advocated similar policies on Russia, and communism at home was not an issue. Nor did other major issues distinguish the CCF sharply from the "old parties." Under these circumstances, what could its members talk about when they met, other than the "business" of their group?

The party responded to this persistent problem by devoting much of its "educational" programme to discussing, in the riding association meetings and on the other special occasions, its election platforms, major policy statements, such as the Winnipeg Declaration, and, above all, the rosters of resolutions for its impending conventions. The following passage is typical:

The provincial election will be used as a means of giving direction to our educational work . . . we can provide ourselves with a revised and dynamic provincial election program and at the same time stimulate the widest possible participation of our members in the formulation of that program. This is perhaps the most effective type of education that we can undertake, since it has a specific objective in view. . . .[24]

From the party's viewpoint, these discussions had the special merit of embodying, at least in form, its cardinal principle of policy formulation by the rank and file and they provided the local groups with a recurrent activity and a strong justification for existence.

The difficulty was that, in the 1950's, few issues aroused much excitement in the CCF. The resolutions stirred little controversy; most were either somewhat technical or reformulations of established policy or both. Others, such as the perennial temperance resolution, had acquired a ritualistic aspect, since their defeat was as inevitable as their appearance, and few, other than their proponents, treated them seriously. Finally, the decline of factionalism reduced the excitement and interest of meetings and conventions.

[23]Peg Stewart, in *CCF News*, May 1957.
[24]"Program of Action" adopted by Provincial Executive, Minutes, Aug. 15, 1953.

This general mood was responsible for incidents such as the following, which occurred at two meetings of a riding association in the mid-1950's:

The resolutions for the forthcoming national convention were the main item on the agenda. But, as usual, the discussion of business had dragged on to a late hour, and the small gathering was slightly dismayed when it saw the bulky folder of convention resolutions.

The chairman, an active and devoted member, asked if anyone wanted to examine the resolutions. There was no answer. She leafed idly through the folder without really looking at the contents—she had probably seen them earlier—and said, "There's nothing much new in here." In the absence of further comments, the meeting soon adjourned.

The main item of "business" at the second meeting was the formulation of the group's educational programme for the new year. The following discussion took place:

Harold J suggested that the program be based "on Saskatchewan." Joan C, a new member of the executive and of the group, spoke for the first time. She had to start several times because Harold J was still recommending an educational programme on the CCF's achievements as the Government of Saskatchewan. He paused several times; each time she began. Then he would resume as if he hadn't heard her, which was probably the case.

She finally got through, on about the fourth try, and made a very earnest plea for a "really interesting" programme, declaring how effective and necessary it was in order to attract and hold members. (It was an unusual effort in its earnest hopefulness, representing almost exactly what one might expect a newcomer to say.)

Mrs. F suggested that, with the federal election on the horizon, the group study the CCF election programme. She pointed out the advantages in canvassing of being well informed about the programme.

Elizabeth G, a top CCF officer of long standing, suggested that the group take a different magazine article for discussion at each monthly meeting. It should not plan the whole year's programme in advance but make one person responsible for the programme of each meeting. She rejected a suggestion that all members read the article in advance because "it makes too great a demand."

The suggestions of the last speaker were adopted but were never implemented.

However, none of these pronouncements, speeches and incidents spanned the whole ideological distance which the party travelled more clearly than did the following brief discussion, which occurred early in 1957 at a CCF educational conference on the Winnipeg Declaration.

The participants were divided into small discussion groups. (These "buzz groups," as they were called, were a favourite CCF discussion technique.) The group of four, whose remarks are recorded here, consisted of a top Ontario leader, two veteran local "leaders," i.e., executive members of riding associations, and one rank and file member. The last fortunately was a member of the left wing minority or the following conversation would never have ensued.

Group chairman (*local leader*): "Now we come to the question of whether we can get rid of inequalities. Can differences in income be eliminated?"

Rank and file member: "We should eliminate these differences. They're getting greater all the time."

Chairman: "I don't think that's necessary or desirable."

Top leader: "What we need is not equality of income. We have to raise the floor of wages."

Rank and file member: "We should have a ceiling on wages. Factory workers make just as great a contribution as any others and they're just as valuable."

Chairman: "No, they're not as valuable and important. It's easy to replace them."

Top leader: "Some people are content on $3,000 a year for example. Others want more and are willing to pay for it in work, education and responsibility."

Rank and file member: "But the factory workers have to have dignity as well, and socialism has to provide it.".

Top leader: "Certainly. That's why we're so in favour of unions. The problem is to get people to take responsibility. Most people don't want more. The more ambitious ones want more and look ahead for it. I can't be horrified by ambition, by people who want to get ahead and become president of the union or of the company."

Rank and file member: "Isn't it our job to protect people from the more powerful?"

Top leader: "Yes, that's what we have to do . . . but we can't prevent leadership or do without it."

Chairman: "Yes, and don't forget the sacrifices the leaders have to make. Their responsibility and worry doesn't end at 5 o'clock. For instance, the president of the company may be phoned late at night because something's gone wrong."

Top leader: "What gives me a pain are these people who don't work but who go to meetings of directors. . . . But we can get at those deadheads through taxation."

Second local leader (*speaking for the first time*): "There can't be complete planning without interfering with personal liberty. The mesh would be too small."

Rank and file member: "Prices are always getting higher. Every time that you go to the store everything is a few cents up."

Perhaps some of these people were pushed a little beyond their beliefs in this situation. Nevertheless, their remarks require no further comment. An interesting sidelight to this episode is that the *New Commonwealth,* the Ontario CCF's newspaper in the 1930's, contained few harsher indictments of capitalism than a series of articles by the chairman of this discussion group.

Thus, as it neared the 1960's, the CCF seemed to be turning into a liberal, reform party. Although it insisted, especially to its members, that its fundamental objectives had not altered, its ideological efforts to establish a new *modus vivendi* followed three main lines: (1) a revision of its official doctrine towards greater tolerance of private enterprise, (2) a heavier emphasis on specific, limited reforms and (3) a heightened concern about explaining the role of a minor, reform party to its members and the public. One long range consequence of this process may be that the term "socialism" will acquire the same symbolic and exalted status and a similarly vague and all-inclusive meaning as the words "liberalism" and "conservatism" have long had in their respective parties.

CCFers were sometimes labelled "Liberals in a hurry," especially by Liberals who were attempting to minimize the difference between the two parties in order to attract the CCF's leaders or voters into their own camp. None the less, that term was one sign that, despite the steady convergence of all parties on the political "centre," the CCF's viewpoint remained at least somewhat distinctive to the very end.

STRUCTURE

For the party's organization, the 1950's were as tranquil as the previous decade had been tempestuous. Instead of the rapid inflation and sudden puncture of the middle phase, the most important developments in the final one took place quietly and steadily behind the scene.

The period began convulsively enough. Whether it was still the aftermath to June 1945 or a reaction to the next disaster, the severe federal setback in 1949, the members resumed their mass departure. In Canada as a whole, one-third left within a year of the latter event. Losses continued everywhere, though on a reduced scale, in 1951, but again they were outweighed by a large gain in Saskatchewan in that year.[25]

The Ontario Section suffered heavy losses too. Although the general pattern there resembled that of 1945 to 1947 (see Table VI), the details differed in certain respects. Table VIII indicates the CCF's deeper penetration, especially on the lower levels of leadership, of the large steel and auto unions of Hamilton, Windsor and Oshawa. (Toronto did not hold as firm this time, but it remained, with Ottawa, well above the provincial average. Most other cities approximated that average.)

---

[25]The Saskatchewan figures fluctuated wildly during these few years. After rallying strongly in 1948, they fell to less than half by 1950 and then increased by over one-third in 1951.

TABLE VIII

CCF MEMBERSHIP IN ONTARIO, 1949–51*

(Membership in June 1949 in each area = 100)

	1949	1950	1951
Ontario	100	74	63
Toronto	100	83	73
Ottawa	100	87	70
Hamilton	100	103	80
Windsor	100	81	90
Oshawa	100	94	82
Northern Ontario	100	64	48
Eastern Ontario†	100	67	46
Central Ontario‡	100	63	55
Western Ontario§	100	69	64

*The 1950 figures are for April and the 1951 for December. By March 1951, the provincial total had fallen to 50 per cent of the June 1949 figure.
†Exclusive of Ottawa.
‡Exclusive of Toronto, Hamilton, and Oshawa.
§Exclusive of Windsor.

In 1951 the exodus finally came to an end; membership figures rallied in that year and again in 1953 and displayed unprecedented stability thereafter.

If the leaders elsewhere resembled those in Toronto, membership stability decreased as one descended the party hierarchy. Of the forty-seven top officers and candidates[26] in Toronto in 1945, 72 per cent were still members a decade later, as were 60 per cent of the city's 173 local officers.[27] Table IX indicates much less fidelity among the rank and file.[28] Retaining the latter continued to be especially difficult in the weaker ridings. In 1952, the Organization Committee reported (in its Minutes, Oct. 4–5), "Apart from these bright spots, the general picture is one of the organizers working hard to maintain the membership at its present level. There it little sign of progress towards the membership goal adopted . . . last May."

[26]In the provincial and federal elections of June 1945.

[27]Members of riding association executives. Increasingly, that came to mean all of the active members.

Of the "non-manual" local officers in 1945, almost three-quarters were still members in 1955 compared to half of the "manual" group. These figures may help to explain the stability of the party's occupational composition during the post-war period despite an apparently heavier recruitment of industrial workers. Although the middle class became poorer recruiting ground, its members seem to have been the more durable.

[28]Although the Toronto membership in 1955 stood at two-thirds of the 1945 level, many of these members had joined after 1945.

TABLE IX

CCF MEMBERSHIP IN ONTARIO, 1949–61
(Membership in June 1945 = 100)

1949	55
1950	41*
1951	35*
1952	36
1953	45
1954	44
1955	47
1956	42
1957	40
1958	46
1959	51
1960	45†
1961	37†

*The 1950 and 1951 figures are for April and December respectively. All others are for June or July. The March 1951 membership percentage stood at 27.

†These figures probably do not represent a real decline but some diversion of recruitment into the New Party Clubs.

Fresh efforts in the next few years produced roughly similar results. For example, throughout the autumn of 1954 the energetic new chairman of the Organization Committee tried to inject new vigour into efforts to expand the membership. She wrote to all riding presidents and secretaries pointing out the tremendous number of lapsed memberships and urging the ridings to make a concentrated attack on the problem of renewals. The letter concluded, "Surely we can all make at least One Call a week for the CCF." A membership secretary of a Toronto riding replied relating the difficulties of getting renewals and concluded with the mild protest:

We do make an effort to keep the renewals up to date. . . . I'll admit that I have been rather tardy about some but will try to get rolling. . . . There really appears to be an alarming amount of lapsed members and I would appreciate any suggestions you have to offer, but it probably boils down to putting more effort and enthusiasm into our work.[29]

In 1954, the Organization Committee launched a well-publicized new scheme, known as "The Pledge," to expand membership.

The committee has drawn up a plan for doubling our membership over the next two years. As part of this plan, it recommends that 200 people in our movement be asked to sign an undertaking that they will each sign up an average of at least two members per month . . . during the period between

[29]Organizing Committee, Records, 1954.

July 1, 1954 and June 30, 1956, and that members of the Executive and Council be the first asked to sign this undertaking so as to give a lead to others in our movement.

This recommendation was approved.[30]

Midway through the two year period, the Organization Committee reported that while the new scheme had brought in many new members, the party was losing two old ones for every three recruits. Shortly after the end of the two years,[31] the Committee reported frustratedly that it

had contacted all ridings urging them to get to work in renewing lapsed memberships. . . . Most of those lapsed memberships could undoubtedly have been renewed if only personal calls had been made. However, in spite of the fact that the committee had sent out two follow-up letters, there had been very little response from the ridings. The chairman said that the committee was at a loss to know what to do about this situation. Memberships could be picked up only by the local organizations, and yet the committee seemed to be up against a stone wall in its attempts to get any activity in all but a few of the local areas.[32]

Despite these difficulties, the CCF roughly balanced its losses. Its recruits seem to have included numerous British immigrants, many with trade union experience and Labour party allegiance.

However, the main reinforcement to the party organization came in another form and from another source—financial assistance from the trade unions. Advocacy of such support had originated many years earlier among the interlocking directors of the party and several large CCL (CIO) unions, but it had taken some time to percolate down and across union hierarchies. According to one CCF leader, "It was never a grass roots reaction; it came from the leaders. In most of the locals that affiliated, the local leaders were old country Labour people —probably most of the members too." The main centres of CCF strength in the trade unions were in several of the major CCL bodies, notably the steel, packinghouse and auto workers.

Their most tangible contribution to the party was the Political Action Committee, known as PAC. Besides financial assistance, the PAC contributed personnel and propaganda on the party's behalf both in the unions and outside, especially in election campaigns. Nevertheless, the CCF and its trade union supporters were disappointed with the results

[30]Provincial Executive, Minutes, June 12, 1954.

[31]When the pledge campaign was over, membership was slightly lower than when it began. See Table IX.

[32]Provincial Council, Minutes, Dec. 8, 1956.

of PAC support. The following CCF assessment of PAC tells why, and accurately forecasts subsequent developments.

PAC has been a matter of great disappointment and soul-searching not only in the CCF, but more particularly among those trade unionists who have been giving it leadership. Results in the recent Ontario election [1951] have shocked all concerned into a re-examination of political action methods. . . . there is emerging in the thinking of PAC leaders an organizational pattern which . . . is most encouraging. I emphasize that much of this is not a matter of official decision, certainly not as yet widely considered and accepted among the rank and file unionists. Trends in the thinking of PAC leaders are as follows:

1. That the ultimate goal is actual affiliation with the CCF on a per capita dues paying basis, similar to the British Labour Party, and thereby providing the movement with a stable financial base. . . .

2. That PAC should be closely integrated with the CCF organizationally, rather than, as originally conceived, an effort paralleling that of the CCF.

3. It follows that the objective is not a high-pressure publicity campaign by PAC which can be used by the daily press to drive away as many middle class and rural votes as it wins from labor, but, rather, a more quiet organization job.

4. In order to integrate CCF and PAC work at the riding and poll committee level, cooperation must be continuous rather than only after an election is called; to achieve this, full-time CCF organizers are necessary, and can be financed only through the pooling of financial resources.

If these trends in PAC thinking become a reality they offer real hope for more effective organization work.[33]

In the nine years before these "trends" materialized in the formation of the New Democratic party, the main form of union support was growing financial assistance. This helped the party to make a rapid and sustained recovery from the financial crisis created by the heavy membership losses immediately after 1949.

The figures shown in Table X, unlike those for earlier periods, do not provide a true picture of the CCF's financial position. They hardly begin to show either its improvement or who was responsible for it. The most direct source was the party's own membership, whose annual per capita fees and donations[34] had risen steadily from about eighty cents in 1935 to just over two dollars in 1945 to almost five and a half dollars in 1960.[35] The experience of the CCF's administrative staff in conducting

[33]National Council, Minutes, March 1–2, 1952.

[34]The term "donations" refers only to money above the membership fee contributed at the time of renewing or taking out membership. It does not include contributions to special appeals, especially for election funds. Sometimes members reduced their donations in election years in anticipation of contributing later to election funds.

[35]Based on estimated median membership for each year.

TABLE X

GROSS RECEIPTS* OF THE ONTARIO CCF, 1949–61
(Gross receipts in 1945 = 100)

1949	65
1950	82
1951	76
1952	85
1953	86
1954	111
1955	110
1956	114
1957	119
1958	122
1959	126
1960	144
1961	83†

*All membership fees and contributions, including the fees of affiliated union members, direct union donations and minor miscellaneous revenues.

†This figure covers only the first seven months of 1961. It does not include substantial union donations which the CCF received annually but which, in 1961, were diverted, by mutual consent, to organizational work for what was then called the New party.

annual financial and membership drives was partly responsible for the gain,[36] but more important was the system of graduated membership fees.[37] Throughout the 1950's, Sustaining and Five Hundred Club members accounted for about half of Ontario's gross receipts. Indeed, so concentrated did these contributions become that, in 1956 for example, the Five Hundred Club—consisting very largely of senior and intermediate leaders, many of them union officers, and accounting for 2.5 per cent of the membership—provided over 40 per cent of gross receipts. Since two-thirds of that 40 per cent came from one-third of the Five Hundred Club members, that meant that the Ontario Section obtained one-quarter of its gross receipts from less than one per cent of its membership.

Despite the greatly increased contributions of its own members, especially the leaders, the Ontario Section's financial position became steadily more dependent on the unions. The latter's main assistance

[36]The annual membership drive was an elaborately organized province-wide affair. It was well publicized, and operated on a complex system of quotas on the basis of which the individual riding associations were encouraged to compete with each other for cash prizes.

[37]For an explanation of this system, see chap. VI, p. 81.

took indirect forms,[38] chiefly through PAC, which they financed. PAC did its own organizing on the party's behalf and published and distributed CCF leaflets. However, its greatest contribution was the assumption of an ever-increasing share of the party's election expenses, chiefly by paying for most of its newspaper advertising. The unions' share of election expenses rose from 10 per cent in the triumphant 1943 campaign to 73 per cent in the 1959 contest.[39] In addition, from 1952 on, two full time CCF organizers in Ontario were on the PAC payroll of a major union.[40]

In the same year, the promise of union funds especially for that purpose permitted the Provincial Council, over strong left wing opposition, to make the post of provincial leader a salaried position. The Provincial Leader, though agreeing with that decision, resigned several months later, after having served for eleven years. His successor, another seasoned, professional CCF administrator and organizer, was voted what was, by CCF standards, a handsome salary, and so, unlike his predecessor, was able to devote full time to the party. During this period the official voluntary leadership also increased substantially. The Provincial Council, which had been expanded from thirty-seven to fifty in 1945, continued to grow in size, reaching seventy-nine in 1955.

Thus, although the CCF's size remained relatively stable, its leadership grew larger, more professional and more dependent on the unions. Indeed, the dominant trend throughout the whole period was the growing role of the trade unions in party affairs and the steady meshing of the two organizations in conducting the operations of the CCF.

This development, which took place behind the scenes, eventually culminated in the open and highly publicized alliance of these bodies.

[38]Direct contributions by the unions, though important, were much less significant. Union donations usually constituted about one-eighth of gross receipts, rising on one or two occasions to about one-fifth. Fees from affiliated union members never exceeded one-eighth of gross receipts and were usually closer to one-tenth. Thus, together, these two sources ordinarily accounted for about one-quarter of gross receipts, the remainder coming almost entirely from the party's own members. (These figures apply only to the post-war period. Before then, union funds were much less important.)

[39]The costs of the two campaigns, at least to the central organization, were approximately equal. Figures from Minutes of Finance Committee, 1943, and Report of Joint OFL (Ontario Federation of Labour)—CCF Election Committee to CCF Provincial Executive, Dec. 15, 1959. According to a senior CCF officer, the union share of expenses in the 1959 campaign was actually about 50 per cent.

[40]In reporting this arrangement to the 1953 Provincial Convention, the Provincial Council added, "The money from [another union] is helping to pay for organizers in the other provinces."

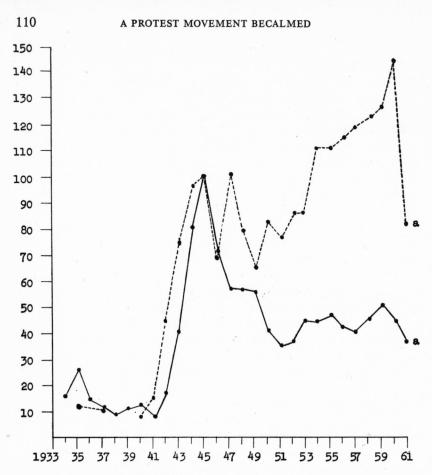

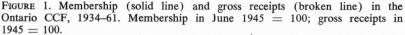

FIGURE 1. Membership (solid line) and gross receipts (broken line) in the Ontario CCF, 1934–61. Membership in June 1945 = 100; gross receipts in 1945 = 100.

ªThe 1961 figures do not represent real declines but the diversion of members and funds to the emerging New Democratic party organization.

In 1956, the Canadian Congress of Labour (affiliated with the CIO) and the Trades and Labor Congress (affiliated with the AFL) merged into the Canadian Labour Congress. The new body's strong CCF sympathies were quickly apparent. The powerful body of CCF supporters in the CCL and the smaller core in the TLC together constituted the best-organized group within the new congress on the subject of political action. At its founding convention, the new labour body passed a resolution on political education—a compromise stand on political action —expressing approval of the CCF, which, for the moment, was all that the latter's strategists sought.[41] In 1958, the party and the congress each called for "a new party," based on the CCF and the unions, a declaration which the two bodies passed overwhelmingly at their respective national conventions in 1960. The final act in this process took place in the summer of 1961 with the formation of the New Democratic party.

The growing prospect of "a new party" in the latter 1950's set aside an administrative and strategic problem which had intensified steadily since 1945. The weakness of so many of its local organizations confronted the CCF with the question of how much of its limited resources of personnel and funds it ought to devote to the obviously hopeless ridings. Support mounted for the alternative of funnelling these resources into the more promising areas in the hope that victories there would enhance the party's status everywhere and thus lead to further gains. The plan had serious drawbacks. It meant neglecting or abandoning the CCF's remaining adherents in many ridings. Furthermore, since parties ordinarily try to run as many candidates as possible in order to impress the public with their strength and with the seriousness of their intentions, a significant reduction in that number would constitute an open and damaging admission of weakness. The final danger was that some other minor party, in particular Social Credit, would contest these ridings federally and thereby injure CCF strength and prestige.

Every party faces these problems. Each must decide how best to use its limited resources. When the CCF was a major party, or at any rate a serious aspirant to that position, it hardly felt it could consider the first alternative of a limited but intensive campaign. However, its decline to the standing of a minor party made the prospect of these equally unsatisfactory choices even more painful until the appearance on the horizon of a "new party" thrust it into the background for the rest of the CCF's life.

To bring the preceding chronicle of structural developments into sharper focus, it must be related to the changes in the CCF's thinking during its last two decades. The party's "moderating" outlook had profound effects on its structure.

The first major change occurred when, after a re-examination of the world's ailments, the CCF altered its prescription from major surgery to heavy medication. The consequent shift in time perspective, it will be recalled, had stimulated the party's quest for power and thus encouraged its growing preoccupation with the effectiveness of its

---

[41]At that convention, the CCF quietly restrained its more ardent adherents from pressing for a stronger stand on the grounds that such a move was premature and that a rebuff at that point would jeopardize further progress.

formal machinery, with "organizational" problems, techniques and nostrums of many kinds (the pledge campaign, for example), and with securing support from the unions.

The decline in ideological distinctiveness contributed to these developments in another way. The more commonplace the CCF's views became, the less able they were to unite and mobilize the membership, and therefore the more the party turned to organizational efficiency and to union support—it has been obvious how closely the two were related—to achieve these ends. A brief comparison of the three phases explains this change.

In the 1930's, their unorthodox convictions had been what linked and aroused the movement's adherents, especially since its administrative apparatus was so flimsy. When the party's differences with society narrowed, during the war, the prospect of an early CCF victory took over the main job of recruitment and mobilization. In the entire postwar period, therefore, with the two former mainsprings of motivation—indignation and anticipation—both seriously run down,[42] the CCF became more dependent than ever on its administrative machinery to hold it together.

Nevertheless, these very changes in its thinking facilitated the attainment of that end because the party's growing moderation helped it to gain substantial union support. Reform was a more congenial cause than socialism to most of the unions and especially to the merged labour body, which helped found the New Democratic party.

INVOLVEMENT

It has been described how, as hopes of being a major party faded, the leaders of the CCF attempted to disseminate a new criterion of political success—the reforms which a strong minor party could obtain indirectly, especially if it held the balance of power. Whatever its effectiveness, this aim was rarely as compelling as either set of the old objectives, as the following incident suggests:

The CCF National Leader addressed a group of election workers whose candidate was a top leader of many year's standing. After his talk, the candidate's wife, herself an extremely active member, remarked privately, "You know that stuff of Coldwell's about old age pensions and unemployment insurance, I don't know . . . but I'm getting tired of hearing that sort of thing. But I suppose it helps to take one or two things and keep pushing them. They develop a line I suppose and stick to it.

[42]The next section shows that where either indignation or anticipation remained strong, it galvanized CCFers into activity.

"That's alright for a political audience and it goes over with them. But for [party] workers you need some crusade. That's what Tommy Douglas does so well—he crusades." Then obviously feeling that she had perhaps gone too far, she concluded, "But of course no one can help being terribly impressed by Coldwell—his sincerity and conviction."

The problem of incentives was especially pronounced in the weaker ridings where victory seemed particularly remote and where nuclei of professional leaders were not to be had. In most of these places the local organizations either died or became dormant. A favourite theme of the CCF's right wing leaders was that lack of proper organization, especially at the local level, was the primary cause of the party's "needless" failures since the war. The Ontario Section's minutes contain countless passages expressing their anguished frustration about the local organizations and, especially, about "poor local leadership." The following passages are typical:

Enthusiasm could not be created synthetically, said [a very prominent national leader]. Our failure in the CCF, to the extent there had been a failure, and in his opinion there had been a failure, was only an organizational lack. In the last two or three years we have gone through a period of public apathy in politics which is a phenomenon throughout the world. . . . Every socialist movement in the world has been affected. To the extent that there has been a failure, it has been on the part of our local organizations throughout the country and in this province. National, provincial and local organizations should concentrate on getting new members into the movement to revive enthusiasm and provide new workers in the movement.[43]

It is generally agreed that if we had won 12 or 15 seats in the last Ontario election, and thus had become the Official Opposition, our present situation would be entirely different. This illustrates dramatically the basic importance of organization, because there can be no doubt that, with good organization, we could have won 12 or 15 seats, notwithstanding a generally unfavourable situation. *In this connection, the key factor of our failure has been lack of local leadership.* It is therefore important that people at the provincial level should make a further sacrifice of their time to get into the ridings to develop local leadership.[44]

It may be argued that leadership worry about rank and file apathy is the natural condition of many organizations and that, furthermore, most Liberal and Conservative riding associations showed no greater signs of life between elections than the CCF's. But there are decisive differences between these parties and the CCF and consequently between their local organizations. The former had a large and stable basis of support in most ridings. Their candidates were either the incumbent members or

[43]Provincial Council, Minutes, Jan. 12, 1952.
[44]Provincial Executive, Minutes, Jan. 10, 1956 (italics added).

else represented the party in power or the main alternative to it and therefore ordinarily had reasonable chances of winning. Consequently, the major parties tended to be less disturbed if their local organizations hibernated between elections. They could usually count on the prospect of victory to revitalize them at election time.

The CCF, however, could not ordinarily take a relaxed view of local lethargy. Where CCF prospects were poor, public interest, funds and prominent candidates were hard to obtain. Nor could it, like a major opposition party, count on profiting from anti-Government senti-ment.[45] Consequently, in these places, it had to depend on its local groups to build the support and organization required for an effective campaign. With no prospects of victory to revive or stimulate these groups, the outlook for the campaign was usually ominous if they were inactive between elections.[46]

The organizers' reports show that they spent most of their time, at elections, working desperately to revive the many weak riding associations by trying to "line up" a candidate and get a campaign under way. Previous passages have revealed the frustration and irrita-tion of the central leadership with these local bodies, whose perennial apathy taxed its personal resources and, it felt, drained the party's. But because success depended on these numerous ridings, the CCF could hardly abandon them, although there was a growing inclination to do so, as was mentioned earlier.

If "poor local leadership" bore the brunt of the official criticism for the party's post-war difficulties, somewhat parallel trends also occurred on the higher levels. As hopes grew fainter with the passing years, many voluntary leaders drifted away from administrative responsibilities in the CCF. Most retained their membership, but heavier career demands, family obligations and other interests gnawed steadily away at the time and energy available for the party.

One significant group among these leaders was the trade union officers who had formed the first solid bridge between the CCF and the unions. For the most part their careers followed a rather similar pattern. They began as ardent CCFers, and the party was their spring-board to careers in the new CIO unions. During the CCF's second period, they were deeply involved in both of these expanding organi-

[45]Several elections indicated that where the CCF did succeed in arousing such sentiments, most of the resulting votes went to the major opposition party.

[46]The CCF did take ridings in which it had virtually no organization. Some of these victories became legendary. But they occurred only when the tide was running very heavily in the party's favour, and these seats were especially hard to hold subsequently.

zations and rose rapidly in both. Subsequently, their union work clearly came first, although their attachment to the party continued. They retained membership, increased their personal and, in some cases, organizational donations and played leading roles first in forming the Political Action Committee and later in bringing the Canadian Labour Congress into the "new party" partnership with the CCF. But they left party administration and candidacy to others, in many cases minor officers in their own unions.

Of the nine senior union officers who occupied top leadership posts in the provincial party organization between 1942 and 1949, only three continued to do so after 1950 and only one after 1954. Nor did any prominent trade unionists become CCF candidates, at least in Ontario, after 1955, although all but one of the nine men above had run previously. Growing reluctance to accept, let alone seek, federal and provincial candidacy was not confined to the trade unionists. Many top voluntary leaders who, in the past, had been the party's first choice to be its parliamentary representatives became unwilling to undertake the rigours of still another apparently hopeless contest. The attitude of one of these men, still active in CCF affairs at the time of this conversation, was probably typical. Explaining why another leader, once a regular candidate, no longer ran, he said,

"He's probably like me. You run two or three times and it's a very wearing business. I'm not *just* going to run again. If I do, it'll be somewhere where there's a good chance of winning. I'm not going to fill a ticket again. . . . There are some who have the professional athlete's attitude towards it. They know they can't win, but it's another time at bat and it has to be done."

A former top leader, who was not a trade unionist, explained the withdrawal of the union men and other voluntary leaders as follows:

"Many of them were people who would have majored in the CCF if the prospect had been more encouraging—especially union people. I'll tell you where it hit us very hard." He said that the number of union people who were CIO organizers and therefore moved frequently had affected the party very adversely because they could not take on lasting administrative responsibilities. "They were very much like travelling salesmen," he suggested. He mentioned that many of them were recruited from the CCF and CCYM.[47] "People wonder why the unions have given us so much support. Well, it's never been any mystery. When I go to one of the union conventions, there are hundreds of people I know through the CCF."

[47]The CCF's Youth Movement, an organization which was usually on the verge of collapse. Some CCF leaders were in the CCYM in the 1930's and thereby gave it vitality and a tradition of being potentially valuable.

In the post-war period, the CCF's senior salaried officers were gripped in a somewhat different tug-of-war than the voluntary leaders. Money and careers were usually the critical considerations for them, as time and energy were for the voluntary leaders, and discouragement was the common factor in both sets of equations. Although party salaries increased substantially over the pre-war pittances, the salaried officers were still unable to live in the style of their middle class associates both inside and outside the CCF, most of whom were in more lucrative professional, business and trade union careers. The struggle for a middle class standard of living on a party salary drove a few deeply into debt. As the party's prospects waned, these CCF officers weighed increasing family responsibilities and attractive career opportunities outside the party against their heavy investment of years, efforts, hopes and ambitions in the CCF. Family obligations were the exit through which most left their political careers, fortified by the feeling that the long years of "sacrifice" merited a respite. (According to one senior officer, the low salaries made it virtually impossible to find suitable replacements for these officials.)

Questioned about these withdrawals from administrative positions, one of the officers concerned explained that countless meetings (of the Provincial Executive and Council, their committees and subcommittees, and the riding associations), speech-making, preparing committee reports and many other duties left no time or energy for any other interests or, in the case of the voluntary leaders, for their careers. He concluded with the cautious observation that these were the factors in his case but that he didn't know how they had affected the others. Most of these officers, after leaving the party's employ, remained active and influential members, some occupying important voluntary positions.

Some CCF representatives followed more individualistic political careers, notably in municipal politics. In many Canadian cities, including Toronto, municipal politics operate on an ostensibly non-party basis even though the party attachments of many politicians are well known. In the early 1940's, at the height of the CCF success in Ontario, a slate of candidates did run on the party's label in Toronto with some success, but the practice was soon abandoned.

Some CCFers, in Toronto and elsewhere, enjoyed continued success in municipal politics. Their political careers, however, tended to draw them away from the party. The CCF did seek their active participation, but ready acquiescence would have limited their opportunities to establish contacts and support in the other associations of the community. However, if they rejected these claims, they were suspected by some

CCF members of seeking too personal a following and perhaps even of expediently turning their backs on the party. The old sectarian alarm that the leaders may become too deeply involved in the outside world was still sounded occasionally by left wing "purists" (as they were scornfully called) though much less audibly in their eventual weakened condition. Many of these observations are embodied in the following remarks of a CCFer, prominent in municipal politics, in an informal conversation.

He began by mentioning his CCF colleagues on the city council and jokingly suggested that I might have heard some derogatory remarks in the CCF about them. The main opposition to them in the party, he said, came from people like X, Y, Z (the last two are left wingers, the first is widely regarded as a crackpot) and others like them, "doctrinaire purists, pro–Regina Manifesto, anti–Winnipeg Declaration; you know the rest of it." But the others in the CCF, especially the leaders, were friendly and supporting. He mentioned, however, that one of them had recently upbraided him, in a friendly way, for not being more active in the CCF.

He admitted that he had become less active in party affairs. (He was very active at one time, as were the colleagues he mentioned. Now none of them are.) Municipal politics, he explained, didn't leave time for CCF activity.

A little later in the discussion he mentioned that he and his colleagues had been approached frequently to accept federal and provincial candidacy, "which is only natural since our names are well known." He was not interested in federal candidacy because his work could not easily be resumed elsewhere.

"I would like to run provincially, but for selfish reasons I wouldn't do so unless it were a good riding, like————. I'd like to run in a safe seat but . . ." (he implied that none exist).

An incident involving another prominent municipal politician, once deeply involved in the CCF and still a member at the time, illustrates the relation between the party and its increasingly distant municipal representatives. This politician, a guest speaker at a CCF meeting, prefaced his address on municipal affairs by saying,

"In a way I am perhaps one of the worst people you could have chosen for such an occasion. I have grown away from the CCF over the last few years." He did not mention the CCF again. Later he was subjected to some hostile questions, several of which got under his skin. (Other questions were much more sympathetic.) Finally, the wife of a top CCF leader, who was herself very active in the party, asked briefly but forcefully for an understanding of the important contribution of people such as the guest speaker.

This incident occurred characteristically at a Toronto and District Council meeting. The T and D, as it was known, had little prestige among the party's top leaders, one of whom voiced a common attitude in describing it as "a haven for second-rate leaders. It's the place for the Toronto leaders who failed to make the Provincial Council or else couldn't keep their place on it but who are, nevertheless, faithful."

The T and D and the CCF's municipal representatives were constant sources of irritation to each other. The friction stemmed from the T and D's insistence that these representatives run on the CCF label and their determination not to. The following passage expresses the annoyance of the T and D executive:

There has been absolutely no co-operation between the [CCF] municipal candidates and the [T & D] Council. . . . there has been no co-operation between the clubs and the T & D either. We were not able to obtain a full list of the [CCF] candidates for the various offices in the Metropolitan area, although it was possible to know the Toronto candidates, since they were well known. The only call we got was from a suburban councillor well known for his Communist sympathies, which is ironic, to say the least. Too many of our CCF candidates seem to be afraid of admitting even to CCFers their political stripe, although we had hoped to be of some assistance to them.[48]

Although most CCFers, including the leaders, endorsed these individualistic careers, the suspicions of the hard-shell minority acted as an irritant and repellent. The party's weakness lessened its value to civic candidates with other sources of support, a fact which probably accounted for the unusual preface of the guest speaker on municipal affairs, and it discouraged these better-known municipal figures from seeking or even accepting provincial or federal nomination. Consequently, the CCF candidates, at least in Toronto,[49] were less likely to be graduates of muncipal politics and extensive community participation than were their Liberal and Conservative opponents. Their relative obscurity tended to reduce the CCF vote and, with it, the party's future expectations and morale, thereby making it even harder to obtain a strong candidate the next time.

One CCFer with a successful political as well as professional career talked about the changed reaction of his professional and academic acquaintances to the party and remarked that on several occasions these people had joked or complained to him about "your CCF." He continued, "I said to P [the person who had complained], 'Why do you say *my* CCF? Why not yours? ' " Such incidents, he explained, indicated

[48]Toronto and District CCF Council, Executive Committee Report to the Annual Meeting, Feb. 15–16, 1957.

[49]According to a top CCF leader, this was the case in Toronto but not in a number of other communities. Data to check this matter adequately were not available.

that these kinds of people were dissociating themselves from the party. "From a prestige point of view," he added, "they won't join." He had asked two acquaintances, whom he named, why they didn't join the CCF to help correct the conditions which provoked their complaints. They had replied that they couldn't jeopardize their jobs, although well-known CCFers had long been employed in the same institutions as they were.

This member's observations reflect one of the most conspicuous aspects of the post-war party—the extent to which it no longer drew on the occupations which had furnished most of its early leaders.[50] An examination of the background of the top CCF leaders in Toronto shows the extent of this change. Four occupations—teaching, law, journalism and welfare work—accounted for twenty-eight of the fifty-one people who first attained senior office in the party before 1945 but for only ten of the forty-three who first reached these positions between 1945 and 1956. The CCF's federal and provincial candidates display an identical pattern. In the first period, twenty-six of the fifty-two in Toronto were in six occupations (the four above, the ministry and medicine), compared to only thirty out of 115 in the last period.[51]

As these figures imply, the number and types of CCF candidates were sensitive indices of how various kinds of members appraised both candidacy and the party's prospects. After 1945, when hopes were highest, the total number of candidates declined steadily (see tables XI and XII), and changes occurred both in social composition as well as in motives in seeking or accepting candidacy.

The steady decrease represented failure to nominate in the weaker ridings rather than deliberate policy, as the chairman of the Organization Committee clearly showed in her report on the 1957 federal election.

She reported . . . on the candidate situation. Candidates have now been nominated in 15 ridings, and the dates of nominating conventions have been

[50]A dramatic incident in this process occurred in 1952, when the long mistrust between the Ontario CCF administration and a group of more independent members, who were dominant in the Woodsworth Memorial Foundation, exploded into open conflict for control of that organization. The issue centred about the control of the valuable property which housed both organizations but which was owned by the latter. The administration won the fight but alienated its opponents; some of the latter quit the party and nearly all became less active. The defeated group had visualized the Foundation's original terms of reference—for research and education—as a mandate to attempt to establish a Canadian counterpart of the Fabian Society. It contained most of the group which controlled the *Canadian Forum*, which was once the chief spokesman for the CCF in Canada but which, in the years preceding the Woodsworth House struggle, had grown steadily more independent and critical of the party.

[51]In the middle period these six occupations accounted for thirty-eight of the eighty-four Toronto candidates.

TABLE XI

CCF Federal Candidates in Canada and Ontario, 1935–58

	Canada			Ontario		
	Ridings	CCF candidates	Ridings contested by CCF %	Ridings	CCF candidates	Ridings contested by CCF %
1935	245	118	48	82	50	61
1940	245	96	39	82	26	32
1945	245	205	84	83	80	96
1949	262	180	69	85	77	91
1953	265	171	65	85	65	76
1957	265	161	61	85	60	71
1958	265	167	63	85	63	75

TABLE XII

CCF Provincial Candidates in Ontario, 1934–59

	Ridings	CCF candidates	Ridings contested by CCF %
1934	90	35	39
1937	90	43	48
1943	90	86	96
1945	90	89	99
1948	90	85	94
1951	90	77	86
1955	98	81	83
1959	98	80	82

set in five others. There are an additional 22 ridings which are almost certain to nominate. This means that we have to get about 20 more candidates if we are to reach our objective of 60. These must come from a group of 27 ridings where the committee believes that candidates may be obtained but only with considerable difficulty. There are 16 ridings where the committee sees no possibility of getting candidates.[52]

A senior CCF officer explained the difficulty of securing candidates in these areas:

There are ridings where it's pretty hard to get candidates. The ones I feel sorry for are those like the farmer, for instance, who is able, successful and popular. He's an active member of the cattle breeders' or fruit growers' association; he knows many people and has lots of friends.

Then he awakes the morning after the election to find he has 800 votes out of about 15,000. He's completely exhausted from the effort, strain and

[52]Provincial Council, Minutes, Dec. 8, 1956.

excitement of the campaign; he's out of pocket a few hundred dollars, and his wife is down on him for being away from home so much of the time during his campaign. Then, when he sees the vote, he figures the whole world hates him.

When the next election comes around, he's not likely to try it again. He's the person I feel sorry for. I can't work up much sympathy for the ones who get beaten in Toronto.

Although the weakest ridings were responsible for the decline in the total number of candidates, significant changes in the types of people that ran occurred even in Toronto, one of the strongest CCF areas in the province. These changes reflected the growing reluctance, noted previously, among the following groups of members to accept candidacy: the most prominent voluntary leaders, including the senior trade union officers; the successful municipal politicians; and, more generally, men of the middle class.

As a result, many more manual workers and women became candidates in the last period. Three facts strongly suggest that, on the whole, these two groups were not the party's first choice for federal and provincial candidacy and consequently were less likely to call forth its support. First, their numbers increased as the party's prospects declined; second, they usually appeared in the weaker ridings; and, finally, they were much more numerous in the federal field, where the CCF was weaker, than in the provincial. Tables XIII and XIV show the steady progression of this trend, and Table XV is a composite of federal and provincial candidates, comparing the proportions of "first" and "second" choice candidates by periods.[53]

The figures in Tables XIII to XV do not reflect changes in the composition of either the general membership or the local leadership, neither of which showed any significant change in the decade that began in 1945.[54] Instead, judging from the number of candidates who were union members (often presidents of their locals) or British immigrants, or both, they suggest that although CCF candidacy no longer carried much prestige in the middle class, it still did in the working class, especially among active trade union members.

Another striking sign of the change in motivation towards candidacy was the location and number of "token" or "sacrifice" candidates, as they were often referred to within the party. Token candidacies were,

[53]The distinction between "first" and "second" choice candidates is a general one that obviously did not fit every instance. One notable exception was Agnes Macphail, four times CCF candidate (and twice winner) in East York between 1943 and 1951 and MP from 1921 to 1940.

[54]See chap. III, p. 30.

TABLE XIII

CCF Federal Candidates in Toronto, 1935–58

	"First choice"	"Second choice"		
	Male, non-manual workers	Women	Male, manual workers	Total
1935	14	1		1
1940	6	1		1
1945	13	1	1	2
1949	12	1	2	3
1953	11	3	4	7
1957	4	5	8	13
1958	3	4	11	15

TABLE XIV

CCF Provincial Candidates in Toronto, 1934–59

	"First choice"	"Second choice"		
	Male, non-manual workers	Women	Male manual workers	Total
1934	9	1	1	2
1937	14		3	3
1943	15	2		2
1945	13	2	2	4
1948	13	1	3	4
1951	13	1	3	4
1955	10	1	9	10
1959	10	2	8	10

TABLE XV

CCF Federal and Provincial Candidates
in Toronto, by Periods*

Candidates	Period I (1934–41)	Period II (1942–49)	Period III (1950–59)
"First choice"	43	69	55
"Second choice"	9	15	60

*Includes by-elections

of course, not confined to the CCF. The strategic importance of fielding as many candidates as possible leads all parties to contest ridings which they know are hopeless, and the CCF, even at its peak, ran many more token candidates than did the Liberals or Conservatives. But, although reliable quantitative information about these condidacies was, by their very nature, non-existent, "sacrificial victims" (an even more private term) increased in number and appeared in former CCF strongholds and in many ridings once contested seriously. In these cases, the candidates were persuaded to stand not so much to fill out a list as to avert the damage that would inevitably result from a failure to nominate in these ridings.

These reasons add to the difficulties of distinguishing "sacrifice" candidates clearly from the rest. The following accounts describe two different sets of reasons for, and ways of, becoming a token, or virtually nominal, candidate.

The informant in the first case, a rising member of the administration, answered a question about the CCF's 1957 federal candidates in Toronto with the seemingly defensive remark that "they've thrown in young punks from the union movement" and contrasted the current situation with "the days when the CCF had a middle class appeal, when there were lots of idealistic people." He then described how Cynthia H,[55] the wife of a top leader, became a candidate:

> I asked her last year and, in a weak moment, she said she would if we couldn't find anyone else. When I called her a couple of weeks ago, she asked if we had approached anyone else. When I read her the list of about fifteen people we had approached and she heard some of those names, she agreed to honour her promise.
>
> Anybody who runs in that riding knows they'll be crucified. So anyone with any really serious political ambitions isn't willing to undertake it except perhaps a person at the very beginning of his career, like Jim C last time, who wants to get his name known.

The second case, witnessed direct, occurred in another riding and another campaign. While the CCF had never won the riding, it had finished second in the four preceding campaigns, twice within promising distance of the winner. The prospect this time, however, was obviously discouraging.

At the nominating meeting two names were put forward. The first was that of a young lawyer, who had been regarded as the probable candidate for some time. The second was that of an industrial worker who had had little formal education, virtually no experience in public speaking and who was above all, a distinct "left winger." But his nomination was a reward for his herculean efforts in canvassing for membership renewals, votes and support.

---

[55]Sacrifice candidacy appears to account for a large part of the increase in women candidates. Many of them were salaried employees of the unions most sympathetic to the CCF, and their candidacies therefore involved a minimum of personal and organizational inconvenience.

The lawyer began with the ominous remark that he had a statement to make. He announced his decision not to run because he had just opened his own office and was threatened with the loss of an important client if he ran for the CCF. Upon his withdrawal, the second nominee, Donald A, was declared the candidate. He worked hard at his campaign but he was virtually unknown in the riding and incapable of mobilizing the membership to help him. He was badly beaten, finishing third.

The result proved too much for him. At the election night gathering, he was very drunk and obstreperous, annoying the party leaders with incessant petty complaints about which they could do nothing. He repeatedly mused aloud, "I don't know whether to stay in the CCF or join the LPP," to which his acquaintances replied, "You won't do that, Don. You've got too much intelligence."

But, pointing to him, one top leader remarked quietly to another, "One of our troubles was that we had some bad candidates, and that's one of them."

Donald A was not a genuine token candidate because (and this was what made his defeat so shattering personally), unlike Cynthia H and others like her, he had been virtually sacrificed without realizing it.[56] Most token candidates fall somewhere between these two extremes of awareness and unawareness, although the term "token" ostensibly applied to the candidates who accepted nomination with the understanding that no more than a token campaign was possible. The cumulative evidence therefore suggests that for many CCFers, but by no means all, candidacy became a chore rather than a prize.

The preceding pages have documented the weakening involvement of the leaders. It will be recalled, however, that this process was even more intense and widespread among the rank and file. One riding leader, long close to some at the top and still active at the time of this conversation, commented on the general reduction in CCF activity.

"Well, you know it's getting more and more hopeless, and they're older, tired and disillusioned. They put their efforts into other organizations, unions, churches and so on."

As he was leaving, he suddenly turned and, from a distance, offered this parting shot, "It's just that we're dying from lack of oomph. The reason is simply that our cause has disappeared."

The following two comments also summarize and explain CCF morale in the last period. In the first instance, an election worker who was almost bursting with exasperation explained to another, " 'They [the CCF's supporters] say that he [the CCF candidate] hasn't got a chance. What they don't realize is that he hasn't got a chance just because they think

[56]He would not have secured the nomination had there been any prospect of winning.

so.' " The second observation was that of a veteran top leader. He began his explanation of the party's difficulties in the usual fashion by attributing it to poor local leadership which, he added, was a problem in all organizations in Ontario. But he elaborated as follows:

"The meetings are too dull and lifeless. They're concerned only with business, which is of interest only to those already involved. They can't attract anyone and they don't help to keep them. . . .
The trouble is that you can't maintain a sense of moral outrage in a time of prosperity. . . . Many ridings depend on one key person. If you lose him, it all goes and has to be rebuilt from scratch."

The election worker's statement expresses in a single sentence the common problem of minor parties while the top leader's explains how the absence of a distinctive viewpoint and of cohesive nuclei affect the local organizations of such a party.

Although the last speaker had the outlying ridings primarily in mind, his remarks fit Toronto's surprisingly well. The changes which occurred in one Toronto riding association, which was described briefly earlier,[57] were typical of most. Revolving about a close group of veteran top leaders, it was, for almost two decades, one of the party's most vigorous and lively, although it was not in a promising CCF area. When the group was first observed, in 1952, it still carried on an active programme, consisting of monthly membership meetings with an attendance of between twenty and twenty-five (out of an official membership of 274);[58] fortnightly executive meetings; two annual weekend seminars; an active project, which continued for some months, of collecting signatures for a national health plan petition by door to door canvassing several evenings a week; an annual Christmas party at the home of one of these top leaders as well as other activities. Although its numbers diminished and its pace slackened perceptibly, the group continued along these general lines for the next three years.[59]

In the spring of 1955, with a provincial election scheduled for June, the group, acting according to custom, nominated two of its members to contest the two provincial ridings which it covered. This time both were badly beaten, finishing third, something which had not occurred in either riding since 1937. That autumn, after the usual summer break, meetings did not resume. The executive met in November and again in January. At the second meeting, it was announced that the group's top

[57]See above, p. 101.
[58]All CCF members in any riding officially belonged to its local association.
[59]Being in the centre of the city, it was severely handicapped by the steady exodus of its members to the suburbs.

leader, who with his extremely "active" wife had been a key member of its nucleus, had decided some months previously to accept federal nomination in a more promising riding and that therefore he and his wife had, at that time, transferred their membership to the other group. Most of the members of the executive attended his nomination meeting as an expression of support, but their own group declined rapidly. Meetings were held irregularly, averaging about three or four a year; they were very poorly attended (the official membership for 1956–57 was down to 117), and other activities ceased. However, a small nucleus of women, employed by the more sympathetic trade unions and by the party, kept the group alive for three more years, until 1958. In the two years thereafter, it virtually confined its activities to the annual spring meeting.

Not only the frequency and size of the meetings changed but also their spirit, as a sense of paralysing weariness gradually overcame the group. During these years, the diminishing band of "the faithful"—a term then heard frequently in CCF circles—spent an increasing amount of the meetings' time lamenting the poor attendance in a manner that grew steadily more resigned and hopeless, and it derived what comfort it could from the customary reports that many other riding associations as well as groups outside the CCF were also afflicted with shrinking attendance. Its members set the date for the next meeting according to an invariable procedure. They mentioned the main events scheduled on the CCF calendar as well as other events, such as holidays, so that the meeting would avoid not only direct conflict with but even proximity to these engagements. A discussion of the most suitable day of the week followed—Friday, Saturday and Sunday were never mentioned—in the faint hope that selection of the right day might stir some response from the great but invisible ranks of the "inactive." When proposed dates clashed with their other meetings, the members usually implied that the latter had priority.

Nevertheless, until about 1958, the group did meet, and it continued to hold its annual meeting thereafter and to communicate occasionally with its membership by mail. Some of its members continued to obtain money and renewals of membership from most of the "inactive" and they still sent delegates to the conventions, nominated federal and provincial candidates and, together with a few inactive members who had been roused and a few potential recruits, conducted a campaign of sorts on behalf of their candidate.

Not all riding associations were as phlegmatic as this one. Some met more often and waged vigorous campaigns. But if some were more enthusiastic, others were even less so, and the morale of this group was not uncharacteristic even in such dependable CCF territory as Toronto. Evidence to that effect is contained in the remarks of a leader to a city-wide club clinic, organized in November 1957 to diagnose and combat sagging interest in the Toronto riding associations. Speaking to a disappointingly small audience of between fifteen and twenty, he first struck the theme that the imminent disintegration of the national Liberal party (it had been defeated several months before) presented a unique opportunity for the CCF to fill the vacuum. Then, turning to the problem of capitalizing on this opportunity, he warmed up to the subject of the meeting.

"We [a Toronto riding] are one of the few ridings who hold regular monthly meetings and send regular notices of these meetings to our members. But we've had very poor success or, I should say, no success since we haven't had any results. We get from ten to fifteen people turning out but we can't attract any new members. The meetings have been fairly interesting (he had previously admitted that he hadn't attended any for the past 12 months), but we can't extend our activities into the riding in this way. No one knows better than I that you can't win elections without poll organizations. But there are no more than two or three ridings here in Toronto which have any kind of poll organization. . . .
"I tell you frankly that I would not send a group of trade unionists to most of the riding associations in Toronto, including my own, because the lack of organization in the riding associations would thwart their efforts and frustrate their energies . . . . if it's the usual humdrum meeting we're used to having, these people (the newcomers) won't come back. . . . One of the complaints that I have about our riding meetings is that politics is the last thing that is discussed at them. Often it doesn't come up at all."
He emphasized the necessity of having interesting meetings "so that people will look forward to these monthly meetings instead of wondering how the hell they can duck them, which many of the lukewarm members—and goodness knows we have an enormous number of them—try to do. . . . We have to revitalize this movement . . . and solve the problems of apathy and indifference. . . . The riding associations have to be strengthened and have to be prepared if we are to be able to integrate the group of potential trade union newcomers."

The cumulative signs of demoralization tempt one to conclude that "nothing fails like failure," as the following *Ottawa Journal* editorial rather floridly explains:

any party kept too long in opposition falls a prey to frustration and despair, its ablest captains tempted to abandon it and younger men discouraged from joining it. Politicians, no matter how determined, weary of "following suns that flame and fade in a day that has no morrow." And young men of ability shrink from joining a party which offers no reward for ambition. Thus in such circumstances an opposition becomes feebler and feebler, drained of the drive it must have if it is to perform its functions adequately.[60]

The growing detachment from the CCF of its adherents has, until now, been attributed to "external" conditions—the party's electoral failures and the members' personal success. The CCF's rapprochement with the world can be more fully understood if one reverses this sequence of cause and effect as well. The adverse effect of this detachment on the party's fortunes has been discussed fully in the preceding pages, but its benign influence on the members' personal fortunes, though less apparent, is not less important.

The world, of course, rather than the party, was always the chief determinant of the members' circumstances, but the world's influence was so great because CCF ideology never repudiated it as thoroughly as did the Communist party's, for example. Unlike the latter, the CCF did not regard its immediate environment as unspeakably loathsome, to be used impersonally, unsentimentally and exclusively in order to attain the "earthly paradise to come." Since its more limited goal did not take precedence over every other consideration, the CCF did not require its personnel to place their lives almost entirely at the disposal of the movement, as do more extreme political and religious groups (as well as the Roman Catholic Church) and, to a lesser degree, military organizations.[61]

Nevertheless, a wide range of alternatives exists between these total claims and the rather irresolute ones which eventually characterized the CCF. Like every group, it was inescapably involved in a ceaseless tug-of-war with the world for the devotion of its members, and any slackening of one side inevitably tightened the hold of the other. It is the theme of this analysis that changes in the CCF's thinking and organization—and not only in its prospects of winning—steadily weakened its hold on its members and, to that extent, freed them for engagement elsewhere. (How

[60]Ironically, this editorial bemoaning the Conservatives' rather than the CCF's fate appeared just before the 1957 federal election, which brought the former back to power after an absence of twenty-two years.

[61]In addition to demanding "the whole of their (members' or functionaries') lives," these organizations characteristically possess authoritarian structures, transcendental causes and doctrines of infallibility. These three elements appear to be logically related. Claims of this kind could hardly be enforced on the members without such a goal, doctrine and structure. Conversely, given that goal, doctrine and structure, these claims seem inevitable.

Perhaps this perspective can be applied to the patriarchal family as well. It seems to share the tendency of these other groups for dissident members to catapult themselves (or be catapulted) out of the group and to hurl themselves against it thereafter with unrelenting fury.

these outside interests, in turn, pulled them away from the party was described in the sections on involvement.)

In the first phase, CCFers were deeply immersed in the movement not simply because they were young and because attractive outside interests, especially jobs, were scarce. Their absorption in the CCF made these other pursuits less attractive and compelling. Accordingly, this was the period of their deepest commitment to the movement and, since it rejected the world most thoroughly then, of its strongest claims upon them.

In the middle phase, these people became less outraged with the world and more active in it. Their more conventional views and looser ties with one another weakened their commitment to the party, and it simultaneously relaxed its hold upon them, facilitating their involvement in other relations and pursuits, especially those of family and career.

Nevertheless, as long as the hope of victory and of political careers remained strong, it provided an effective counterweight to the growing attraction of these other pursuits. But as that hope faded and the networks of personal ties dissolved, the pressures and incentives to participate in the CCF weakened correspondingly, and the members were pulled more easily in other directions. An increasingly conventional viewpoint contributed to that movement by reducing involvement in the party and perhaps too by facilitating participation in the institutions of "capitalist" society. The result of this whole process was an over-all reduction in the members' commitments to the party and in its claims upon them.

In cumbersome language, the foregoing was the story of many CCFers and former members. They were the "angry, young men" for whom the CCF had once been "mother, father and the church."[62] But as their fortunes waxed and the party's waned, they became less angry—and, incidentally, less young—drifted away from their CCF friends and associates and grew more absorbed in their own affairs and less in the party's. It may well be that, as a former top leader expressed it, "many of them were people who would have majored in the CCF if the prospect had been more encouraging."[63] But the "internal" changes in the party also contributed to their growing involvement and success in other interests and organizations at the expense of the CCF. These people were so numerous, influential and, in many cases, still sufficiently attached to the CCF that in their personal progress in the world they not only pulled themselves away from the party but helped to draw it after them.

This sequence of events repeated an old and familiar pattern. Unrespectable social movements seem to flourish among the ambitious and

[62]See chap. IV, p. 53. [63]See above, p. 115.

respectable poor, and the CCF was but one of many which moved into the world as their adherents moved up in it.

The preceding pages have dwelt on detachment and demoralization. Not every sign, however, pointed in that direction. The CCF's stable membership, improving financial position and the remarkably slow shrinkage in its popular support indicate a substantial measure of continued vigour and enthusiasm.

In the places where the party had been most successful, its members usually remained sufficiently involved to maintain its strength. Many top leaders continued to be strongly motivated and to radiate confidence in their exhortations to the "faithful." More money permitted the increasing substitution of paid for voluntary effort. Small nuclei often continued to function where the formal riding associations no longer did. Recruitment among immigrant British trade unionists, as was mentioned before, provided a fresh source of energetic members. A casual impression suggests that, among the veteran members, the left wingers, although greatly reduced in number, were the most active. And, finally, the prospect of "the new party" buoyed up many hopes. Taken together, these events generated sufficient enthusiasm to keep the CCF on an almost even keel until the end.

The elections of the 1950's showed that where the prospect of victory remained bright, the CCF usually mobilized considerable effort from its local membership. The over-all pattern in these elections was the maintenance of CCF strength in the ridings where it had previously won or been a close contender[64] but an even further weakening in the rest.

The top leadership, it was noted earlier, displayed the greatest fidelity of all.[65] Despite their reduced participation, most of the top leaders of the mid-1940's were, a decade later, not simply members, but often involved ones, some still in senior leadership positions. They included parliamentary representatives, who were held by considerations of career, livelihood and friendship as well as by expectations of continued personal success; full time party and union officers on salary, who were linked both personally and professionally; as well as others who were also closely involved in these networks of personal relations but had careers

---

[64]For example, in the three Ontario federal ridings which the CCF captured in 1957, it had finished second in every election from 1945 on. (It retained all three seats in 1958 with increased margins.) Similarly, in the two provincial ridings which it gained in 1959, it had finished either first or second in all the contests from 1943 on, winning both seats in that year and again in 1948. The same pattern carried over into the New Democratic party's first federal campaign, at least in Ontario, and accounted for the three seats which it gained in Toronto.

[65]See above, p. 104.

quite separate from politics. Thus, many who had withdrawn from CCF office and candidacy none the less continued to work very actively on the party's behalf, especially in inter-union politics.

The top leaders were naturally eager, and in any case were expected, to generate enthusiasm among their adherents. Accordingly, they always tried to strike an optimistic and exhortative note, whether at the conventions or at riding association meetings at which their visits, as guest speakers, were the special occasions.[66] In the last decade these speeches followed an almost invariable pattern.

They dwelt on the CCF's enormous contribution to Canada's welfare legislation not only as a source of pride to the party but as an indication of the vital role which it could continue to play in the public service. They acknowledged that the times had been unfavourable but invariably discerned the unmistakable signs of a change which offered great possibilities to the CCF. Unless these solid potentialities were exploited, they warned, the consequences would be disastrous for the public and perhaps for the party. The opportunity was there, but its realization required work and more work, organization and more organization. The CCF must rededicate itself to its ideals. A rousing affirmation that the members would be equal to that challenge formed the conclusion.

The National Chairman, David Lewis, opened the 1956 National Convention with the following observations:

"New things have been happening recently on the Canadian scene. One of the most important for the future of the people's movement in Canada was the merging of the two great labor congresses into one united and powerful Canadian Labor Congress." (*applause*)

"There have also been other developments. There have been developments on the farm front where more and more and stronger farm organizations both in the federation and in the farmers' unions have been created and they are showing greater awareness and a greater militancy in social and political affairs, as well as in the economic affairs of the organization.

"I suggest . . . that these developments on the front of labor and the ferment taking place among the farmers of this country and the tremendous searching which is characteristic of the French Canadian people of the province of Quebec, and elsewhere, for a philosophy and principles and a party that will meet their basic beliefs in social justice, that all of these things now taking place in our country necessarily and inevitably mean a strengthening of the forces within and behind the CCF." (*applause*)[67]

The top leaders were cast in the role of chief morale boosters. In 1956, the Provincial Leader told the Ontario Convention, in essentially

[66]The nuclei who kept these groups alive considered the top leaders the best potential drawing card for the large, inactive membership. Guest speakers from outside the party were rare.

[67]National Convention, Report, 1956.

the same terms as he constantly had the riding associations, that "Today we stand on the threshold of a political groundswell. . . . The last time this kind of groundswell built up was about 14 or 15 years ago." The moral of his message and that of the preceding speaker, Hazen Argue, MP, was "the need to work and organize in the hustings," referring particularly to the forthcoming province-wide finance drive. At the next Provincial Convention, he spoke again of "the imminent [CCF] resurgence in Ontario." The role tended to carry over into less official situations.

On election night 1955, after all the results were in, several CCF candidates in Toronto and their chief lieutenants gathered at the home of the Provincial Leader. Their common lot—all but the Provincial Leader had lost—and the release from the wearying pressures of the campaign and from the almost unbearable suspense of election day all contributed to an atmosphere in which talk was spontaneous, lively and full of wry but exhilarating and comforting humour.

At 1 A.M. the Provincial Leader left the room to answer a long distance call. He returned and, after shouting over the hubbub for attention, excitedly exclaimed, "Who says we're licked? That call came from Kenora. They're starting in tomorrow to nominate a candidate and get set for the next election."

Someone asked, "How did they do?" "Badly," he replied, momentarily crestfallen.

Despite endless official reassurances, within their own ranks some leaders grew less optimistic about CCF prospects. At the National Council's major reassessment of the party's position and strategy in January 1956,[68] one of the most prominent, whose unique position facilitated a measure of detachment, began as follows:

This meeting of the National Council will only have value if we are prepared to look at the situation frankly without any false optimism. We have to look very realistically over the period of the last 10 to 15 years and recognize that we have lost ground. The best indication of our weakness is that the old-line parties are no longer afraid of us. The average person on the street doesn't keep backing a fighter who has been knocked out five or six times in a row and has no prospect of ever becoming champion. You have to have a party that looks as though it is going somewhere, a party that is increasing its prestige and its strength, and frankly I don't think we are. . . .

Therefore I think the picture is much more difficult now. We are facing now a changed economic set-up; we are facing a group of people who are better aware of the dangers of depression, a group of people who have mastered, as we haven't, the techniques of publicity and public relations to

[68]See above, p. 86.

defend their privileged position. And we, at the present moment, like socialist parties all over the western world, are on the defensive.

What is our role in this situation? Is there a place for the CCF in the political scene? Let us go back and read from the preamble to the Regina Manifesto. . . .

That indictment of capitalism is still basically true, but it is not as apparent as it was in 1933 and it is harder to sell.

Having opened on so depressing a note, he became steadily more encouraging and concluded on a note of qualified optimism:

I think there are indications that the tide may be starting to turn again. . . .

In 1932–33 we had as our objective a federation of farmer, labor and socialist organizations. It was a good objective. I'm not completely without hope that if the tide begins to turn, the farm, co-operative and labor organizations might . . . come in with the CCF, or merged in some alignment of which the CCF would be the dynamic core—a new type of federation or the same type of federation enlarged for a genuine farmer-labor-socialist movement in Canada, a movement with people at the center who know where they're going, what they want, and have a philosophy, and ideology, supported by mass movements.

I think that there are definitely hopeful signs in Canada, but I'm not foolishly optimistic. I think that unless we can intensify our efforts, unless we can change some of our techniques, adopt better techniques and adopt them fast, unless we can close our own ranks and create public confidence, unless we can stimulate and direct some of the mass movements to which I have referred, unless we can do all these things I think we will continue to be a diminishing group, a small, well-respected, highly-thought-of minority, with increasingly less influence. But the possibilities are here, they're here if we're prepared to do something about it. The doing of it will require sacrifice, require hard work, require above all a unity of purpose, and I think that is the task to which we should apply ourselves.[69]

Widespread evidence of some continued hope and interest persisted on the local level as well. Even where formal riding associations collapsed, small, informal groups often remained sufficiently involved to recruit some new members, nominate candidates (sometimes only after outside urging and help), conduct election campaigns, select convention delegates and obtain membership renewals and often even more money from the inactive. (Most of the latter renewed their membership, if asked.)

Within some of these enduring local groups, the left wing members (as has already been mentioned), though in the minority, seemed the most energetic and the least discouraged. The top leader who related the difficulty of retaining the party's boom period recruits after 1945[70]

[69]National Council, Minutes, Jan. 13–15, 1956.   [70]See chap. VI, p. 83.

went on to contrast these departing members with the core of "old time" socialists, a greater percentage of whom were left wing.

The old group were more durable; they stuck with the movement. There were always some who worked harder when things got worse, perverse types who thrived at such times. There were many in the party who didn't want to win in '43. They didn't have the will to power. That's been the trouble in BC too.

One of the most indefatigable workers was an elderly but very lively woman with decidedly left wing views who delighted in telling, " 'I joined the Independent Labour party in 1923 on the day that the UFO [United Farmers of Ontario] was voted out of office and,' she added, with a contented chuckle, 'I've been backing lost causes ever since.' "

Whether or not a penchant for lost causes was involved, it was by no means the only source of the left wingers' greater ability to absorb the shock of defeat. Their indignation and their time perspective, which was still oriented towards a more remote fulfilment, were, of course, another. Besides, defeat continually renewed their hope that the CCF would finally recognize the futility of a "me too" policy and realize that uncompromising, open adherence to "basic socialist principles" was the only avenue to lasting success.

If this sounds like the right wing Republicanism of the last two decades, especially as epitomized by the slogan that it would be "better to lose with Taft than win with Ike," the resemblance is no coincidence. The two groups had much in common. Each was its party's defeated and unheeded minority; each saw itself as the guardian of the party's ideological integrity, which the majority had allegedly sacrificed in the interests of expediency. When the voters rejected these "departures from principle," it was hardly surprising that the minority found some comfort in that fact. These views were, of course, not limited to these two parties. Their counterparts can be found in any party and indeed wherever factionalism exists.

Several new incentives can be identified, in the CCF, in the latter 1950's. They were, in ascending order of importance, the defeat of the federal Liberal party, a growing reliance on paid instead of voluntary effort and the prospect of "the new party." All were, more accurately, variations or extensions of older patterns.

The fall of the Liberal Government in 1957 and its smashing defeat in 1958 gave a new twist to an old CCF hope. Instead of expecting, as it had for almost two decades, to replace the stagnating Conservatives as Canada's second major party, it pinned its new hope on a Liberal collapse. This theme was widely circulated immediately after the 1957 election.[71] It was explained by the CCF Premier of Saskatchewan as follows:

Premier Douglas foresees the time when the CCF party will form the core of one group in a realignment of Canadian political forces into a two-party system.

The Saskatchewan Premier, addressing the CCF Party's annual provincial convention, said he predicted in 1954 that there one day would be a Canadian right-wing government supported by the Progressive Conservative, Social Credit and the Quebec National Union Parties.

He predicted the Liberal Party will disintegrate. The right wing would join the Conservatives and allies, while the left wing members would find their way into the CCF movement of farmer, labor and progressive groups.

This had happened in England, Australia, New Zealand and the Scandinavian countries, Mr. Douglas said.

"If the CCF provides the right kind of leadership, I believe it can rally the farmers, organized labor and the progressive elements of Canada behind its banner," he added.[72]

Monetary incentives also seem to have gained in importance. In his presidential address to the first CCF National Convention, J. S. Woodsworth had alluded only briefly to finances in the following words:

Finances, perhaps, have been our weakest spot. Talk of "financing on a shoe-string!" We began without a dollar—and we have almost held our own! We have had what money could not buy—self-sacrificing service and boundless enthusiasm; a realization that we are working in a great cause and that each must do his bit. That spirit has carried us further than could a big budget.[73]

But as these two conditions became reversed—voluntary effort growing feebler while the party grew more prosperous—the CCF relied increasingly on paid effort.[74] Some of these changes on the senior level

[71]See above, p. 127.

[72]*Montreal Gazette*, July 19, 1957.

[73]MacInnis, *A Man to Remember*, p. 278.

[74]Michels (*Political Parties*, pp. 80, 36) describes the same process in other socialist parties as follows:

"In the infancy of the socialist party, when the organization is still weak, when its membership is scanty, and when its principal aim is to diffuse a knowledge of the elementary principles of socialism, professional leaders are less numerous than are leaders whose work in this department is no more than an accessory occupation. But with the further progress of the organization, new needs continually arise, at once within the party and in respect of its relationships with the outer world. Thus the moment inevitably comes when neither the idealism and enthusiasm of the intellectuals, nor yet the goodwill with which the proletarians devote their free time on Sundays to the work of the party, suffice any longer to

were described previously.[75] Even more significant was the evidence of greater discussion and use of financial incentives to replace and supplement voluntary effort at lower levels of the organizational hierarchy. As early as 1951, a senior professional organizer wrote to the Provincial Executive suggesting that "we build up strong poll organizations, even if we have to pay the poll workers." When his proposal was discussed,

> The Provincial Leader said the failure [in the election of that year] was largely organizational but he doubted if we could solve the problem by substituting paid workers for voluntary workers. He said we should not make the mistake of thinking that the Conservative organization was entirely paid for. They have innumerable voluntary workers who work just as hard as our people. The fact remains that our vote did not get to the polls.[76]

The organizer replied in a conciliatory fashion but added, "We must have one worker in every poll even if we have to pay some of them a nominal fee."

The practice of paying election workers, which was well established in the "old parties," probably did not become prevalent in the CCF in part because the latter lacked the money and in part because the taboos against doing so openly were still too strong. Nevertheless, money did seem to find its way into the hands of more election workers, as the following conversation (in the 1950's) with a campaign manager suggests.

> *Author*: "Who'll be here [at the committee room] tomorrow?"
> *Paul* (the Campaign Manager): "Harold H. He's being paid for it. I'm disappointed in him. . . ."
> *Author*: "Who else is being paid?"
> *Paul*: "Don't let this get any farther—Robert C. He was a special case. There were three reasons in his case. First, he was out of work and needed the money. Secondly, he's the hardest worker at canvassing that we've got.

---

meet the requirements of the case. The provisional must then give place to the permanent, and dilettantism must yield to professionalism. . . .

"The more solid the structure of an organization becomes in the course of the evolution of the modern political party, the more marked becomes the tendency to replace the emergency leader by the professional leader. Every party organization which has attained to a considerable degree of complication demands that there should be a certain number of persons who devote all their activities to the work of the party."

[75]The implementation in 1956 of a pension plan to cover all of the party's full time employees, a series of wage increases and the official adoption of other conventional conditions of employment represented the same tendency on the clerical level.

[76]Provincial.Executive, Minutes, Dec. 1, 1951.

Third, [the candidate] arranged with him that he'd get $200 for seven weeks, but that it would be OK if he got a job in the meantime. Well, right off the bat he landed a job and Harold H was swung in on his job. Then there's Freddy G. He needed a job during his vacation. [The candidate's] very high on him. He's a good worker but not especially sharp.

"I think our paid workers were a mistake. If it ever gets out that some of them were paid, there's likely to be lots of hard feelings. . . . It should either be done openly by having a meeting of the election committee and arranging it there and have everyone know about it or else not have any paid workers at all."

The secrecy of these arrangements rendered it impossible to gauge their extent.

Once the proposal for a "new party" came into the open, in 1958, it increasingly dominated the CCF's attention. Numerous conferences and meetings were organized to discuss it, as CCF leaders, on all levels, attempted to use the prospect of a new and much stronger party to generate a widespread revival of enthusiasm throughout the ranks. Because the close observation of the party was terminated before the introduction of this new incentive, its effect on the rank and file cannot be assessed here in any detail.

Taken together, the many aspects of CCF morale suggest that the party's limited claim on most of its members and their memory of a deeper commitment were important sources both of the CCF's strength and weakness in the 1950's. Unlike more radical groups, which obtain a stronger hold on the lives and emotions of their members, the CCF's claims were more limited and its hold weaker, and therefore the emotional breaks common in church and party life did not occur. Many CCF members either did not become seriously involved or else drifted steadily away from the party but still retained membership and some attachment to it. But for others, these claims and commitments remained sufficiently strong to motivate them—a slowly diminishing band of the faithful—to serve as candidates and campaign workers, to give larger donations and to wring from the less active majority renewals of membership, money and occasional participation.

Perhaps the members who had given time, energy and enthusiasm more freely in the days when money was scarce eventually found money more plentiful but time and interest in short supply. Possibly they honoured the obligations they still felt and eased their conscience by contributing in cash what they could no longer give in active participation. By doing so, they helped to keep the party's finances and membership stable and its popular support almost so until the very end.

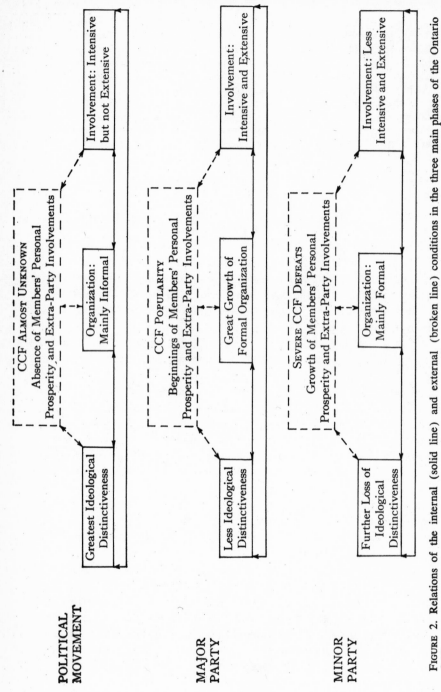

FIGURE 2. Relations of the internal (solid line) and external (broken line) conditions in the three main phases of the Ontario CCF.

PART IV

Conclusion

VIII. How the CCF Was Distinctive

"WHATEVER HAS HAPPENED TO THE CCF?" During the fifties I was asked that question constantly. What the questioners had in mind was the party's disappearance from the limelight or, less often, the conventionality of its viewpoint. This study as a whole suggests a simple answer —both the country and the party changed substantially after the 1930's. Prosperity and welfare legislation stifled the public's interest in the CCF, while changes in the views and lives of the party's members made them more conservative and politically apathetic.

The result was a somewhat unusual occurrence among political movements—the CCF kept diminishing in popularity but growing in "worldliness." Indeed, its character eventually became sufficiently conventional to permit another answer to the question above. If one steps away from the party and looks about at other groups, one might well reply, "Nothing very remarkable happened to the CCF. It simply went the way of all organizations." In technical language, it became institutionalized.

The CCF's changes parallel those of many bodies which have undergone this process. Both the party and the world came a long way towards meeting each other. The former's urge to "shatter to bits this sorry scheme of things entire" subsided and its vision of the form into which it would remould it faded. The public and the "old parties" came to accept many CCF ideas which they had once rejected as unthinkable. Although the viewpoints of the party and the world remained apart, they ceased to do violence to one another. Indeed, their proximity became a serious threat to the CCF's existence, though only because the party was so weak.

As the CCF's initial struggle for acceptance drew to an end, the usual changes occurred. The excitement subsided and the host of enthusiastic amateurs turned their main attention elsewhere (although most of them retained some allegiance), leaving the party's direction increasingly to the professionals, attached to the central offices, who had begun emerging in the meantime. The latter gained influence not simply by default but because they were more deeply involved. Their livelihood and careers were at stake, and, like their counterparts anywhere, they considered themselves more competent than any amateur, however zealous, could be. They developed techniques for the management of the organization that were suited to its more settled and less personal character. These methods included those which any professional group employs in an organization where amateurs have the final say. This dependence on the party for a living and career had important consequences too because the personal circumstances of the paid officers became closely tied to the over-all electoral fortunes of the party, a consideration which hardly encouraged the professionals to steer the CCF away from the society in which it functioned.

Some of the amateurs continued to hold meetings, as they do in most voluntary organizations; but, as elsewhere, these meetings gradually became less frequent, more sparsely attended and almost exclusively devoted to conducting the "business" of the local branch. In fact, though not in form, they usually considered fundamental policy as established and received rather than as "issues" which required local determination.[1]

This description might apply, however roughly, to most groups which begin with a new and unacceptable idea—religious denominations, welfare bodies, and perhaps even business organizations—as they and their members secure comfortable places in the world. It is just this process in radical political movements that Michels describes so well and illustrates so profusely, though perhaps with an excessive flavour of disenchantment and of exposé.[2]

What makes the CCF distinctive, however, was that it acquired the characteristics described above without having achieved a comparable place in society and, indeed, while it was slipping from the modest position which it had attained. In brief, its character grew more worldly while its position[3] became more precarious. This combination of character and position departs not only from the usual pattern of socialist and other parties but also from the conventional "institutionalization cycle"

[1]For a description of the corresponding groups in the British Labour party, see McKenzie, *British Political Parties*, pp. 539–58.

[2]Michels, *Political Parties*.

[3]"Position" is used here to refer to the group's strength, as determined by popular support, rather than to an ideological stand.

suggested by Dawson and Gettys,[4] which presumably applies much more widely. However, to explain this departure it is first necessary to show how political parties differ from other organizations, and then, how minor parties differ from both political movements and major parties.

All organizations whose membership is predominantly voluntary, including political parties,[5] share certain hazards and conditions of existence which differentiate them from non-voluntary bodies. The chief one is harnessing their membership in the absence of some of the main devices that are available to other types of organization. Because voluntary members are not moved by the usual bread-and-butter incentives, these groups must do without this central mechanism of human control.

Instead, they depend all the more heavily on their members' inner convictions and concern about the approval of their fellows, so that a weakening of either is particularly damaging to voluntary groups. At best, regular routines of work and participation are difficult to establish in organizations of this type and are, therefore, often sources of anxious preoccupation. Frequently, the mobilization of its voluntary members, through whom the group reaches the public, consumes much of its money and effort.

Political parties encounter special problems in getting and holding a clientele and membership. They are the only bodies which cannot (legally) provide a direct return for patronage (votes),[6] and only the winner(s), by controlling the government, can provide an indirect return. (One can argue, however, that any party which makes a significant show of strength may do so as well.)

Because only the winner can "pay off," many a voter concludes that his ballot will be "wasted" if it is cast for a party which has "no chance." Thus, if he votes at all, it will probably be for a party which he likes less but whose prospects make him feel that his ballot is not meaningless; and that of course, is why all parties try to convince the electorate of their strength at least as much as of their intelligence and virtue. They all know that unless a political party appears to have a reasonably good chance of "going somewhere," it is unlikely to maintain even a steady level of existence.[7] Because other kinds of organization

[4]*An Introduction to Sociology*, pp. 689–709.

[5]This entire discussion of political groups applies only where elections are free.

[6]The secret ballot, of course, deliberately conceals patronage.

[7]This tendency accounts for most of the difficulties which new parties encounter and for the special importance of the "bandwagon" in politics. It helps to keep the major parties strong and the minor ones weak.

can prosper or at least maintain a stable clientele even though they have no prospect of overtaking their larger rivals, they can lead more settled and less hazardous lives than can political parties.[8]

In a major party, these uncertainties are offset by the numerous ballots which it obtains from people who do not regard it as their first preference but vote for it nevertheless either to remove its main rival from office or to prevent it from getting there. This tendency is sufficiently extensive to make most major parties seem virtually indestructible.

Minor parties lack this form of built-in insurance, and, except where the proportional representation system protects them,[9] they have a much higher mortality rate than do major parties or even radical movements. Several conditions make minor parties more susceptible to the rule of "up or out" than are other political (as well as non-political) organizations.

The first is that the special relation, described above, between a political party and the electorate also exists, although the details differ, between the party and its own members. Though the members' hope may last longer than the public's, and they usually obtain other rewards, the fundamental similarity of the relation remains. The members invest far more in the party than do the voters, giving it their energy, time, money and, possibly, career. The party cannot yield a return on that investment unless it wins, so if the members conclude that it cannot win, they are likely to cut their losses by withdrawing their investment. Thus, the decisions of the members and officers of a political party resemble those of investors. This study as a whole demonstrates how greatly the withdrawal of their investments affects the party's fortunes and how much their decisions depend on the hope of *winning* the contest of popularity.

[8]Premier W. A. C. Bennett of British Columbia made this point very simply in a newspaper interview (*Globe and Mail Magazine*, June 23, 1962):
"You and I can both be successful hardware merchants, my friend. You and I can both be successful lawyers. You and I can both be successful surgeons. But you and I can't both be successful politicians.
"In politics, only one of us can win."
[9]The proportional representation system, which is so prevalent in Europe, is much kinder to minor parties and less helpful to major ones than is the system which prevails in the English-speaking world. (Indeed, it tends to make the distinctions between "major" and "minor" less clear.) These facts account both for the multiplicity of parties where proportional representation is used and for the high correlation between the strength of parties and their attitudes to these two types of electoral system.
The remainder of this discussion deals with minor parties in the simple-plurality, single ballot system. For a detailed discussion of how that system affects political parties and especially the minor ones, see Duverger, *Political Parties*.

Ideologically, the minor parties are in a difficult position. Political movements usually possess a clearer *raison d'être* in their highly distinctive viewpoint. The major parties, though rather alike in viewpoint because their strength and proximity to power make them representative of and sensitive to many shades of public opinion, also possess a more obvious self-justification than do the minor parties—the possession or imminent prospect of power.

Each of these positions provides an effective basis for claiming support from the public as well as from party ranks. Protest movements demand support on the grounds of a transcendental moral justification rather than those of impending victory. Major parties are less outraged by the state of things and less utopian in their promises, but they seek support on the grounds of their immediate prospect of holding office. Both of these positions provide obvious, if very different, justifications for existence in the struggle for political survival.

The position of minor parties is uneasy, by contrast, for they cannot press either of these claims for support very effectively. Because the world does not outrage them and visions of utopia are absent they can do little more than intone the rituals of crusade, while their remoteness from power renders the other claim for support virtually unusable. Establishing a *raison d'être* which is both comprehensible and compelling seems to be an inherent problem of minor parties. The difficulty becomes compounded when doctrinal differences become blurred, as they have been in the recent past and still are, and when, like the CCF, the minor party must search for a place within a cherished two-party system.

Structurally, minor parties occupy an intermediate position between the proselytizing movements which are more personal and tightly knit, and the major parties, which are held together more loosely and formally. Although they are more firmly planted in the world than are the political movements, they are less deeply and intricately rooted in it than are the large, conventional parties.

If the CCF's case is typical, membership may be greater at the minor party stage than it was in the earlier, more sectarian period. But a larger proportion of it is less involved, maintaining little more than a formal connection and refusing to be stirred into active participation, no matter what efforts the party makes.[10] This is even more characteristic of the major parties. But they can be stirred with greater ease and, once aroused, they reach farther because the anticipation of power enables

[10]For a study of the difficulties experienced by some minor American parties in maintaining membership loyalty and participation, see Kornhauser, "Organizational Loyalty."

them to marshal leaders and followers, candidates and funds both from their own ranks and from many other groups.

Emotionally, the minor party cannot draw heavily on the driving power either of a crusading movement or of a major party. Fear and indignation are the chief fuel of the former, and utopian hopes are the sparks which ignite them. These elements cannot exist without a sense of great danger (for example, "capitalism's inherent depressions and tendency towards fascism") and a stirring vision of the future (an abundant and classless society, for instance). But as the minor party's villains and vision recede, so does the energy which they generate. Despite their resemblance to their major rivals, the minor parties cannot harness the latter's main source of energy either: the anticipation of worldly achievements, for self and others, which is ignited by the prospect of impending victory. The remoteness of that prospect deprives the minor parties of most of this motive power.

In summary, minor parties differ from political movements and major parties in the following ways:

	Political movement	Major party
Raison d'être	more distinct	better understood
Organization	more personal	more firmly rooted in the world
Membership motivation	greater involvement	more easily activated (at elections)

Minor parties lack the character to which radical movements chiefly owe their survival as well as the position to which the major parties owe theirs. This does not necessarily mean that minor parties live in the worst of all possible worlds. The CCF, for instance, drew more popular support in its final than in its initial phase, and nearly all its major relatives went through a minor party stage. However, they entered that stage with their sectarian character very much intact and, while in it, their steady progress brought victory within sight. But, without the protest movement's sustaining faith in ultimate triumph or the major party's assurance of taking office as soon as the public tires of its main rival, a minor party is especially susceptible to the rule of "up or out" once its character comes to resemble that of the old and secure members of the establishment.

That susceptibility, in turn, plays back upon the minor party's character, accentuating the tendency towards demoralization, weakening its structure and its confidence in its own approach and viewpoint.

Thus, in our electoral system, minor parties seem destined to a more precarious existence than are other political groups or non-political bodies of comparable strength and worldliness. These considerations account, in brief, for the high mortality rate of "third" parties in the English-speaking nations, the rarity with which they displace their major rivals and the sense of doom which frequently hangs over them.

We can now return to the question of why the CCF, although unsuccessful, none the less acquired a worldly character. Why did it not become either a major, worldly party or an inconsequential, other-worldly sect?

One might argue that only those socialist parties which achieved a minimal degree of momentum fairly early in their career were able to achieve major party status by the democratic process. The evidence for this argument is that every social democratic party which did attain that momentum climbed steadily to power or to the threshold of power and remained a major party. The failure of the United States Socialist party might therefore be attributed to its inability to achieve that minimal degree of propulsion.[11]

Whatever the plausibility of this argument, it obviously does not apply to the CCF. The latter acquired as much momentum, in the early 1940's,[12] as any socialist party ever did, but its progress was quite uncharacteristically arrested and abruptly reversed. This departure from so ubiquitous a pattern gives another twist to the query, "Whatever happened to the CCF?" Why was the march forward reversed so sharply in Canada, and only there, once it had got so well under way?

The most obvious explanation seems to lie in the general political system which Canada shares with most of the English-speaking world. That system, we have observed, does not provide comfortable accommodation for more than two parties at a time. New parties, because of their regional bases, have challenged the established tenants more successfully in the provincial field than in the federal. (At the time of writing, late 1963, Canada's three most westerly provinces are in Social Credit or CCF hands.) But the dominance of the Liberals and Conservatives nationally has remained unbroken since Confederation, despite several attempts by other parties.

The CCF and Social Credit have been the most recent and, in an important sense, the most unusual aspirants. Other new parties were

[11]At the height of its popularity, in 1912, the Socialist party won only 6 per cent of the presidential vote and only one seat in Congress. Since then it has been sidelined in all but name from the main political arena.

[12]See App. A, Table XVIII.

either popular or persistent, but never both. Some, like the Progressive party of the early 1920's, or the Reconstruction party of the mid-1930's, blossomed suddenly and even spectacularly, but faded almost as rapidly —the common fate of most new parties that originate by splitting off from the established major ones.[13] Other political groups, such as the Communists, the Trotskyites (despite several splinterings) and the followers of Daniel de Leon, have survived for decades on the dark outer fringes of the political scene. Only the CCF and Social Credit were able to combine popularity with durability.

The success of other social democratic parties, and particularly of the British Labour party, is decisive evidence that small, third parties are not inevitably doomed to that status and suggests that the formal political system does not in itself account adequately for the CCF's weak position. Canada's distinctive history and character did, of course, make the CCF different from other socialist parties. For example, unlike most of its European counterparts, it arrived on the scene too late to participate in the main battles for political liberty, the franchise and trade union legitimacy. The prior achievement of these goals undoubtedly contributed, in turn, to the CCF's late start and to its lack of a massive trade union base, both of which handicapped it severely, although probably neither was an insurmountable obstacle in itself.

Although every major socialist party, except those in the new nations, was formed by the beginning of the twentieth century, age by itself did not guarantee success, as the United States Socialist party[14] and others demonstrate. Nor were formal alliances (collective affiliations) with trade unions essential to the success of socialist parties, as the evidence from continental Europe indicates.[15]

---

[13]In origin and type of life cycle these parties had less in common with the CCF than with such third parties in the United States as the Bull Moose, the two Progressive parties and the Dixiecrats. These also began by springing full bodied from the major parties, following unsuccessful efforts to win control of them, disintegrated after only one genuine trial of strength, and were largely reabsorbed by their original parties.

The Canadian Progressives had a somewhat more independent origin and after the party disintegrated its radical minority was instrumental in founding the CCF. (See Morton, *The Progressive Party in Canada*.)

[14]Formed in 1902, only two years after the British Labour party, it was never as strong as even the CCF.

[15]Formal collective affiliation exists only in the Swedish and Norwegian parties and, in both cases, only on the local level, in contrast to the practice in the British Labour party. In Norway, these affiliations constitute only about 35 per cent of the present Labour party membership. (For a more detailed discussion of these arrangements and of the main types of relations between the trade unions

But if these socialist parties did not need the industrial workers' membership to succeed, they did need, and got, their votes. The CCF's failure to duplicate that feat stemmed, according to F. H. Underhill and others, from North America's distinctive political conditions.

socialism [in Canada] . . . was obviously an importation, partly from Marxians in continental Europe, and partly from the more moderate parliamentary socialists, the Fabian socialists, of England. It obviously didn't originate in Canada; the CCF was an attempt to adapt these European ideas, primarily the Fabian ideas, to Canadian conditions. . . .
    I feel the CCF was an attempt to set up a British-type of party system, a division between left and right. We [the CCF] were defeated by Mr. King because he was a good North American and he saw that our politics wasn't likely to work that way.[16]

A definitive explanation of the CCF's failure requires a thorough examination of its environment, a task which lies beyond the scope of the present study. One point may be noted here, however. The special North American or Canadian environment may explain the party's weakness, but it does not account for the CCF's departure from the usual paths taken by political movements which have felt rejected. The fate of the CCF was especially unusual for North America, where reform parties, if successful, tend to blow away or shrink into purely regional groups, and where radical movements, if the climate is uninviting, seem to shrivel and crawl back into a hard, sectarian shell. The CCF did neither. Instead, it became a minor national party but retained and developed the wordly character which had begun to blossom during its great expansion. The distinctiveness of that combination, at least among socialist parties, as well as the explanation of it, emerge from a comparison of the CCF with the numerous "left wing" movements of the last hundred years.

    That comparison reveals one significant difference between the history of the CCF and that of its major relatives.[17] Once the latter had reached the height of popularity attained by the CCF in the early 1940's, none

and the socialist parties of the democratic nations of continental Europe, see "Structural Relationships between Trade Unions and Labour Parties," the series of three articles by Paul Malles, Assistant to the Director of Organization, ICFTU.

[16]Underhill, *The Radical Tradition.* For a similar explanation of the Progressive party's failure see Morton, *The Progressive Party in Canada,* p. 270.

    These views leave unexplained, however, how close the CCF did come to attaining power or becoming the official Opposition. The timing of its upsurge, mid-way between, rather than just before, elections, was perhaps a chance factor in its failure to achieve either of these objectives.

[17]For the record of the popular support of these parties, see App. C.

suffered a serious reversal before attaining at least second party status.[18] The full significance of that difference was demonstrated by the combination of defeat and change. When these other socialist parties finally met misfortune, each had already secured a very different *modus vivendi*—it had become a major party and was still the chief alternative to the one in power, a position which insured it heavily against the hazards of defeat and change. When defeat taught its adherents that they were participating in the conventional political process rather than in an irreversible crusade, the prospect of forming the next government continued to arouse them to action. That same prospect provided an effective and easily understood *raison d'être* when their socialism became less clear and ardent. And it enabled the party, when defeated, to hold together the organization and alliances which it had built during its long and steady rise.

The CCF, in contrast, was badly hurt by the combination of defeat and change. Defeat led to hopelessness, which sapped the energies of many members and deflated the interest of the public. And when the party's faith in utopian socialism withered, no stimulating *raison d'être* was available as a replacement. Consequently, these twin losses—of hope in present victory and of certainty in ultimate triumph—inflicted critical, and in some areas fatal, injuries to the party's organization. They left the CCF neither a major party nor a political movement, defeat demolishing the former mode of existence and change the latter.

Instead of following the typical protest movement–minor party–major party sequence of its stronger socialist confrères, the CCF's career came closer to a protest movement–major party–minor party order. Two sets of events account for this unusual sequence. First, the CCF was catapulted into the world, became deeply involved in it and experienced a profound change of character, a change that was of course common to many socialist parties. Unlike them, the CCF was unable to establish a secure place in that world because its propulsion failed to carry it into at least second place, as theirs invariably did. Instead, the CCF was the only one of these parties to encounter severe reversals before reaching the safe haven of second place but after leaving the shelter of sectarianism. This was the departure from the typical process of institutionalization that twisted the CCF out of the usual socialist forms.

If its position distinguished the CCF from the major socialist parties, its character separated it from the lesser groups of the "left," for example from the United States Socialist party. The latter's outstanding features

[18]Many of them had held or shared office before meeting that reversal.

in the forties and fifties were its extremely unorthodox views and its almost total rejection by the public, both of which it shared with numerous other "left wing" groups. Many of the latter either repudiated or were unconcerned with the more conventional forms of the contest for power. Instead, much more than the CCF ever did, they rejected the world, looked towards its utopian successor and awaited the cataclysm which, under their leadership, would usher in a better life.

There are still other socialist (and non-socialist) groups which are essentially parties-in-exile but which have little hope of returning to the scene of their original endeavours and little desire to do so. They maintain their ideology and some aspects of their structure with surprisingly little change. But their stability also stems from the absence of a deep involvement in the issues of here and now. Their hearts, instead of dwelling in the remote future, live in the past and in another place. The Communist party also looks elsewhere, a fact which governs most of its behaviour, including its time perspective.

Thus, their perspectives of time and place seem to divide the socialist and other "left wing" parties in the democratic countries into two broad categories, which correspond closely to their strength (position). The first consists of the parties whose main concern is with the present and with their immediate surroundings and which are generally quite popular. The other category contains the parties whose primary orientation is to another time or place or both, parties which, except for the Communist party in Italy, France and pre-Nazi Germany, have had little following. In sum, there are the strong parties of here and now and the weak ones of another time and place.

In which category did the CCF belong? Because its character and position were moving in opposite directions, it did not belong wholly in either category. Its character steadily approached that of a major party, while its position slipped gradually towards that of a minor sect (although it remained very much stronger than any of the latter). In fact, the CCF's most distinctive feature, at least among the many movements which arose out of a somewhat common ideological heritage, was that, in the last half of its life, its perspective of time and place and its strength headed simultaneously in opposite directions, the former towards that of a major party and the latter towards that of a minor sect. This unusual concurrence, which resulted from the party's peculiar pattern of success and failure, provides the last answer to the question, "Whatever happened to the CCF?"

Another relevant question concerns something that did not happen: Why did the CCF not revert to its original character after its reversals?

The answer lies in the state of the world since the war and in the magnitude of the CCF's and its individual members' involvement in it. The post-war world was hard on the party, but it was kind to individual members of the party and to the public at large. A drastic change in conditions might have led either the contemporary CCFers to reject the world once again, thereby recapturing for the party the character of a militant political movement, or to a wholesale turnover of personnel, with the same result.[19] Since extreme change did not occur, the CCF's worldly character continued to grow despite the weakening position of the party in the world.

One cannot help wondering how long these two opposing trends could have continued without tearing the party asunder. During the 1950's, the CCF based its hopes for a solution to this problem on two main possibilities, the arrival of strong trade union reinforcements and a drastic change in the political climate, each of which, it felt, would reverse its downward trend. The New Democratic party now holds out the promise of the first of these possibilities, although it is perhaps still too early to judge the strength or effectiveness of the trade union reinforcements.

Even in its new form, the CCF may find itself on the same path as the United States Socialist party did after its two peaks of strength, in 1912 and 1932. If a rival leader emerges with the magnetic appeal of a Woodrow Wilson or a Franklin Roosevelt, or, as seems more likely in the Canadian political system, if a sufficiently controversial issue arises, one of the major parties may draw off a substantial segment of the New Democratic party, those whose views have moved farthest into the world. The distance that these people would have to travel is no longer very great, and they may find themselves in the same position as did the Socialist party stalwarts who became supporters of the New Deal.

The more militant and utopian minority could then ride off unfettered in the opposite direction, as it did in the Socialist party. By reducing the party to a fraction of its present strength and returning its time perspective to the more remote future, such a development would restore the "natural" order of the socialist world. It is partly to ward off just such an eventuality that the CCF's leaders are now striving so desperately to build their new party.

[19]For a description of just such a change in the United States Socialist party in the early 1930's see Bell, "Marxian Socialism [in the United States]," pp. 369 ff.

The formation of the CCF resulted from the same kind of membership influx and character change in the Canadian socialist movement at exactly the same period.

APPENDIXES

APPENDIX A

CCF Dates and Statistics

1932
  JANUARY: League for Social Reconstruction formed by groups from Toronto and Montreal
  MAY: Ginger Group of MPs, under leadership of J. S. Woodsworth, meets in Ottawa to plan the formation of a new party
  AUGUST: Decision to form CCF taken at Western Labour Conference in Calgary
1933
  JULY: First CCF National Convention adopts Regina Manifesto
1941
  OCTOBER: CCF obtains plurality of votes in British Columbia provincial election
1942
  FEBRUARY: CCF defeats Conservative National Leader in South York, Toronto, by-election
1943
  AUGUST: CCF wins 34 seats in Ontario provincial election; none held in preceding legislature
  SEPTEMBER: Canadian Congress of Labour (affiliated with CIO) endorses CCF "as political arm of labour." Gallup Poll records high point of CCF popular support in Canada
1944
  JUNE: CCF comes to power in Saskatchewan, winning 47 of 52 seats in provincial election
1945
  JUNE 4: CCF representation in Ontario legislature reduced from 34 to 8 in provincial election
  JUNE 11: CCF obtains only 28 seats and 16 per cent of vote in national election
1956
  JULY: CCF National Convention adopts Winnipeg Declaration
1958
  MARCH: CCF representation in Parliament reduced from 25 seats to 8 in national election
  APRIL: Canadian Labour Congress adopts proposal to co-operate with CCF in forming a new party
  JULY: CCF National Convention adopts proposal to co-operate with CLC in forming a new party
1961
  AUGUST: Founding convention of the New Democratic party

CCF POPULAR SUPPORT IN CANADA

All but one of the tables below record the support which the CCF has obtained in national elections. The exception, Table XVIII, is perhaps the most significant; it portrays the party's dramatic rise and decline between the federal elections of 1940 and 1945.

TABLE XVI
NATIONAL ELECTIONS, 1935–63: SEATS WON BY PARTIES

	1935	1940	1945	1949	1953	1957	1958	1962	1963
Liberal	171	178	125	190	170	105	49	100	130
Conservative	39	39	67	41	51	111	208	116	94
CCF	7	8	28	13	23	25	8	19*	17*
Social Credit	17	10	13	10	15	19	0	30	24
Others	11	10	12	8	6	5	0	0	0
	245	245	245	262	265	265	265	265	265

*New Democratic party.
SOURCE: *Canadian Parliamentary Guide.*

TABLE XVII
NATIONAL ELECTIONS, 1935–63: PERCENTAGE OF POPULAR VOTE, BY PARTIES

	1935	1940	1945	1949	1953	1957	1958	1962	1963
Liberal	44	55	41	50	49	40	33	37	41
Conservative	30	31	28	30	31	40	54	37	33
CCF	9	9	16	13	11	11	10	13*	14*
Social Credit	4	3	4	2	5	6	2	12	12
Others	13	2	10	5	4	3	1	0	0
	100	100	99	100	100	100	100	99	100

*New Democratic party.

TABLE XVIII
CCF POPULAR SUPPORT IN CANADA, 1940–45

		CCF	Lib.	Cons.	Bloc populaire	Others
1940	March (election)	9	55	31	—	5
1942	Jan.	10	55	30	—	5
	Sept.	21	39	23	—	17
1943	Feb.	23	32	27	7	11
	Sept.	29	28	28	9	6
1944	Jan.	24	30	29	9	8
	Sept.	24	36	27	5	8
1945	Jan.	22	36	28	6	8
	April	20	36	29	6	9
	May	19	38	29	6	8
	June 2	19	40	27	5	9
	June 9	17	39	29	5	10
	June 11 (election)	16	41	28	3	12

SOURCE: Gallup Poll, reported in McHenry, *The Third Force in Canada*, p. 136.

TABLE XIX

	S*	1935	1940	1945	1949	1953	1957	1958
Newfoundland	7							
Prince Edward Island	4							
Nova Scotia	12		1	1	1	1		
New Brunswick	10							
Quebec	75							
Ontario	85				1	1	3	3
Manitoba	14	2	1	5	3	3	5	
Saskatchewan	17	2	5	18†	5	11	10	1
Alberta	17							
British Columbia	22	3	1	4	3	7	7	4
Yukon–NWT	2							
	265	7	8	28	13	23	25	8

*Provinces' seats in the House of Commons, 1957.
†Saskatchewan had 21 seats in 1945.

CCF POPULAR SUPPORT IN ONTARIO

The tables below record the support which the CCF has received in Ontario in both federal and provincial elections. Tables XX and XXI report on the federal balloting and tables XXII to XXIV on the provincial; the latter show that the party is stronger in Ontario's provincial politics.

TABLE XX

NATIONAL ELECTIONS, 1935–58:
PERCENTAGE OF CCF VOTE IN CANADA AND ONTARIO

	Canada	Ontario
1935	8.9	8.0
1940	8.5	3.8
1945	15.6	14.6
1949	13.4	15.5
1953	11.3	11.4
1957	10.6	12.6
1958	9.7	10.6

TABLE XXI

NATIONAL ELECTIONS, 1935–58: INDICES OF CCF STRENGTH IN ONTARIO

	Ridings	CCF candidates	Won by CCF	CCF second
1935	82	50	0	1
1940	82	26	0	0
1945	82	80	0	5
1949	83	77	1	3
1953	85	65	1	3
1957	85	60	3	4
1958	85	63	3	3

TABLE XXII

ONTARIO PROVINCIAL ELECTIONS, 1934–63: SEATS WON BY PARTIES

	1934	1937	1943	1945	1948	1951	1955	1959	1963
Liberal	66	63	15	11	13	7	10	22	23
Conservative	17	23	38	66	53	79	83	71	78
CCF	1	0	34	8	21	2	3	5	7*
Others	6.	4	3	5	3	2	2	0	0
	90	90	90	90	90	90	98	98	108

*New Democratic party.

TABLE XXIII

ONTARIO PROVINCIAL ELECTIONS, 1934–63:
PERCENTAGE OF POPULAR VOTE, BY PARTIES

	1934	1937	1943	1945	1948	1951	1955	1959	1963
Liberal	51	52	31	30	29	31	33	37	35
Conservative	40	40	36	45	41	49	47	46	49
CCF	7	7	32	22	27	19	17	17	16*
Others	2	1	1	3	3	1	3	0	0
	100	100	100	100	100	100	100	100	100

*New Democratic party.

TABLE XXIV

ONTARIO PROVINCIAL ELECTIONS, 1934–59: INDICES OF CCF STRENGTH

	Ridings	CCF candidates	Won by CCF	CCF second
1934	90	35	1	0
1937	90	43	0	0
1943	90	86	34	10
1945	90	89	8	22
1948	90	85	21	13
1951	90	77	2	22
1955	98	81	3	18
1959	98	81	5	6

CCF POPULAR SUPPORT IN METROPOLITAN TORONTO

As the preceding figures showed that the CCF in Ontario is stronger in provincial than in federal politics, so Table XXV records the fact that it has always obtained better support in metropolitan Toronto than in the province as a whole.

TABLE XXV

ONTARIO PROVINCIAL ELECTIONS, 1934–59: PERCENTAGE
OF CCF VOTE IN ONTARIO, TORONTO, AND ONTARIO
EXCLUDING TORONTO

	Ontario	Toronto	Ontario excluding Toronto
1934	7	14	6
1937	7	$12\frac{1}{2}$	5
1943	32	$36\frac{1}{2}$	$30\frac{1}{2}$
1945	22	29	20
1948	27	39	22
1951	19	30	$15\frac{1}{2}$
1955	17	26	14
1959	17	26	14

CCF Documents

CO-OPERATIVE COMMONWEALTH FEDERATION PROGRAMME

Adopted at First National Convention Held at Regina, Sask., July, 1933

[REGINA MANIFESTO]

The CCF is a federation of organizations whose purpose is the establishment in Canada of a Co-operative Commonwealth in which the principle regulating production, distribution and exchange will be the supplying of human needs and not the making of profits.

We aim to replace the present capitalist system, with its inherent injustice and inhumanity, by a social order from which the domination and exploitation of one class by another will be eliminated, in which economic planning will supersede unregulated private enterprise and competition, and in which genuine democratic self-government, based upon economic equality will be possible. The present order is marked by glaring inequalities of wealth and opportunity, by chaotic waste and instability; and in an age of plenty it condemns the great mass of the people to poverty and insecurity. Power has become more and more concentrated into the hands of a small irresponsible minority of financiers and industrialists and to their predatory interests the majority are habitually sacrificed. When private profit is the main stimulus to economic effort, our society oscillates between periods of feverish prosperity in which the main benefits go to speculators and profiteers, and of catastrophic depression, in which the common man's normal state of insecurity and hardship is accentuated. We believe that these evils can be removed only in a planned and socialized economy in which our natural resources and the principal means of production and distribution are owned, controlled and operated by the people.

The new social order at which we aim is not one in which individuality will be crushed out by a system of regimentation. Nor shall we interfere with cultural rights of racial or religious minorities. What we seek is a proper collective organization of our economic resources such as will make possible a much greater degree of leisure and a much richer individual life for every citizen.

This social and economic transformation can be brought about by political action, through the election of a government inspired by the ideal of a Co-operative Commonwealth and supported by a majority of the people. We do not believe in change by violence. We consider that both the old parties in Canada are the instruments of capitalist interests and cannot serve as agents of social reconstruction, and that whatever the superficial differences between them, they are bound to carry on government in accordance with the dictates of the big business interests who finance them. The CCF aims at political power in order to put an end to this capitalist domination of our political life. It is a democratic movement, a federation of farmer, labor and socialist organizations, financed by its own members and seeking to achieve its ends solely by constitutional methods. It appeals for support to all who believe that the time has come for a far-reaching reconstruction of our economic and political institutions and who are willing to work together for the carrying out of the following policies:

1. PLANNING

The establishment of a planned, socialized economic order, in order to make possible the most efficient development of the national resources and the most equitable distribution of the national income

The first step in this direction will be setting up of a National Planning Commission consisting of a small body of economists, engineers and statisticians assisted by an appropriate technical staff.

The task of the Commission will be to plan for the production, distribution and exchange of all goods and services necessary to the efficient functioning of the economy; to co-ordinate the activities of the socialized industries; to provide for a satisfactory balance between the producing and consuming power; and to carry on continuous research into all branches of the national economy in order to acquire the detailed information necessary to efficient planning.

The Commission will be responsible to the Cabinet and will work in co-operation with the Managing Boards of the Socialized Industries.

It is now certain that in every industrial country some form of planning will replace the disintegrating capitalist system. The C.C.F. will provide that in Canada the planning shall be done, not by a small group of capitalist magnates in their own interests, but by public servants acting in the public interest and responsible to the people as a whole.

2. SOCIALIZATION OF FINANCE

Socialization of all financial machinery—banking, currency, credit, and insurance, to make possible the effective control of currency, credit and prices, and the supplying of new productive equipment for socially desirable purposes

Planning by itself will be of little use if the public authority has not the power to carry its plans into effect. Such power will require the control of finance and of all those vital industries and services, which, if they remain in private hands, can be used to thwart or corrupt the will of the public authority. Control of finance is the first step in the control of the whole economy. The chartered banks must be socialized and removed from the control of private profit-seeking interests; and the national banking system thus established must have at its head a Central Bank to control the flow of credit and the general price level, and to regulate foreign exchange operations. A National Investment Board must also be set up, working in co-operation with the socialized banking system to mobilize and direct the unused surpluses of production for socially desired purposes as determined by the Planning Commission.

Insurance Companies, which provide one of the main channels for the investment of individual savings and which, under their present competitive organization, charge needlessly high premiums for the social services that they render, must also be socialized.

3. SOCIAL OWNERSHIP

Socialization (Dominion, Provincial or Municipal) of transportation, communications, electric power and all other industries and services essential to social planning, and their operation under the general direction of the Planning Commission by competent managements freed from day to day political interference

Public utilities must be operated for the public benefit and not for the private profit of a small group of owners or financial manipulators. Our natural resources must be developed by the same methods. Such a programme means the continuance and extension of the public ownership enterprises in which most governments in Canada have already gone some distance. Only by such public ownership, operated on a planned economy, can our main industries be saved from the wasteful competition of the ruinous over-development and over-capitalization which are the inevitable outcome of capitalism. Only in a regime of public ownership and operation will the full benefits accruing from centralized control and mass production be passed on to the consuming public.

Transportation, communications and electric power must come first in a list of industries to be socialized. Others, such as mining, pulp and paper and the distribution of milk, bread, coal and gasoline, in which exploitation, waste, or financial malpractices are particularly prominent must next be brought under social ownership and operation.

In restoring to the community its natural resources and in taking over industrial enterprises from private into public control we do not propose any policy of outright confiscation. What we desire is the most stable and equitable transition to the Co-operative Commonwealth. It is impossible to decide the policies to be followed in particular cases in an uncertain future, but we insist upon certain broad principles. The welfare of the community must take supremacy over the claims of private wealth. In times of war, human life has been conscripted. Should economic circumstances call for it, conscription of wealth would be more justifiable. We recognize the need for compensation in the case of individuals and institutions which must receive adequate maintenance during the transitional period before the planned economy becomes fully operative. But a CCF government will not play the role of rescuing bankrupt private concerns for the benefit of promoters and of stock and bond holders. It will not pile up a deadweight burden of unremunerative debt which represents claims upon the public treasury of a functionless owner class.

The management of publicly owned enterprises will be vested in boards who will be appointed for their competence in the industry and will conduct each particular enterprise on efficient economic lines. The machinery of management may well vary from industry to industry, but the rigidity of Civil Service rules should be avoided and likewise the evils of the patronage system as exemplified in so many departments of the Government today.

Workers in these public industries must be free to organize in trade unions and must be given the right to participate in the management of the industry.

4. AGRICULTURE

Security of tenure for the farmer upon his farm on conditions to be laid down by individual provinces; insurance against unavoidable crop failure; removal of the tariff burden from the operations of agriculture; encouragement of producers' and consumers' co-operatives; the restoration and maintenance of an equitable relationship between prices of agricultural products and those of other commodities and services; and improving the efficiency of export trade in farm products

The security of tenure for the farmer upon his farm which is imperilled by the present disastrous situation of the whole industry, together with adequate social insurance, ought to be guaranteed under equitable conditions.

The prosperity of agriculture, the greatest Canadian industry, depends upon a rising volume of purchasing power of the masses in Canada for all farm goods consumed at home, and upon the maintenance of large scale exports of the stable commodities at satisfactory prices or equitable commodity exchange.

The intense depression in agriculture today is a consequence of the general world crisis caused by the normal workings of the capitalistic system resulting in: (1) Economic nationalism expressing itself in tariff barriers and other restrictions of world trade; (2) The decreased purchasing power of unemployed and under-employed workers and of the Canadian people in general; (3) The exploitation of both primary producers and consumers by monopolistic corporations who absorb a great proportion of the selling price of farm products. (This last is true, for example, of the distribution of milk and dairy products, the packing industry, and milling.)

The immediate cause of agricultural depression is the catastrophic fall in the world prices of foodstuffs as compared with other prices, this fall being due in large measure to the deflation of currency and credit. To counteract the worst effect of this, the internal price level should be raised so that the farmers' purchasing power may be restored.

We propose therefore:

(1) The improvement of the position of the farmer by the increase of the purchasing power made possible by the social control of the financial system. This control must be directed towards the increase of employment as laid down elsewhere and towards raising the prices of farm commodities by appropriate credit and foreign policies.

(2) Whilst the family farm is the accepted basis for agricultural production in Canada the position of the farmer may be much improved by: (a) The extension of consumers' co-operatives for the purchase of farm supplies and domestic requirements; and (b) The extension of co-operative institutions for the processing and marketing of farm products.

Both of the foregoing to have suitable state encouragement and assistance.

(3) The adoption of a planned system of agricultural development based upon scientific soil surveys directed towards better land utilization, and a scientific policy of agricultural development for the whole of Canada.

(4) The substitution for the present system of foreign trade, of a system of import boards to improve the efficiency of overseas marketing, to control prices, and to integrate the foreign trade policy with the requirements of the national economic plan.

5. EXTERNAL TRADE

The regulation in accordance with the National plan of external trade through import and export boards

Canada is dependent on external sources of supply for many of her essential requirements of raw materials and manufactured products. These she can obtain only by large exports of the goods she is best fitted to produce. The strangling of our export trade by insane protectionist policies must be brought to an end. But the old controversies between free traders and protectionists are now largely obsolete. In a world of nationally organized economies Canada must organize the buying and selling of her main imports and exports under public boards, and take steps to regulate the flow of less important commodities by a system of licenses. By so doing she will be enabled to make the best trade agreements possible with foreign countries, put a stop to the exploitation of both primary producer and ultimate consumer, make possible the co-ordination of internal processing, transportation and marketing of farm products, and facilitate the establishment of stable prices for such export commodities.

6. CO-OPERATIVE INSTITUTIONS

The encouragement by the public authority of both producers' and consumers' co-operative institutions

In agriculture, as already mentioned, the primary producer can receive a larger net revenue through co-operative organization of purchases and marketing. Similarly in retail distribution of staple commodities such as milk, there is room for development both of public municipal operation and of consumers' co-operatives, and such co-operative organization can be extended into wholesale distribution and into manufacturing. Co-operative enterprises should be assisted by the state through appropriate legislation and through the provision of adequate credit facilities.

7. LABOR CODE

A National Labor Code to secure for the worker maximum income and leisure, insurance covering accident, old age, and unemployment, freedom of association and effective participation in the management of his industry or profession

The spectre of poverty and insecurity which still haunts every worker, though technological developments have made possible a high standard of living for everyone, is a disgrace which must be removed from our civilization. The community must organize its resources to effect progressive reduction of the hours of work in accordance with technological development and to provide a constantly rising standard of life to everyone who is willing to work. A labor code must be developed which will include state regulation of all wages, equal reward and equal opportunity of advancement for equal services, irrespective of sex; measures to guarantee the right to work or the right to maintenance through stabilization of employment and through unemployment insurance; social insurance to protect workers and their families against the hazards of sickness, death, industrial accident and old age; limitation of hours of work and protection of health and safety in industry. Both wages and insurance benefits should be varied in accordance with family needs.

In addition workers must be guaranteed the undisputed right to freedom of association, and should be encouraged and assisted by the state to organize themselves in trade unions. By means of collective agreements and participation in works councils, the workers can achieve fair working rules and share in the control of industry and profession; and their organizations will be indispensable elements in a system of genuine industrial democracy.

The labor code should be uniform throughout the country. But the achievement of this end is difficult so long as jurisdiction over labor legislation under the B.N.A. Act is mainly in the hands of the provinces. It is urgently necessary, therefore, that the B.N.A. Act be amended to make such a national labor code possible.

8. SOCIALIZED HEALTH SERVICES

Publicly organized health, hospital and medical services

With the advance of medical science the maintenance of a healthy population has become a function for which every civilized community should undertake responsibility. Health services should be made at least as freely available as are educational services today. But under a system which is still mainly one of private enterprise the costs of proper medical care, such as the wealthier members of society can easily afford, are at present prohibitive for great masses of the people. A properly organized system of public health services including medical and dental care, which would stress the prevention rather than the cure of illness should be extended to all our people in both rural and urban areas. This is an enterprise in which Dominion, Provincial and Municipal authorities, as well as the medical and dental professions can co-operate.

9. B.N.A. ACT

The amendment of the Canadian Constitution, without infringing upon racial or religious minority rights or upon legitimate provincial claims to autonomy, so as to give the Dominion Government adequate powers to deal effectively with urgent economic problems which are essentially national in scope; the abolition of the Canadian Senate

We propose that the necessary amendments to the B.N.A. Act shall be obtained as speedily as required, safeguards being inserted to ensure that the existing rights of racial and religious minorities shall not be changed without their own consent. What is chiefly needed today is the placing in the hands of the national government of more power to control national economic development. In a rapidly changing economic environment our political constitution must be reasonably flexible. The present division of powers between Dominion and Provinces reflects the conditions of a pioneer, mainly agricultural, community in 1867. Our constitution must be brought into line with the increasing industrialization of the country and the consequent centralization of economic and financial power—which has taken place in the last two generations. The principle laid down in the Quebec Resolution of the Fathers of Confederation should be applied to the conditions of 1933, that "there be a general government charged with matters of common interest to the whole country and local governments for each of the provinces charged with the control of local matters to their respective sections".

The Canadian Senate, which was originally created to protect provincial rights, but has failed even in this function, has developed into a bulwark of capitalist interests, as is illustrated by the large number of company directorships held by its aged members. In its peculiar composition of a fixed number of members appointed for life it is one of the most reactionary assemblies in the civilized world. It is a standing obstacle to all progressive legislation, and the only permanently satisfactory method of dealing with the constitutional difficulties it creates is to abolish it.

10. EXTERNAL RELATIONS

A Foreign Policy designed to obtain international economic co-operation and to promote disarmament and world peace

Canada has a vital interest in world peace. We propose, therefore, to do everything in our power to advance the idea of international co-operation as represented by the League of Nations and the International Labor Organization. We would extend our diplomatic machinery for keeping in touch with the main centres of world interest. But we believe that genuine international co-operation is incompatible with the capitalist regime which is in force in most countries, and that strenuous efforts are needed to rescue the League from its present condition of being mainly a League of capitalist Great Powers. We stand resolutely against all participation in imperialist wars. Within the British Commonwealth, Canada must maintain her autonomy as a completely self-governing nation. We must resist all attempts to build up a new economic British Empire in place of the old political one, since such attempts readily lend themselves to the purposes of capitalist exploitation and may easily lead to further world wars. Canada must refuse to be entangled in any more wars fought to make the world safe for capitalism.

11. TAXATION AND PUBLIC FINANCE

A new taxation policy designed not only to raise public revenues but also to lessen the glaring inequalities of income and to provide funds for social services and the socialization of industry; the cessation of the debt-creating system of Public Finance

In the type of economy that we envisage, the need for taxation, as we now understand it, will have largely disappeared. It will nevertheless be essential during the transition period, to use the taxing powers, along with the other methods proposed elsewhere, as a means of providing for the socialization of industry, and for extending the benefits of increased Social Services.

At present capitalist governments in Canada raise a large proportion of their revenues from such levies as customs duties and sales taxes, the main burden of which falls upon the masses. In place of such taxes upon articles of general consumption, we propose a drastic extension of income, corporation and inheritance taxes, steeply graduated according to ability to pay. Full publicity must be given to income tax payments and our tax collection system must be brought up to the English standard of efficiency.

We also believe in the necessity for an immediate revision of the basis of Dominion and Provincial sources of revenues, so as to produce a co-ordinated and equitable system of taxation throughout Canada.

An inevitable effect of the capitalist system is the debt creating character of public financing. All public debts have enormously increased, and the fixed interest charges paid thereon now amount to the largest single item of so-called uncontrollable public expenditures. The CCF proposes that in future no public financing shall be permitted which facilitates the perpetuation of the parasitic interest-receiving class; that capital shall be provided through the medium of the National Investment Board and free from perpetual interest charges.

We propose that all Public Works, as directed by the Planning Commission, shall be financed by the issuance of credit, as suggested, based upon the National Wealth of Canada.

12. FREEDOM

Freedom of speech and assembly for all; repeal of Section 98 of the Criminal Code; amendment of the Immigration Act to prevent the present inhuman policy of deportation; equal treatment before the law of all residents of Canada irrespective of race, nationality or religious or political beliefs

In recent years, Canada has seen an alarming growth of Fascist tendencies among all governmental authorities. The most elementary rights of freedom of speech and assembly have been arbitrarily denied to workers and to all whose political and social views do not meet with the approval of those in power. The lawless and brutal conduct of the police in certain centres in preventing public meetings and in dealing with political prisoners must cease. Section 98 of the Criminal Code which has been used as a weapon of political oppression by a panic-stricken capitalist government, must be wiped off the statute book and those who have been imprisoned under it must be released. An end must be put to the inhuman practice of deporting immigrants who were brought to this country by immigration propaganda and now, through no fault of their own, find themselves victims of an executive department against whom there is no appeal to the courts of the land. We stand for full economic, political and religious liberty for all.

13. SOCIAL JUSTICE

The establishment of a commission composed of psychiatrists, psychologists, socially minded jurists and social workers, to deal with all matters pertaining to crime and punishment and the general administration of law, in order to humanize the law and to bring it into harmony with the needs of the people

While the removal of economic inequality will do much to overcome the most glaring injustices in the treatment of those who come into conflict with the law, our present archaic system must be changed and brought into accordance with a modern concept of human relationships. The new system must not be based as is the present one, upon vengeance and fear,· but upon an understanding of human behaviour. For this reason its planning and control cannot be left in the hands of those steeped in the outworn legal tradition; and therefore it is proposed that there shall be established a national commission composed of psychiatrists, psychologists, socially minded jurists and social workers whose duty it shall be to devise a system of prevention and correction consistent with other features of the new social order.

14. AN EMERGENCY PROGRAMME

The assumption by the Dominion Government of direct responsibility for dealing with the present critical unemployment situation and for tendering suitable work or adequate maintenance; the adoption of measures to relieve the extremity of the crisis such as a programme of public spending on housing, and other enterprises that will increase the real wealth of Canada, to be financed by the issue of credit based on the national wealth

The extent of unemployment and the widespread suffering which it has caused, creates a situation with which provincial and municipal governments have long been unable to cope and forces upon the Dominion government direct responsibility for dealing with the crisis as the only authority with financial resources adequate to meet the situation. Unemployed workers must be secured in the tenure of their homes, and the scale and methods of relief, at present altogether inadequate, must be such as to preserve decent human standards of living.

It is recognized that even after a Co-operative Commonwealth Federation Government has come into power, a certain period of time must elapse before the planned economy can be fully worked out. During this brief transitional period, we propose to provide work and purchasing power to those now unemployed by a far-reaching programme of public expenditure on housing, slum clearance, hospitals, libraries, schools, community halls, parks, recreational projects, reforestation, rural electrification, the elimination of grade crossings, and other similar projects in both town and country. This programme, which would be financed by the issuance of credit based on the national wealth, would serve the double purpose of creating employment and meeting recognized social needs. Any steps which the government takes, under this emergency programme, which may assist private business, must include guarantees of adequate wages and reasonable hours of work, and must be designed to further the advance towards the complete Co-operative Commonwealth.

Emergency measures, however, are of only temporary value, for the present depression is a sign of the mortal sickness of the whole capitalist system, and this sickness cannot be cured by the application of salves. These leave untouched the cancer which is eating at the heart of our society, namely, the economic system in which our natural resources and our principal means of production and distribution are owned, controlled and operated for the private profit of a small proportion of our population.

No C.C.F. Government will rest content until it has eradicated capitalism and put into operation the full programme of socialized planning which will lead to the establishment in Canada of the Co-operative Commonwealth.

WINNIPEG DECLARATION OF PRINCIPLES (1956) OF THE CO-OPERATIVE COMMONWEALTH FEDERATION / PARTI SOCIAL DEMOCRATIQUE DU CANADA

The aim of the Co-operative Commonwealth Federation is the establishment in Canada by democratic means of a co-operative commonwealth in which the supplying of human needs and enrichment of human life shall be the primary purpose of our society. Private profit and corporate power must be subordinated to social planning designed to achieve equality of opportunity and the highest possible living standards for all Canadians.

This is, and always has been, the aim of the C.C.F. The Regina Manifesto, proclaimed by the founders of the movement in 1933, has had a profound influence on Canada's social system. Many of the improvements it recommended have been wrung out of unwilling governments by the growing strength of our movement and the growing political maturity of the Canadian people. Canada is a better place than it was a generation ago, not least because of the cry for justice sounded in the Regina Manifesto and the devoted efforts of CCF members and supporters since that time.

CANADA STILL RIDDEN BY INEQUALITIES

In spite of great economic expansion, large sections of our people do not benefit adequately from the increased wealth produced. Greater wealth and economic power continue to be concentrated in the hands of a relatively few private corporations. The gap between those at the bottom and those at the top of the economic scale has widened.

Thousands still live in want and insecurity. Slums and inadequate housing condemn many Canadian families to a cheerless life. Older citizens exist on pensions far too low for health and dignity. Many too young to qualify for pensions are rejected by industry as too old for employment, and face the future without hope. Many in serious ill-health cannot afford the hospital and medical care they need. Educational institutions have been starved for funds and, even in days of prosperity, only a small proportion of young men and women who could benefit from technical and higher education can afford it.

In short, Canada is still characterized by glaring inequalities of wealth and opportunity and by the domination of one group over another. The growing concentration of corporate wealth has resulted in a virtual economic dictatorship by a privileged few. This threatens our political democracy which will attain its full meaning only when our people have a voice in the management of their economic affairs and effective control over the means by which they live.

THE FOLLY OF WASTED RESOURCES

Furthermore, even during a time of high employment, Canada's productive capacity is not fully utilized. Its use is governed by the dictates of private economic power and by considerations of private profit. Similarly, the scramble for profit has wasted and despoiled our rich resources of soil, water, forest and minerals.

This lack of social planning results in a waste of our human as well as our natural resources. Our human resources are wasted through social and economic conditions which stunt human growth, through unemployment and through our failure to provide adequate education.

THE CHALLENGE OF NEW HORIZONS

The C.C.F. believes that Canada needs a program for the wise development and conservation of its natural resources. Our industry can and should be so operated as to enable our people to use fully their talents and skills. Such an economy will yield the maximum opportunities for individual development and the maximum of goods and services for the satisfaction of human needs at home and abroad.

Unprecedented scientific and technological advances have brought us to the threshold of a second industrial revolution. Opportunities for enriching the standard of life in Canada and elsewhere are greater than ever. However, unless careful study is given to the many problems which will arise and unless there is intelligent planning to meet them, the evils of the past will be multiplied in the future. The technological changes will produce even greater concentrations of wealth and power and will cause widespread distress through unemployment and the displacement of populations.

The challenge facing Canadians today is whether future development will continue to perpetuate the inequalities of the past or whether it will be based on principles of social justice.

CAPITALISM BASICALLY IMMORAL

Economic expansion accompanied by widespread suffering and injustice is not desirable social progress. A society motivated by the drive for private gain and special privilege is basically immoral.

The CCF reaffirms its belief that our society must have a moral purpose and must build a new relationship among men—a relationship based on mutual respect and on equality of opportunity. In such a society everyone will have a sense of worth and belonging, and will be enabled to develop his capacities to the full.

SOCIAL PLANNING FOR A JUST SOCIETY

Such a society cannot be built without the application of social planning. Investment of available funds must be channelled into socially desirable projects; financial and credit resources must be used to help maintain full employment and to control inflation and deflation.

In the co-operative commonwealth there will be an important role for public, private and co-operative enterprise working together in the people's interest.

The CCF has always recognized public ownership as the most effective means of breaking the stranglehold of private monopolies on the life of the nation and of facilitating the social planning necessary for economic security and advance. The CCF will, therefore, extend public ownership wherever it is necessary for the achievement of these objectives.

At the same time, the CCF also recognizes that in many fields there will be need for private enterprise which can make a useful contribution to the development of our economy. The co-operative commonwealth will, therefore, provide appropriate opportunities for private business as well as publicly-owned industry.

The CCF will protect and make more widespread the ownership of family farms by those who will till them, of homes by those who live in them, and of all personal possessions necessary for the well-being of the Canadian people.

In many fields the best means of ensuring justice to producers and consumers is the co-operative form of ownership. In such fields, every assistance will be given to form co-operatives and credit unions and to strengthen those already in existence.

BUILDING A LIVING DEMOCRACY

The CCF welcomes the growth of labour unions, farm and other organizations of the people. Through them, and through associations for the promotion of art and culture, the fabric of a living democracy is being created in Canada. These organizations must have the fullest opportunity for further growth and participation in building our nation's future.

In the present world struggle for men's minds and loyalties, democratic nations have a greater responsibility than ever to erase every obstacle to freedom and every vestige of racial, religious or political discrimination. Legislation alone cannot do this, but effective legislation is a necessary safeguard for basic rights and a sound foundation for further social and educational progress.

Therefore, the CCF proposes the enactment of a Bill of Rights guaranteeing freedom of speech and of expression, the right of lawful assembly, association and organization, equal treatment before the law, freedom to worship according to one's own conscience and the enjoyment of all rights without distinction of race, sex, religion or language.

BASIS FOR PEACE

The solution of the problems facing Canada depends, in large part, on removing the international dangers which threaten the future of all mankind. Therefore no task is more urgent than that of building peace and of forging international policies which will banish from the earth the oppressive fear of nuclear destruction. Only if there is a determined will to peace and if every part of the world is free from the fear of aggression and domination, can progress be made toward a lasting settlement of outstanding differences.

Throughout the years the CCF has maintained that there has been too much reliance on defence expenditures to meet the threat of communist expansion. One of the urgent needs for building a peaceful world and for extending the influence and power of democracy is generous support of international agencies to provide assistance to under-developed countries on a vast scale.

The hungry, oppressed and underprivileged of the world must know democracy not as a smug slogan but as a dynamic way of life which sees the world as one whole, and which recognizes the right of every nation to independence and of every people to the highest available standard of living.

SUPPORT OF UN

The CCF reaffirms full support for the United Nations and its development into an effective organization of international co-operation and government. The world must achieve a large measure of international disarmament without delay and evolve a system of effective international control and inspection to enable the prohibition of nuclear weapons.

The CCF believes in full international co-operation which alone can bring lasting peace. The practices of imperialism, whether of the old style or the new totalitarian brand, must disappear. The CCF strives for a world society based on the rule of law and on freedom, on the right to independence of all peoples, on greater equality among nations and on genuine universal brotherhood.

CONFIDENCE IN CANADA

The CCF has confidence in Canada and its people who have come from many lands in search of freedom, security and opportunity. It is proud of our country's origins in the British and French traditions which have produced our present parliamentary and judicial systems.

The CCF believes in Canada's federal system. Properly applied in a spirit of national unity, it can safeguard our national well-being and at the same time protect the traditions and constitutional rights of the provinces. Within the framework of the federal system the CCF will equalize opportunities for the citizens of every province in Canada. True national unity will be achieved only when every person from the Atlantic to the Pacific is able to enjoy an adequate standard of living.

SOCIALISM ON THE MARCH

In less than a generation since the CCF was formed, democratic socialism has achieved a place in the world which its founders could hardly have envisaged. Many labour and socialist parties have administered or participated in the governments of their countries. As one of these democratic socialist parties, the CCF recognizes that the great issue of our time is whether mankind shall move toward totalitarian oppression or toward a wider democracy within nations and among nations.

The CCF will not rest content until every person in this land and in all other lands is able to enjoy equality and freedom, a sense of human dignity, and an opportunity to live a rich and meaningful life as a citizen of a free and peaceful world. This is the Co-operative Commonwealth which the CCF invites the people of Canada to build with imagination and pride.

CONSTITUTION OF THE CO-OPERATIVE COMMONWEALTH FEDERATION (ONTARIO SECTION)

With amendments adopted by Provincial Conventions up to and including the Convention of April, 1955

ARTICLE I. NAME

The name of the organization shall be the Co-operative Commonwealth Federation (CCF), Ontario Section.

ARTICLE II. OBJECT

The CCF is dedicated to the establishment in Canada of a Co-operative Commonwealth which shall replace the present capitalist system, with its inherent injustice and inhumanity, by a social order from which the domination and exploitation of one class by another will be eliminated, in which economic planning will supersede unregulated private enterprise and competition, and in which genuine democratic self-government based upon economic equality will be possible.

ARTICLE III. MEMBERSHIP

1. The Co-operative Commonwealth Federation, Ontario Section, shall consist of:

    (*a*) Persons who have agreed to subscribe to the principles and policies of the CCF as set out in decisions of the national and provincial conventions, to abide by the terms of this constitution, and whose application for membership has been approved in accordance with the provisions of section 2 below.

    (*b*) Economic organizations, such as trade unions, farmers' organizations or co-operative societies, cultural or educational organizations, who have applied for affiliation and whose affiliation has been accepted as set out in section 3.

2. Individual membership applications may be received by the local units and sent on to the provincial office after being approved; or by the provincial general secretary direct, provided that in the latter case notice of such application shall be sent to the secretary of the constituency association in which the applicant resides. On receipt of this notice the constituency secretary shall notify the provincial secretary of any objection there may be locally to the application being granted. Where no reply is received within twenty-one days it shall be assumed

that no such objection exists. In all cases actual membership dates from the time at which the membership card is issued from the provincial office, and the provincial council may at its discretion refuse to accept any person as a member.

3. Applications from economic or cultural groups shall be received by the provincial council, which shall have power to accept or reject such application, and the terms of affiliation shall be such as are from time to time laid down by the provincial convention.

4. No member of the CCF shall be a member of any other political party nor shall any affiliated body be affiliated to another political party, or any organization ancillary thereto, and such membership or affiliation in another party shall cancel membership in, or affiliation to, the CCF.

ARTICLE IV. PROVINCIAL CONVENTION

1. A convention, to be known as the annual provincial convention, shall be held once a year at such time and place as the provincial council shall determine; and the provincial council may call such other conventions as it deems necessary, and shall call such a further convention if requested to do so in writing by 50 per cent of the organized constituencies.

2. Subject to the national constitution of the CCF, and the decisions of the national conventions, the convention of the CCF, Ontario Section, is the supreme governing body of the movement in Ontario. It shall have power to make decisions, rules, and regulations which shall govern and regulate the policies and activities of the movement. It shall also have the power to amend this constitution, subject to the provisions of section 14 below.

3. The Convention shall consist of: (a) Delegates elected by the constituency associations; (b) Delegates from affiliated organizations; (c) Members of the provincial council.

4. The provincial council shall have the power to determine the number of delegates which units and affiliated organizations are entitled to send and this number shall be in proportion to membership, provided, however, that the council shall maintain a reasonable ratio between constituency associations on the one hand and affiliated organizations on the other hand.

5. Every delegate must be a member of the CCF, or in the case of affiliated organizations, a properly qualified representative of such organization, must have paid his delegate fee, filed his credential or authority proving his election as delegate, signed by the president or secretary of the unit he represents.

6. The provincial council shall determine the amount of the fee to be paid by each delegate, and may provide for all or part of the travelling expenses of delegates.

7. At least ninety days' notice of the date of the annual convention, and of the place where it is to be held, shall be given to each unit and each affiliated organization.

8. Membership for the purposes of representation shall be the number of members appearing on the records of the provincial office thirty days before the date of the convention and credentials shall be issued on this basis.

9. The unit of representation under 3 (*a*) above shall be the constituency association, but for purposes of representation University CCF clubs will at their request be regarded as constituency associations. Every constituency association shall ensure that any club or clubs within the boundaries of the constituency are given a fair share of the constituency's representation, having regard to the membership of the club or clubs.

10. Each riding association, regardless of its membership, shall be entitled to a minimum of one delegate.

11. Resolutions to be submitted to the annual convention shall have been proposed:

    (*a*) by a constituency association or club or organization entitled to representation; copy of these resolutions must be submitted in writing to the provincial office at a date determined by the provincial council but not later than sixty days before the convention date;

    (*b*) or by the provincial council who shall see that copies of these resolutions, as well as of those proposed under (*a*), are communicated to all units and affiliated organizations not later than thirty days before the convention date.

    The provincial council may, however, with the consent of the convention, submit to the convention emergency resolutions.

12. The convention shall itself elect a resolutions committee to which emergency resolutions from member bodies and organizations may be referred. Such emergency resolutions shall be submitted to the convention only on the recommendation of the resolutions committee. The question on this recommendation shall be put without debate.

13. An emergency resolution is one dealing with a matter of emergency which has arisen since the date for agenda resolutions and could not, therefore, be included on the regular agenda. Further, emergency resolutions are not subject to amendment by the convention, and must not involve any reversal of previously established policy.

14. All decisions of the convention shall be by majority vote, except that this constitution can be amended only by a two-thirds majority.

15. A report of proceedings of the annual convention shall be sent to each delegate who attended the convention, and to all units and affiliated organizations as soon as possible after the close of the convention.

ARTICLE V. PROVINCIAL COUNCIL

1. The Provincial council shall consist of:

    (*a*) A president, a provincial leader, and five vice-presidents, elected by the annual convention.

    (*b*) The immediate past president, for a period of one year after his retirement.

(*c*) Such others as may have been elected to the national council by the provincial convention, and those residing in Ontario and elected to the national council by the national convention.

(*d*) Twenty members elected by the convention without geographical restrictions.

(*e*) Such members as are elected by constituency associations or groups of constituency associations on the following basis: (i) one member from each of the following groups of constituencies in the Toronto metropolitan area: High Park, Parkdale and Davenport; Trinity and Spadina; St. Paul's and Rosedale; Broadview and Greenwood; Danforth and York-Scarborough; York East and Eglinton; York Centre and York South; York-Humber and York West; (ii) one member from each other constituency having at least 50 members, but the convention may designate a constituency as a rural constituency, and such constituency shall thereupon be entitled to one member of the council if it has at least 25 members.

The term of office of a member elected under this clause shall be from the conclusion of the annual convention until the conclusion of the immediately succeeding annual convention, and if his successor has not been elected, for one additional council meeting.

(*f*) The president and one additional member elected by the Ontario CCF Youth.

(*g*) The chairman elected by the Provincial Women's Conference.

(*h*) The chairman elected by the annual trade union and farm conferences.

2. A vacancy occurring between conventions in the office of president, vice-president or national council member elected by the provincial convention shall be filled by the provincial council from among its own members, but the Provincial Leader shall always be elected by regular or special convention.

3. No person may be nominated for any office unless his consent to nomination has been obtained.

4. The election of officers and council members shall be by secret ballot.

5. Constituency associations and city organizations shall, wherever possible, elect their candidates for the council and forward their names to the provincial secretary at least ten days before the provincial convention.

6. Each constituency with 50 or more members, shall be assessed $10 per year to defray the transportation expenses of the council members selected by the city and constituency organizations.

7. One-third of the members shall constitute a quorum at the meetings of council.

8. The provincial council shall have the power and authority to:

(*a*) Accept or reject any application for membership or affiliation.

(*b*) Expel or suspend from membership or affiliation any individual, group or organization who (or which) acts contrary to the fundamental principles and policies of the CCF, or the obligations of membership or affiliation imposed by this constitution, or who (which) persistently refuses to co-operate in projects for the advancement of the CCF which have been authorized or initiated by the provincial council;

provided that no disciplinary action shall be taken under this section until written charges have been made and delivered to the accused individual or organization and proven at a hearing at which the accused shall have the right to adduce evidence and be heard personally or represented by another member.

(c) Make rules and regulate the manner in which the provisions of this constitution and the decisions of the convention shall be carried out, but such rules and regulations shall not alter the substance of any such provision or decision.

(d) Supervise the publication of books, newspapers, pamphlets, leaflets, articles, and general publicity on behalf of the movement.

(e) Appointment committees and delegate to them such powers as it deems advisable.

(f) Make regulations to govern the transaction of its business and that of its committees.

(g) Subject to previous decisions of the convention, and appeal to the convention, take such other action, as it deems necessary to the fulfilment of the purposes of the organization.

9. The provincial council shall meet not less than five times a year.
10. The provincial council shall submit to the annual convention succeeding that at which it was elected, a report in writing of the acts done by it in the exercise of its powers and authority conferred by this constitution. This report shall be sent to the secretaries of all CCF units in this province and of all affiliated organizations not less than thirty days before the date of the annual convention.

ARTICLE VI. PROVINCIAL EXECUTIVE

1. The provincial council, at its first meeting, shall appoint from its own members an executive committee to transact the business of the council between the meetings of council. This meeting shall also elect a chairman of the executive.
2. The executive shall consist of the president, the provincial leader, the vice-president, and twelve others. Six members shall constitute a quorum.
3. Any member of the executive who is absent from three consecutive meetings, without having shown at the time of those meetings any satisfactory reason for absence accepted as such by the executive, shall automatically cease to be a member of the executive, and his place shall be filled by the council at its next meeting.
4. All provincial council members shall be notified of the time and place of executive meetings, and such as are not members of the executive shall be given voice but no vote at executive meetings. Failure to notify other than executive members shall not however, invalidate the transaction of business at any meeting of the executive.

ARTICLE VII. CONSTITUENCY ASSOCIATIONS

1. All members residing within the boundaries of a federal electoral district shall, as soon as is practicable, establish a constituency association for such district.

2. All members of the CCF residing in the district shall be deemed members of the constituency association for the purpose of nominating conventions.

3. The purpose of each constituency association shall be to organize its electoral district for educational and election purposes, and generally to undertake on behalf of the provincial council the furthering of the CCF within its particular district.

4. Subject to the provisions of this constitution and the national constitution, and the decisions of national and provincial conventions, and of the provincial council properly made and adopted, each constituency association has the authority to do all it deems necessary in order that its purposes shall be fulfilled.

5. Each constituency association may elect delegates to the provincial convention, and may submit resolutions for the consideration of the convention.

6. Each constituency association may adopt its own constitution and regulations subject to approval of the provincial council.

7. The constituency association shall have the right to suspend or expel any member for good cause subject to appeal to the provincial council.

8. CCF members in any locality with the approval of the constituency association or the provincial council may form themselves into a CCF club for social, educational and political purposes, hold meetings, elect officers and raise from among themselves the necessary monies to carry on such local activities, provided that, for the purposes of electing candidates and fighting election campaigns, members of all clubs in the constituency shall act through the constituency association.

9. CCF clubs may also be formed by members in any industrial unit or affiliated organization for the same purposes as outlined in Section 8 above.

10. The expression "CCF unit" in this constitution refers both to clubs and to constituency associations.

ARTICLE VIII. MUNICIPAL ELECTORAL MACHINERY

1. The members residing within the limits of any municipality in the province of Ontario may constitute a municipal association for such municipality.

2. The municipal association may set up a council within the municipality, which shall consist of representatives from units in the district.

3. The purpose of a municipal association through its council and member organizations shall be to undertake the work of the movement within the municipality insofar as such work relates to municipal affairs and not otherwise, except where general organizational projects may be delegated to it as being the most convenient organization for such projects, by agreement with the provincial council and the federal constituency associations in that district.

4. Any program or policy adopted by a municipal association or council which the association proposes to submit to the voters at any municipal election shall, before being so submitted, be communicated to the

federal constituency association or associations in that district and, if approved by the constituency association or associations, be in turn communicated by them to the provincial council for final approval.

5. A municipal association may adopt a constitution in a form approved by the federal constituency association or associations and the provincial council, and make such rules as are necessary to the proper conduct of its meetings.

ARTICLE IX. ELECTIONS

1. For the purpose of contesting an election, the constituency association may call a nominating convention for the purpose of selecting a candidate to represent the movement in such election and shall do so as soon as an election is imminent.
2. Where no constituency association is in existence, or where the association, for whatever reason, has failed to call such a nominating convention, the provincial council may call a nominating convention.
3. All members of the CCF residing within the boundaries of the electoral district shall receive notice of such a convention at least ten days before it is held, unless, in the opinion of the provincial council, special circumstances make the application of this rule inadvisable and the constituency association has been advised to this effect.
4. All members of the CCF residing within the electoral district, and only members so residing, shall have a vote at a nominating convention, unless the constitution of the constituency association provides for a delegate convention.
5. Any CCF member qualified to vote at a nominating convention shall have the right to propose a member for nomination.
6. For the purpose of nomination conventions, membership lists shall be closed one month before the nomination is held, unless, in the opinion of the provincial council special circumstances make the application of this rule inadvisable and the constituency association has been notified to this effect.
7. Any person selected as a candidate by a nominating convention must be endorsed by the provincial council and the council has the right to refuse this endorsation.
8. Where the CCF is contesting municipal elections, municipal councils shall have the same authority in municipal elections as is possessed by the provincial council in federal or provincial elections, subject to appeal to the provincial council.
9. The constituency association may, with the approval of the provincial council, provide for a delegate convention or for nomination and selection by referendum.
10. A meeting of members or of an affiliated organization shall not endorse any candidate for election except candidates selected in accordance with the provisions of this constitution.
11. Any member who offers himself for election in opposition to a candidate or candidates selected as CCF candidates as provided for in this constitution shall forthwith cease to be a member upon the public announcement of his candidature.

12. Any member may be a candidate for election in a municipality independently of the CCF, provided the members in the municipal electoral district concerned have failed to select a candidate or candidates for such election; but such member shall not advocate measures contrary to the principles and policies of the CCF, and shall be responsible to the municipal and/or provincial councils for the proper conduct of his campaign.

ARTICLE X. DUES

1. Membership dues shall be fixed from time to time by resolution of the provincial convention.
2. Affiliated organizations shall pay monthly such dues as are fixed from time to time by convention resolution.
3. Each member shall receive all regular issues of the CCF News without further charge.
4. Any member who, or affiliated organization which, is three months in arrears of dues or has not renewed an annual subscription within three months of its falling due shall be deemed to have forfeited membership in, or affiliation with, the CCF.

SUPPLEMENTARY RESOLUTIONS

TRADE UNION AFFILIATION

1. Numbers on which dues and representation shall be calculated shall be the numbers on which dues are paid to the congress with which the union is affiliated. (This has been amended to allow for "Contracting out".)
2. Representation at the provincial convention shall be based on the average paid-up membership of the union with the CCF for the three months preceding the convention call.
3. The per capita dues of a union to the CCF shall be 2 cents per member per month, of which 1 cent shall be paid to the national office and 1 cent to the provincial office.
4. The basis of representation at provincial conventions shall be one delegate for the first 100 members, one additional delegate for each additional 500 members or major fraction thereof up to a total of 5,100 members, and one additional delegate for each additional 1,000 members or major fraction thereof, with a minimum of one delegate for any one local union.
5. The affiliated body may decide how its representation to provincial conventions shall be allocated among its local unions on the basis of their membership, but the delegates shall, as far as possible, be chosen by the local unions themselves.
6. An affiliated local union shall be entitled to representation to all constituency meetings and conventions in accordance with the number of its members residing in the constituency on the basis of one delegate per 100 members or major portion thereof, with a minimum of one delegate. Where there are a number of ridings in one district or region, such

as in Greater Toronto, the affiliated unions in that district or region should have representation on the CCF district council on a basis arranged in consultation with that council.

7.　　(a) Every delegate must individually accept and conform to the constitution, program, principles, and policy of the CCF;

　　(b) Delegates must be bona fide members or paid permanent officials of the organization appointing them;

　　(c) Persons acting as candidates or supporting candidates in opposition to duly endorsed CCF candidates will not be eligible as delegates;

　　(d) Persons who are members or active supporters of political parties other than the CCF which are not in affiliation with the CCF shall not be eligible as delegates.

UNION MEMBERSHIP

Industrial democracy is an integral part of the CCF program; the CCF has always advocated the organization of workers in bona fide unions and has expected all its members to give full support to such unions; therefore where an industrial establishment or other bargaining unit is covered by a bona fide union contract, any person who is eligible and refuses to join the union is unfit to hold membership in the CCF.

MEMBERSHIP FEE

Whereas the National Convention has adopted a national membership fee of $1.00 a year;

Be it resolved that the membership fee of the Ontario CCF remain at $2.00, which, with the national fee, will make a total of $3.00 which shall be the minimum fee for membership in the CCF in Ontario.

FAMILY MEMBERSHIP

That this convention hereby establish a family membership in the Co-operative Commonwealth Federation (Ontario Section) to apply to husband, wife and children living in the same household, and that the subscription for such family members be: For the first member $3.00; for each subsequent member $1.00 up to a maximum of $5.00 for the family; it being understood, however, that such members are entitled to only one copy of the CCF News for the family, and of such other communications as may from time to time be sent to members from the provincial office.

PROVINCIAL COUNCIL

The number of members of the Federal and Provincial Parliaments elected to the Provincial Council shall not be greater than one-third of the Council, minus two.

APPENDIX C

Election Statistics
of Other Socialist Parties

All figures refer only to general elections to
the lower houses or to single chambers

AUSTRALIA

	Lab.*	Lib. (United Australia)		Country (Cons.)	Others
1901	16	34		25	—
1903	25†	26		24	—
1906	26	17		32	—
1910	44		29		2
1913	37		38		—
1914	42		32		1
1917	20	(35	plus‡	18)	—
1919	27	(27	plus	19)	2
1922	29		46?		—
1925	23	38		14	
1928	31				
1929	46	14		10	5
1931	14	39		16	6
1934	18	32		15	9
1937	29	(29	plus	16)	1
1940	36	23		14	2
1943	48	12		13	2
1946	43	18		11	3
1949	48	(57	plus	17)	1
1951	54	(52	plus	17)	—
1954	59	(47	plus	17)	—
1955	49	(57	plus	18)	—
1958	47	(58	plus	19)	—
1961	60		62		

PERCENTAGE OF POPULAR VOTE

	Lab.*	Lib. (United Australia)		Country (Cons.)	Others
1901	9				
1903	30				
1906	36				
1910	50				
1913	50				
1914	51				
1917	45				
1919	42	(45	plus	9)	4
1922	44	(38	plus	13)	5
1925	45				
1928	45				
1929	49				
1931	38				
1934	42				
1937	43	(36	plus	13)	8
1940	48	31		14	8
1943	50	19		12	18
1946	50	33		11	6
1949	46	40		11	4
1951	43		46		11
1954	50		48		3
1955	51				

*Formed in 1901.
†First took office in 1904.
‡"Plus" stands for coalition.

AUSTRIA

	Soc. Dem.*	Christian Soc.	German Nat.	United Bohmn.	Poles	Ukrain.	Croat Slav	Czech Nat. Soc.	Others
1897	14								
1901	10								
1907†	87	96							
1911	82	73	100	84	70	28	27	9	56

	Soc. Dem.	Christian Soc.	Pan-German (Nat. Econ.)	Heimatblock	Others
1919‡	72	69	27		2
1920	69	85	28		1
1923	68	82	15		—
1927	71	85	9		—
1930	72	66	19	8	—
PERCENTAGE OF POPULAR VOTE					
1919	41	36	21		2
1920	36	42	17		5
1923	40	45	13		3
1927	42	49	6		3
1930	41	36	12	6	5

	Soc. Dem.	People's	League of Indep. (Freedom)	Communist	Others
1945	76	85		4	—
1949	67	77	16	5	—
1953	73	74	14	4	—
1956	74	82	6	3	—
1959	78	79	8	—	—
1961	76	81	8	—	—
PERCENTAGE OF POPULAR VOTE					
1945	45	50		5	—
1949	39	44	12	5	—
1953	42	41	11	5	—
1956	43	46	7	4	—
1959	45	44	8	3	—

*Formed in 1888.
†First election held under universal manhood suffrage.
‡Proportional representation adopted.

BELGIUM

	Lab.*	Cath.	Lib.	Others
1886	—	98	40	—
1888	—	98	40	—
1890	—	94	44	—
1892	—	92	60	—
1894	34†	104	14	—
1896	28	111	13	—
1898	27	112	13	—
1900§	33	86	32	1
1902	34	96	34	2
1904	29	93	42	2
1906	30	89	46	1
1908	35	87	43	1
1910	35	86	44	1
1912	39	101	44	2
1914	40‡	99	45	2
1919	70	73	34	9
1921	68	80	33	15
1925	78	78	23	8
1929	70	76	28	13
1932	73	79	24	11
1936	70	63	23	46
1939	64	73	33	32
1946	66	92	16	28
1949	66	105	29	12
1950	73	108	20	11
1954	82	95	24	11
1958	81	104	20	7
1961	84	96	20	12

PERCENTAGE OF POPULAR VOTE‖

1894	19	51	26	4
1896–98	22	47	25	5
1900	23	48	23	6
1912	22	51	25	2
1919	37	37	18	3
1925	40	38	15	6
1929	36	38	17	8
1932	37	39	14	9
1936	32	39	12	17
1939	30	33	17	21
1946	32	43	9	16
1949	30	44	15	11
1950	36	47	12	5
1954	38	41	13	7
1958	36	47	11	6

*Formed in 1885.
†First contested elections in 1894. Election in that year was the first under manhood suffrage.
‡First held office in 1914, as part of a coalition.
§Proportional representation adopted.
‖Percentages from 1894 to 1912 incl. are rough approximations.

DENMARK

	Soc. Dem.*	"Left Groups" (Lib., Agrar., Ref.)	Cons.	Others
1884	2	81	19	—
1887	2	73	27	—
1890	2	76	24	—
1892	2	68	32	—
1895	8	80	25	1
1898	12	86	16	—
1901	14	92	8	—
1903	16	85	12	1

	Soc. Dem.	Agrar.	Lib.	Cons.	Single Tax	Communist	Others
1906	24	66	11	12			1
1909	24	49	20	21			—
1910	24	57	20	13			—
1913	32	44	31	7			—
1918	39	44	33	22	—		1
1920	42	48	17	28	—	—	4
1920†	48	51	18	27	—	—	4
1924	55‡	44	20	28	—	—	1
1926	53	46	16	30	2	—	1
1929	61	43	16	24	3	—	1
1932	62	38	14	27	4	2	1
1935	68	28	14	26	4	2	6
1939	64	30	14	26	3	3	8
1943	66	28	13	31	2	—	8
1945	48	38	11	26	3	18	4
1947	57	49	10	17	6	9	—
1950	59	32	12	27	12	7	—
1953	61	33	13	26	9	7	—
1953	74	42	14	30	6	8	1
1957	70	45	14	30	9	6	1
1960	76	38	11	32	—	—	18

PERCENTAGE OF POPULAR VOTE

	Soc. Dem.	Agrar.	Lib.	Cons.	Single Tax	Communist	Others
1906	25	39	14	21	—	—	—
1909	29	32	18	20	—	—	1
1910	28	34	19	19	—	—	—
1913	29	29	19	22	—	—	1
1918	29	29	21	19	—	—	3
1920	29	34	12	20	—	—	5
1920	32	34	12	18	—	—	3
1924	37	28	13	19	1	1	2
1926	37	28	11	21	1	—	1
1929	42	28	11	17	2	—	1
1932	43	25	9	19	3	1	1
1935	46	18	9	18	3	2	5
1939	43	18	10	18	2	2	7
1943	45	19	9	21	2	—	6
1945	33	23	9	18	2	13	3
1947	40	28	7	12	5	7	2
1950	40	21	8	18	8	5	—
1953	41	22	9	17	6	5	1
1953	41	23	8	17	4	4	3
1957	39	25	8	17	5	3	3
1960	42	21	6	18	2	1	10

*Formed in 1878.
†Proportional representation adopted.
‡First took office, 1924.

FINLAND

	Soc. Dem.*	Agrar.	Finnish	Young Finnish	Swedish People's	Others
1907†	80	9	59	26	24	2
1908	83	9	54	27	25	2
1909	84	13	48	29	25	1
1910	86	17	42	28	26	1
1911	86	16	43	28	26	1
1913	90	18	38	29	25	—
1916	103	19	33	23	21	1
1917	92	26	32	24	21	5

PERCENTAGE OF POPULAR VOTE

	Soc. Dem.	Agrar.	Finnish	Young Finnish	Swedish People's	Others
1907	37	6	27	14	13	4
1908	38	6	25	14	13	3
1909	40	7	24	15	12	3
1910	40	8	22	14	14	2
1911	40	8	22	15	13	2
1913	43	8	20	14	13	2
1916	47	9	17	13	12	2
1917	45	12	30		11	2

	Soc. Dem.	Agrar.	Nat. Coalit.‡	Nat. Prog.§	Swedish People's	Fi. People's Dem. Union‖	Com-munist	Others
1919	80	42	28	26	22			2
1922	53	45	35	15	25		27	—
1924	60	44	38	17	23		18	—
1927	60	52	34	10	24		20	—
1929	59	60	28	7	23		23	—
1930	66	59	42	11	20		—	2
1933	78	53	18	11	21			19
1936	83	53	20	7	21			16
1939	85	56	25	6	18			10
1945	50	49	28	9	14	49		1
1948	54	56	33	5	14	38		—
1951	53	51	28	10	15	43		—
1954	54	53	24	13	13	43		—
1958	48	48	29	8	14	50		3
1962	38	53	32	13	14	47		3

PERCENTAGE OF POPULAR VOTE

	Soc. Dem.	Agrar.	Nat. Coalit.‡	Nat. Prog.§	Swedish People's	Fi. People's Dem. Union‖	Com-munist	Others
1919	38	20	16	13	12			2
1922	25	20	18	9	12		15	—
1924	29	20	19	9	12		10	—
1927	28	23	18	7	12		12	—
1929	27	26	15	6	11		13	1
1930	34	27	18	6	10		1	4
1933	37	23	17	7	10			5
1936	39	22	10	6	11			11
1939	40	23	14	5	10			9
1945	25	21	15	5	8	23		2
1948	26	24	17	4	8	20		1
1951	27	23	15	6	8	22		1
1954	26	24	13	8	7	22		—
1958	23	23	15	6	7	23		3

*Formed in 1899 as the Labour party.
†First general election. Proportional representation adopted. Previously there were four chambers in the Diet, one each of the nobles, clergy, burgesses and farmers.
‡Formed in 1918 by monarchists in the two Finnish parties.
§Formed in 1918 by republicans in the two Finnish parties.
‖Formed in 1945 by a coalition of the Communist and Socialist Unity parties.

FRANCE

	Soc.	Indep.; Mod.; Rep. Lib.	Rad.; Rad. Soc.; Left Rep.	MRP	Communist	Gaullist	Others
1893	40						
1906	54						
1910	76						
	71						
1914	103						
1919	68						
1924	105				27		
1928	112		109		15		
1932	129		157		10		
1936	149	199	147	23	72		18
1945*	139	53	60	150	159	—	25
1946	129	58	53	167	153	—	26
1946	93	65	59	160	168	9	15
1951	104	98	94	85	103	118	25
1956	94	95	57	73	149	21	95
1958	66	136	16	57	10	189	72
1962	66	55†	39	—	41	223	58

PERCENTAGE OF POPULAR VOTE

	Soc.	Indep.; Mod.; Rep. Lib.	Rad.; Rad. Soc.; Left Rep.	MRP	Communist	Gaullist	Others
1936	16	33	21	5	16		3
1945	23	16	11	24	26		
1946	21	13	12	28	26		
1946	18	17	11	26	28		
1951	15	13	12	12	27	22	
1956	12	12	12	9	21	—	14
1958							

*Proportional representation adopted.   †Includes MRP.

GERMANY

	Soc. Dem.*	Centre	German Cons.	Free Cons.	Lib.	Other major groups
1871	2	63	55	39	152	46
1874	9	91	22	33	158	49
1877	12	93	40	38	128	35
1878	9†	94	59	57	99	26
1881	12	100	50	28	47	106
1884	24	99	78	28	51	67
1887	11	·89	80	41	99	32
1890	35	106	73	20	42	66
1893	44	96	72	28	53	37
1898	56	102	56	23	46	41
1903	81	100	54	21	51	31
1907	43	105	60	24	54	42
1912	110	91	43	14	45	42

*Formed in 1863.   †Socialist activities banned in 1878.

	Soc. Dem.	Centre	German Cons.	Free Cons.	Lib.	Other major groups
			PERCENTAGE OF POPULAR VOTE			
1871	3	19	23		30	17
1874	7	28	14		30	10
1877	9	25	18		27	10
1878	8	23	27		23	11
1881	6	23	24		15	23
1884	10	23	22		18	19
1887	7	22	25		22	14
1890	20	19	19		16	18
1893	23	19	19		13	15
1898	27	19	15		13	11
1903	32	20	14		14	9
1907	29	19	14		14	11
1912	35	16	12		14	12

	Soc. Dem.	Centre	German Nat. People's	German People's	Dem.	Com-munist	Nat. Soc.	Others
1919‡	165–22§	91	44	19	75	—	—	4
1920	102–84	85	71	65	39	4	—	4
1924	100	81	95	45	28	62	32	10
1924	131	88	103	51	32	45	14	17
1928	153	78	78	45	25	54	12	23
1930	143	87	41	30	20	77	107	23
1932	133	98	37	8	4	89	230	—
1932	121	89	51	11	2	100	196	1
1933	120	92	52	2	5	81	288	—
			PERCENTAGE OF POPULAR VOTE					
1919	38–8	20	10	4	19	—	—	1
1920	22–18	18	15	14	8	2	—	1
1924	20–1	17	20	9	6	13	7	4
1924	26	18	20	10	6	9	3	5
1928	30	15	14	9	5	11	3	9
1930	25	15	7	5	4	13	18	9
1932	22	16	6	1	1	14	37	—
1932	20	15	8	2	1	17	33	—
1933	18	14	8	1	1	12	44	—

	Soc. Dem.	Christian Dem.	Free Dem.	German	Communist	Others
1949	131	139	52	17	15	48
1953	151	244	48	15	—	29
1957	169	270	41	17	—	—
1961	190	242	67	—	—	—
		PERCENTAGE OF POPULAR VOTE				
1949	29	31	12	4	6	18
1953	29	45	10	3	2	11
1957	32	50	8	3	—	7

‡Proportional representation adopted.
§Social Democrats divided until 1922 into Majority Socialists and Independent Socialists.

ITALY

	Soc.*	Consti- tutionalist	Cath.	Rad.	Communist	Fascist	Others
1886	3						
1890	5						
1892	10						
1895	12						
1900	32						
1904	27						
1909	42	420	.	54			14
1913†	52–23–8	318	24	70			13
1919‡	156	189	100	36			27
1921	123	275	107		16		15
1924§	46	45	39		19	375	11

	Soc.	Christian Dem.	Monarchist	Lib.	Communist	Ital. Soc.	Others
1946	115	207	16	41**	104		73
1948	51‖–33#	306	13	15	132		24
1953	76–19	261	39	14	142	23	16
1958	84–22	273	25	17	140	24	11

*Formed in 1892.
†First election held under universal manhood suffrage.
‡Proportional representation adopted. Statistics for earlier elections are less reliable, referring mainly to looser groups than parties.
§Election held under new Fascist Constitution of 1923.
‖The Socialist party, the "left wing" majority after the split.
#The Social Democratic party, the "right wing" minority after the split.
**The National Democratic Union.

NETHERLANDS

	Soc. Dem. Lab.*	Cath.	Lib. and Rad.	Anti- Revolu- tionary	Christian Historical	Communist	Others
1894	—	25	60	15	—	—	—
1897	3	22	52	17	6	—	—
1901	7	25	35	23	9	—	1
1905	7	25	45	15	8	—	—
1909	7	25	33	25	10	—	—
1913	19	25	35	11	10	—	—
1917	15	25	39	11	10	—	—
1918§	22	30	15	13	7	2	9
1922	20	32	16	16	11	2	3
1925	24	30	16	13	11	1	5
1929	24	30	15	12	11	2	6
1933	22	28	13	14	10	4	9
1937	23†	31	10	17	8	3	8
1946	29	32	6	13	8	10	2
1948	27	32	8	13	9	8	3
1952	30	30	9	12	9	6	4
1956‡	50	49	13	15	13	7	3
1959	48	49	19	14	12	3	5

*Formed in 1894.   †First held office in 1939, as part of a coalition.
‡Total number of seats increased from 100 to 150.
§Proportional representation adopted.

NEW ZEALAND

	Lab.*	Ref. Cons.	Nat.	United Lib.	Others
1902	—	19		47	10
1905	1	15		55	6
1908	1	25		47	3
1911	4	39		33	4
1914	7	40		33	—
1919	10	48		18	4
1922	17	38		25	—
1925	14	53		11	2
1928	19	28		29	4
1931	24	30		21	5
1935	53†		20		7
1938	53		25		2
1943	45		34		1
1946	42		38		—
1949	34		46		—
1951	30		50		—
1954	35		45		—
1957	41		39		—
1960	35		45		—

PERCENTAGE OF POPULAR VOTE

	Lab.*	Ref. Cons.	Nat.	United Lib.	Others
1902	2	21		52	25
1905	1	30		54	15
1908	4	28		59	9
1911	9	35		41	15
1914	10	47		43	—
1919	24	36		29	11
1922	25	40		26	9
1925	27	47		20	6
1928	27	35		30	8
1931	35		44		21
1935	47		31		22
1938	56		40		4
1943	48		43		9
1946	51		49		—
1949	47		52		—
1951	45		54		—
1954	44		44		11
1957	48		44		7
1960	44		48		9

*Formed in 1904.
†First took office in 1935.

NORWAY

	Lab.*	Cons.	Lib.	Agrar.	Communist	Others
1894	—	55	59			—
1897	—	25	79			10
1900	—	37	77			—
1903	4	47	50			16
1906†	10	45	68			—
1909	11	64	48			—
1912	23	24	70			6
1915	19	22	74			7
1918	18	50	54	3		1
1921‡	29 + 8	57	37	17		2
1924	24 + 8	54	34	22	6	—
1927	59§	30	32	26	3	1
1930	47	40	37	25	—	1
1933	69	30	25	23	1	2
1936	70	36	23	18	—	3
1945	76	25	20	10	11	8
1949	85	23	21	12	—	9
1953	77	27	15	14	3	14
1957	78	29	15	15	1	12
1960	74	29	14	16	—	17

PERCENTAGE OF POPULAR VOTE

	Lab.*	Cons.	Lib.	Agrar.	Communist	Others
1894	0.3	49	50			—
1897	0.6	47	53			—
1900	3	41	54			2
1903	10	45	43			3
1906	16	33	50			1
1909	22	42	36			—
1912	26	33	40			1
1915	32	29	37			2
1918	32	30	31			7
1921	21 + 9	33	20	13	—	3
1924	18 + 9	33	19	14	6	2
1927	37	26	19	15	4	—
1930	32	?	?	?	—	?
1933	40	22	18	14	2	5
1936	43	23	16	12	—	7
1945	41	17	14	8	12	8
1949	46	18	14	7	6	9
1953	47	18	10	9	5	11
1957	48	17	10	9	3	13

*Formed in 1887 as the Social Democratic party.

†First parliamentary election after the union with Sweden was dissolved. Statistics for earlier elections are less reliable, referring mainly to looser groups than parties.

‡Proportional representation adopted.

§First took office in 1928.

SWEDEN

	Soc. Dem.*	Cons.	Lib.	Peasant	Communist
1890	—				
1893	—				
1896	1				
1900	4				
1903	17		106		
1908	33				
1911†	64	65	101	—	—
1914	73	86	71	—	—
1914	87	86	57	—	—
1917	86‡	59	62	12	11
1920	75	70	48	30	7
1921	93	62	41	21	13
1924	104	65	33	23	5
1928	90	73	32	27	8
1932	104	57	25	36	8
1936	112	44	27	36	11
1940	134	42	23	28	3
1944	115	39	26	35	15
1948	112	23	57	30	8
1952	110	31	59	25	5
1956	106	42	58	19	6
1958	111	45	38	32	5
1960	114	39	40	34	5

PERCENTAGE OF POPULAR VOTE

1911	29	31	40	—	—
1914	30	38	32	—	—
1914	37	37	27	—	—
1917	31 + 8	25	28	8	?
1920	30 + 6	28	22	14	?
1921	36 + 3	26	19	11	5
1924	41	26	17	11	5
1928	37	29	16	11	6
1932	42	24	12	14	8
1936	46	18	13	14	8
1940	54	18	12	12	4
1944	47	16	13	14	10
1948	46	12	23	12	6
1952	46	14	24	11	4
1956	47	17	24	9	5
1958	46	20	18	13	3
1960	48	17	18	14	5

*Formed in 1889.
†Proportional representation adopted, 1911–14. Beginning of genuine party system. No reliable statistics available for preceding elections.
‡First held office in 1917, as part of a coalition.

SWITZERLAND

	Soc. Dem.*	Rad. Dem.	Cath. Cons.	Farmers, Workers and Middle Class	Lib. Dem.	Indep.	Others
1890	1						
1899	3						
1902	7						
1905	2						
1908	7						
1911	17	110	38		14		10
1914	18						
1919†	41	61	41	29	9		8
1922	43	58	44	34	10		9
1925	49	59	42	31	7		10
1928	50	58	46	31	6		7
1931	49	52	44	30	6		6
1935	50	48	42	21	7	7	12
1939	45	52	43	22	6	10	9
1943	56	47	43	22	8	6	12
1947	48	52	44	21	7	9	13
1951	49	51	48	23	5	10	10
1955	53	50	47	22	5	10	9
1959	51	51	47	23	3	10	9

*Formed in 1888.
†Proportional representation adopted. No reliable statistics available for prceeding elections.

UNITED KINGDOM

	Lab.*	Cons.		Lib.	Others
1900	2	334		186	150
1906	29	167		377	83
1910	40	273		275	82
1910	42	272		272	84
1918	57		526		118
1922	142	346		115	12
1923	191†	258		159	7
1924	151	419		40	5
1929	288	260		59	8
1931	52	521		37	5
1935	154	431		21	9
1945	394	212		12	22
1950	315	298		9	3
1951	295	321		6	3
1955	277	345		6	2
1959	258	365		6	1

PERCENTAGE OF POPULAR VOTE

1900	1	55		44	
1906	6	46		48	
1910	8	47		45	
1910					
1918	24	46		15	15
1922	30	38		29	3
1923	31	38		30	2
1924	33	48		18	1
1929	37	38		23	1
1931	31	50		15	2
1935	38	54		6	2
1945	48	40		9	3
1950	46	44		9	3
1951	49	48		3	1
1955	46	50		3	1
1959	44	49		6	1

*Formed in 1900.
†First took office in 1923.

BIBLIOGRAPHY

BOOKS

BEER, MAX. *A History of British Socialism*. 3rd ed. 2 vols. London: Allen and Unwin, 1953.

BURNET, JEAN R. *Next Year Country*. Toronto: University of Toronto Press, 1951.

CANTRIL, H. *The Psychology of Social Movements*. New York: John Wiley and Sons, 1941.

CLARK, S. D. *Church and Sect in Canada*. Toronto: University of Toronto Press, 1948.

COLDWELL, M. J. *Left Turn, Canada!* New York: Duell, Sloan and Pearce. 1945.

CROSSMAN, R. H. S., ed. *The God That Failed*. London: Hamish Hamilton. 1950.

DAWSON, C. A., and GETTYS, WARNER E. *An Introduction to Sociology*. 3rd ed. New York: Ronald, 1948.

DEETS, L. E. *The Hutterites*. Gettysburg: Gettysburg, Pa. Times and News Publishing Co., 1939.

DUVERGER, MAURICE. *Political Parties*. Translated by BARBARA and ROBERT NORTH. London: Methuen and Co., 1954.

EGBERT, DONALD D., and PERSONS, STOW, eds. *Socialism and American Life*. 2 vols. Princeton: Princeton University Press, 1952.

FUSILIER, RAYMOND. *Le Parti socialiste suédois*. Paris: Les Editions Ouvrières, 1954.

GOULDNER, A., ed. *Studies in Leadership*. New York: Harper and Brothers, 1950.

HEBERLE, R. *Social Movements*. New York: Appleton-Century-Crofts, Inc., 1951.

HOFFER, ERIC. *The True Believer*. New York: Harper and Brothers, 1951.

HUTCHISON, BRUCE. *The Incredible Canadian*. Toronto: Longmans, Green, and Co., 1952.

HOMANS, GEORGE C. *The Human Group*. New York: Harcourt, Brace and Co., 1950.

IRVING, JOHN. *The Social Credit Movement in Alberta*. Toronto: University of Toronto Press, 1959.

KING, C. W. *Social Movements in the United States*. New York: Random House, 1956.

KOESTLER, ARTHUR. *Darkness at Noon*. Translated by DAPHNE HARDY. London: Macmillan Co., 1941.

LAIDLER, H. W. *Social-Economic Movements*. New York: Thomas Y. Crowell Co., 1946.

LEWIS, DAVID, and SCOTT, FRANK. *Make This Your Canada*. Toronto: Central Canada Publishing Co., 1943.

LIPSET, S. M. *Agrarian Socialism*. Berkeley: University of California Press, 1950.

McHenry, Dean E. *The Third Force in Canada*. Berkeley: University of California Press, 1950.

MacInnis, Grace. *A Man to Remember*. Toronto: Macmillan Co., 1953.

McKenzie, R. T. *British Political Parties*. London: William Heinemann, 1955.

McNaught, K. *A Prophet in Politics*. Toronto: University of Toronto Press, 1959.

Macpherson, C. B. *Democracy in Alberta*. Toronto: University of Toronto Press, 1953.

Mann, W. E. *Sect, Cult and Church in Alberta*. Toronto: University of Toronto Press, 1955.

Michels, Robert. *Political Parties*. Translated by Eden and Cedar Paul. London: Hearst's International Library Co., 1915.

Morton, W. L. *The Progressive Party in Canada*. Toronto: University of Toronto Press, 1950.

Nash, Howard P., Jr. *Third Parties in American Politics*. Washington, D.C.: Public Affairs Press, 1959.

Rolph, W. K. *Henry Wise Wood of Alberta*. Toronto: University of Toronto Press, 1950.

Rossi, A. (pseudonym). *A Communist Party in Action*. Translated and edited by W. Kendall. New Haven: Yale University Press, 1949.

Sharp, P. F. *The Agrarian Revolt in Western Canada*. Minneapolis: University of Minnesota Press, 1948.

Truman, David B. *The Governmental Process*. New York: Alfred A. Knopf, Inc., 1951.

Wach, J. *Sociology of Religion*. Chicago: University of Chicago Press, 1944.

Weber, Max. *Theory of Social and Economic Organization*. Translated by A. M. Henderson and Talcott Parsons. Glencoe: Free Press, 1947.

ARTICLES, PARTS OF BOOKS, AND PAMPHLETS

Bell, Daniel. "Marxian Socialism [in the United States]" in *Socialism and American Life*, edited by Donald D. Egbert and Stow Persons. Princeton: Princeton University Press, 1952.

Blumer, H. "Morale" in *American Society in Wartime*, edited by W. F. Ogburn. Chicago: University of Chicago Press, 1943.

———— "Collective Behavior" in *Principles of Sociology*, edited by A. M. Lee. New York: Barnes and Noble, 1955.

Borsook, B. "The Workers Hold a Conference," *Canadian Forum*, XII (Sept. 1932).

Brewin, A. "Democracy Comes to Life in Ontario," *Canadian Forum*, XXII (May 1942).

———— "What the CCF Needs," *ibid.*, XXV (Feb. 1946).

Cole, G. D. H. "The Future of Socialism," *New Statesman and Nation*, Jan. 15 and 22, 1955.

Corbett, J. "Canadian Labor Makes Up Its Mind," *Canadian Forum*, XVII (Nov. 1937).

Coser, Lewis. "Sects and Sectarians," *Dissent*, Autumn 1954.

FARIS, ELLSWORTH. "The Sect and the Sectarian" in *Personality and the Social Group*, edited by E. W. BURGESS. Chicago: University of Chicago Press, 1929.

GOULDNER, A. "Attitudes of 'Progressive' Trade Union Leaders," *American Journal of Sociology*, LII (March 1947).

GRUBE, GEORGE. "The Issue Is: Jobs," *Canadian Forum*, XXV (June 1945).

HALL, OSWALD. "The Informal Organization of the Medical Profession," *Canadian Journal of Economics and Political Science*, XX (Nov. 1954).

KING, CARLYLE. "Democracy at Work," *Canadian Forum*, XXIV (May 1944).

——— "The CCF Sweeps Saskatchewan," *ibid.*, XXIV (July 1944).

LEWIS, DAVID. *A Socialist Takes Stock*. Toronto: Ontario Woodsworth Memorial Foundation, 1956.

MALLES, PAUL. "Structural Relationships between Trade Unions and Labour Parties," a series of three articles in *Canadian Labour*, Oct., Nov. and Dec. 1959.

MARSHALL, J. "On to Ottawa—Or Back to the People," *Canadian Forum*, XXIV (Dec. 1944).

PEMBERTON, R. E. K. "The CCF Should Get Wise to Itself," *Canadian Forum*, XXV (Oct. 1945).

SCHLESINGER, ARTHUR M., JR. "The U.S. Communist Party," *Life*, July 29, 1946, pp. 84–96.

THOMPSON, LESLIE. "The CCF and Communism," *Canadian Forum*, XXVIII (Sept. 1948).

UNDERHILL, F. H. "L.S.R.," *Canadian Forum*, XII (April 1932).

——— "The CCF," *ibid.*, XII (Sept. 1932).

——— "The Party System in Canada" in *Papers and Proceedings of the Canadian Political Science Association*, 1932.

——— "Political Parties in Canada" in *Encyclopedia of the Social Sciences*, XI, 1933.

——— "The Canadian Party System in Transition," *Canadian Journal of Economics and Political Science*, IX (Aug. 1943).

——— "The Development of National Parties in Canada," *Canadian Historical Review*, XVI (Dec. 1945).

——— *The Radical Tradition: A Second View of Canadian History*, published transcript of two broadcasts on the CBC Television series, "Explorations," June 8 and 15, 1960. Toronto: CBC Publications, 1960.

POLITICAL JOURNALS AND NEWSPAPERS

Canadian Forum. Toronto, 1932–1961.
New Commonwealth. Toronto, 1934–1943.
CCF News. Toronto, 1943–1961.

UNPUBLISHED MATERIAL

ENGELMANN, FREDERICK C. "The Cooperative Commonwealth Federation of Canada: A Study of Membership Participation in Party Policy-Making." Ph.D. dissertation, Yale University, 1954.

GUSFIELD, JOSEPH R. "Organizational Change: A Study of the W.C.T.U." Ph.D. dissertation, Dept. of Sociology, University of Chicago, 1954.
KORNHAUSER, WILLIAM. "Organizational Loyalty: A Study of Liberal and Radical Political Careers." Ph.D. dissertation, Dept. of Sociology, University of Chicago, 1953.

SOURCES OF ELECTION STATISTICS

ARNESON, BEN A. *The Democratic Monarchies of Scandinavia.* Toronto: D. Van Nostrand Co., 1939.
BUTLER, DAVID E. *The Electoral System in Britain, 1918–1951.* Oxford: Clarendon Press, 1953.
Canadian Parliamentary Guide. Edited and published by PIERRE G. NORMANDIN. Ottawa, published annually.
COLE, TAYLOR, ed. *European Political Systems.* New York: Alfred A. Knopf, Inc., 1953.
CRISP, L. F. *The Australian Federal Labour Party.* London: Longmans, Green and Co., 1955.
FINER, HERMAN. *Theory and Practice of Modern Government.* Rev. ed. New York: Henry Holt and Co., 1949.
LEISERSON, AVERY. *Parties and Politics.* New York: Alfred A. Knopf, Inc., 1958.
LIPSON, LESLIE. *The Politics of Equality.* Chicago: University of Chicago Press, 1948.
MARX, FRITZ M., ed. *Foreign Governments.* New York: Prentice-Hall, Inc., 1952.
Political Handbook of the World, 1928–1960. Edited by WALTER H. MALLORY for Council on Foreign Relations. New York: Harper and Brothers, published annually.
PUNTILA, L. A. *The Evolution of the Political Parties in Finland.* Helsinki: 1953.
RUSTOW, D. A. *The Politics of Compromise.* Princeton: Princeton University Press, 1955.
SCHUMAN, FREDERICK L. *Germany since 1918.* New York: Henry Holt and Co., 1937.
SMELLIE, K. B. *A Hundred Years of English Government.* London: Duckworth, 1937.
The House of Commons, 1950. London: The Times, 1950.
The House of Commons, 1951. London: The Times, 1951.
The Statesman's Year Book, 1900–60. Edited by S. H. STEINBERG. London: Macmillan Co., published annually.
THOMAS, NEVILLE P. *A History of British Politics from the Year 1900.* London: Herbert Jenkins, 1956.
TREUE, WOLFGANG. *Deutsche Parteiprogramme, 1861–1954.* Gottingen: Wissenschaftlicher Verlag, 1954.
VAN RAALTE, E. V. *The Parliament of the Kingdom of the Netherlands.* The Hague: The Hansard Society for Parliamentary Government, 1959.

INDEX

62, 72, 98; in final period, 86–90, 103, 133

Structure (Ontario CCF): official, 6, 23–24; local autonomy, 6, 23n, 42–43, 46, 49–51, 66; the administration, 22n, 27–30, 65; the inner circle, 25–27; the slate, 22n, 28–30; .ethnic composition, 30–31; finances, 3, 6, 45–46, 63, 64, 76–77, 81–82, 107–10, 126, 130, 135–37; membership statistics, 30, 44–45, 62–63, 75–76, 81, 103–6, 110; in first period, 41–51; in middle period, 62–67, 68, 75–82; in final period, 103–12; changes summarized, 70, 111–12, 138, 142, 145–46, 152

Sustaining membership, 81n, 108

TEMPLE, WILLIAM, 49–50
Thomas, Norman, 55
Tories. *See* Conservative party
Toronto, 3, 5, 6, 7, 24, 25, 30, 31, 36, 75–76, 81, 87n, 103, 104, 116–27, 130n, 132
Toronto and District Council (CCF), 117–18
Toronto Labour party, 44n
Toronto Telegram, 94
Trade unions: attitude to socialism, 37, 112; financial assistance to CCF, 46, 77, 106–9, 115; influence in CCF, 67, 142; official relations with CCF, 23, 55, 67, 106–7, 109–11; unofficial relations with CCF, 3, 45–46, 67, 103, 106–7, 109. *See also* individual unions by name
Trades and Labor Congress, 110
Trotskyites, 18, 99, 148

UNDERHILL, FRANK H., 4, 149
Union Nationale party, 135
Union of Soviet Socialist Republics, 17n, 21, 38, 58, 91, 97–98, 100
United Auto Workers, 106
United Church, 36
United Electrical Workers, 79
United Farmers: of Alberta, 43n; of Canada, 43n; of Ontario, 44, 134
United Front, 47–50
United Mine, Mill and Smelter Workers, 78n
United Packinghouse Workers, 106
United Steel Workers, 96, 106

VOLUNTARY ORGANIZATIONS, 143
Voters. *See* Popular support

WESTERN CONFERENCE OF LABOUR POLITICAL PARTIES, 43n
Williams, G. H. 16n, 43n
Wilson, Woodrow, 152
Winch, Ernie, 92
Winch, Harold, 71n
Windsor, 75, 76, 103, 104
Winnipeg Declaration, 14–15, 61, 93–97, 98, 100, 101, 117
Women: as CCF candidates, 121–23; place in CCF, 26, 28, 30n, 35
Woodsworth, J. S., 12, 18–19, 20, 21, 43n, 44, 53–54, 88, 135
Woodsworth House, 119n
Woodsworth Memorial Foundation (Ontario), 119n
Working class, 96, 98; CCF candidates, 121–23; CCF local leaders, 30, 104n; recruitment to CCF, 59, 104n

YMCA, 79